BREAD FOR THE DAY

DAILY BIBLE READINGS AND PRAYERS

2026

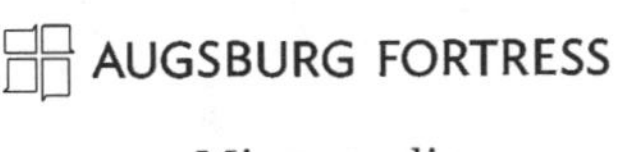

Minneapolis

BREAD FOR THE DAY 2026
Daily Bible Readings and Prayers

Editor: Rebecca Ajer Frantz
Cover design: Laurie Ingram
Cover and interior art: Mary Button

Contributors to the weekday prayers: Philip Ruge-Jones, Eau Claire, Wisconsin (January); Reed Fowler, Saint Paul, Minnesota (February); Liesl Spitz, Minneapolis, Minnesota (March); Laurie K. Stumme-Diers, Bainbridge Island, Washington (April); Kent Narum, Saint Peter, Minnesota (May); Matthew Folkemer-Leonard, York, Pennsylvania (June); Wilbert "Wilk" Miller, Essex, Connecticut (July); Stacey Nalean-Carlson, Decorah, Iowa (August); Mytch Pierre-Noel Dorvilier, Dakar, Senegal (September); Colleen Hetrick, Roanoke, Virginia (October); Ben W. Siebert, Arendtsville, Pennsylvania (November); Fanya Burford-Berry, Chicago, Illinois (December). Table Prayers for Time after Epiphany, The Three Days, Pentecost, Autumn, and Thanksgiving by Meta Herrick Carlson, and for Lent, Easter, Summer, November, and Christmas by Phil Ruge-Jones.

ACKNOWLEDGMENTS
Scripture quotations are from the New Revised Standard Version Updated Edition. Copyright © 2021 National Council of Churches of Christ in the United States of America. Used by permission. All rights reserved worldwide.

Hymn suggestions and prayers of the day for Sundays and festivals are from *Evangelical Lutheran Worship,* © 2006 Evangelical Lutheran Church in America, *This Far by Faith,* © 1999 Augsburg Fortress, *Pastoral Care* © 2008 Evangelical Lutheran Church in America, and *All Creation Sings,* © 2020 Augsburg Fortress.

Materials prepared by the Consultation on Common Texts (CCT), published in *Revised Common Lectionary* © 1992 and *Revised Common Lectionary* Daily Readings © 2005. Used by permission.

"A prayer to begin the work day," "A prayer to begin the school day," "Morning blessing," and "Evening blessing" from *Reformation 500 Sourcebook: Anniversary Resources for Congregations,* © 2016 Augsburg Fortress.

Materials prepared by the English Language Liturgical Consultation (ELLC), published in *Praying Together,* © 1988: "Blessed are you, Lord" and "My soul proclaims the greatness of the Lord." Used by permission.

pISBN:9798889835936
eISBN: 9798889835943

Manufactured in the USA

Contents

Prayers to Accompany Your Reading 5
Introduction 6

January

Prayer List for January 8
Blessing for a Home at Epiphany 14
Time after Epiphany 17
Table Prayer for Epiphany and the Time after Epiphany 17

February

Prayer List for February 43
Lent 61
Table Prayer for the Season of Lent 61

March

Prayer List for March 73
Holy Week 102
Prayer for Placing Palms in the Home 102

April

Prayer List for April 106
The Three Days 108
Table Prayer for the Three Days 108
Easter 113
Table Prayer for the Season of Easter 113

May

Prayer List for May 139
Pentecost 163
Table Prayer for Pentecost 163
Thanksgiving for the Holy Spirit 163
Time after Pentecost—Summer 171
Table Prayer for Summer 171

June

Prayer List for June 173

July

Prayer List for July 204

August

Prayer List for August 236

September

Prayer List for September 268
Time after Pentecost—Autumn 269
Table Prayer for Autumn. 269

October

Prayer List for October. 300

November

Prayer List for November 332
Time after Pentecost—November 333
Table Prayer for November 333
Remembering Those Who Have Died. 334
Reading and Prayer for Thanksgiving Day 360
Advent 364
The Advent Wreath 364
An Evening Service of Candlelight for Advent 365
Lighting the Advent Wreath, week 1. 365
Table Prayer for Advent 367

December

Prayer List for December 370
Lighting the Advent Wreath, week 2 376
Lighting the Advent Wreath, week 3 384
Lighting the Advent Wreath, week 4 392
Christmas 397
Table Prayer for the Twelve Days of Christmas 397
Lighting the Christmas Tree. 398
Blessing of the Nativity Scene 398

Additional Resources

Lesser Festivals and Commemorations. 407
Anniversary of Baptism (abbreviated) 416
Prayers for Various Situations 419
Morning Blessing 423
A Simplified Form for Morning Prayer. 424
A Simplified Form for Evening Prayer 427
Evening Blessing 430
Night Prayers with Children. 430
Suggestions for Daily Reflection 431

Prayers to Accompany Your Reading

Morning Devotions

Be with me as I worship, O Lord. Come open my heart and let me sing harmony to your tune. Let your voice vibrate a new string and your words awaken a lost language. Be with me as I worship, O Lord. Stir me from my slumbers. When I awake, I am still with you. Be with me as I worship, O Lord. Amen.

Scripture

Author of all creation, we give you thanks for inspiring the writers of the Bible, your holy Word, to share your word. Help us to turn to it through all the many days of our lives so that we may find guidance for our living. Amen.

Community

Loving God, as we read your word, help us to discern its meaning for the life of our community. May it empower us to witness to your love in the world in many new ways. Amen.

Discipleship

O God, may we be like Samuel who, when you called him, said, "Here I am!" Empower us to listen to your word and to hear your call to us so that we might more fully live out our vocation as your disciples in the world. Amen.

Devotions

O God, you are our loving parent who gave everything for us so that we might come to know the depth of your love for us. As we read your word and meditate on it, use it to deepen our relationship with you so that we might truly grow in faith. Amen.

Introduction

Daily prayer is an essential practice for those who seek to hear God's voice and cultivate an inner life. Whether you pray alone or with others, with brevity or in sustained meditation, the rhythm of daily prayer reveals the life-sustaining communion to which God invites all human beings. Such prayer is a serene power silently at work, drawing us into the ancient yet vital sources of faith, hope, and love.

The guiding principle of the selection of daily readings in *Bread for the Day* is their relationship to the Sunday readings as presented in the Revised Common Lectionary (a system of readings in widespread use across denominations). The readings are chosen so that the days leading up to Sunday (Thursday through Saturday) prepare for the Sunday readings. The days flowing out from Sunday (Monday through Wednesday) reflect on the Sunday readings.

How this book is organized

- Each day's page is dated and named in relationship to the church's year. Lesser festivals are listed along with the date as part of the day heading. Commemorations are listed just below in smaller type. Notes on those commemorated can be found on pages 407–415.
- Several verses from the New Revised Standard Version Updated Edition (NRSVue) of one of the appointed scripture texts are printed. The full text citation is provided. In addition, two or three additional reading citations with short descriptions are provided.
- Two psalms are appointed for each week: one psalm for Monday through Wednesday and a second psalm for Thursday through Saturday. In this way the days leading up to Sunday or flowing

out from Sunday have a distinct relationship with one another in addition to their relationship with the Sunday readings.
- Following the scripture text is a hymn suggestion from *Evangelical Lutheran Worship* (ELW), *All Creation Sings* (ACS), or *This Far by Faith* (TFF) and a prayer that incorporates a theme present in one or more readings.
- Household prayers and blessings appropriate to the changing seasons are placed throughout the book. Simplified forms of morning and evening prayer, morning and evening blessings, and prayers with children can be found on pages 423–430.

How to use this book

- Use the weekday readings to prepare for and reflect on the Sunday readings.
- Use the questions printed on page 431 to guide your reflection.
- Use the resources for household prayer placed throughout the book. See the Contents on pages 3–4 for a complete list.
- Record prayer requests on the first page for each month.
- In addition to being used to guide individual prayer, this book may be used to guide family prayer, prayer in congregational or other settings during the week, prayer with those who are sick or homebound, or prayer with other groups.

Even though Christians gather on the Lord's day, Sunday, for public worship, much of our time is spent in the home. We first learn the words, gestures, and songs of faith in the home. We discover our essential identity as a community of faith and mark significant transitions of life in the home. To surround and infuse the daily rhythm of sleeping and waking, working, resting, and eating with the words and gestures of Christian prayer is to discover the ancient truth of the gospel: The ordinary and the human can reveal the mystery of God and divine grace. Like planets around the sun, our daily prayer draws us to the Sunday assembly where we gather for the word and the breaking of the bread in the changing seasons of the year. From the Sunday assembly, our daily prayer flows into the week.

Prayer List for January

Thursday, January 1, 2026

Name of Jesus

Philippians 2:5-11

God takes on human form

Let the same mind be in you that was in Christ Jesus,
who, though he existed in the form of God,
did not regard equality with God
as something to be grasped,
but emptied himself,
taking the form of a slave,
assuming human likeness.
And being found in appearance as a human,
he humbled himself
and became obedient to the point of death—
even death on a cross. (Phil. 2:5-8)

Psalm

Psalm 8
How exalted is your name

Additional Readings

Numbers 6:22-27
The Aaronic blessing

Luke 2:15-21
The child is named Jesus

Hymn: All Hail the Power of Jesus' Name! ELW 634

Eternal Father, you gave your incarnate Son the holy name of Jesus to be a sign of our salvation. Plant love in every heart for the Savior of the world, Jesus Christ our Lord, who lives and reigns with you and the Holy Spirit, one God, now and forever.

Friday, January 2, 2026

Ninth Day of Christmas

Johann Konrad Wilhelm Loehe, renewer of the church, died 1872

Hebrews 11:1-12

Abraham's faith

Now faith is the assurance of things hoped for, the conviction of things not seen. Indeed, by faith our ancestors received approval. By faith we understand that the worlds were prepared by the word of God, so that what is seen was made from things that are not visible. (Heb. 11:1-3)

Psalm

Psalm 20

Answer us when we call

Additional Reading

Genesis 12:1-7

Abram and Sarai

Hymn: Faith of Our Fathers, ELW 813

Creating God, you have made the wonderful world that greets us every new day. May we be moved by the faith of our ancestors as your word resonates within us, generating faith and bringing us into your unfolding future.

Saturday, January 3, 2026

Tenth Day of Christmas

Psalm 72

Prayers for the king

Give the king your justice, O God,
  and your righteousness to a king's son.
May he judge your people with righteousness,
  and your poor with justice. . . .
May the kings of Tarshish and of the isles
  render him tribute,
may the kings of Sheba and Seba
  bring gifts.
May all kings fall down before him,
  all nations give him service. (Ps. 72:1-2, 10-11)

Additional Readings

Genesis 28:10-22
Jacob's ladder

Hebrews 11:13-22
Abraham, Isaac, and Jacob act on faith

Hymn: May the God of Hope Go with Us, ACS 984

God of justice, you call the leaders of the world to attend to the needs of those who are most vulnerable. When they waver in commitment, raise our voices to defend those in danger and at risk.

Sunday, January 4, 2026

Second Sunday of Christmas

John 1:[1-9] 10-18

God with us

He was in the world, and the world came into being through him, yet the world did not know him. He came to what was his own, and his own people did not accept him. But to all who received him, who believed in his name, he gave power to become children of God, who were born, not of blood or of the will of the flesh or of the will of man, but of God.

And the Word became flesh and lived among us, and we have seen his glory, the glory as of a father's only son, full of grace and truth. (John 1:10-14)

Psalm

Psalm 147:12-20
Praising God in Zion

Additional Readings

Jeremiah 31:7-14
Joy as God's scattered flock gathers

Ephesians 1:3-14
The will of God made known in Christ

Hymn: Love Has Come, ELW 292

Almighty God, you have filled all the earth with the light of your incarnate Word. By your grace empower us to reflect your light in all that we do, through Jesus Christ, our Savior and Lord, who lives and reigns with you and the Holy Spirit, one God, now and forever.

Monday, January 5, 2026

Twelfth Day of Christmas

Hebrews 11:32—12:2

Surrounded by a cloud of witnesses

Therefore, since we are surrounded by so great a cloud of witnesses, let us also lay aside every weight and the sin that clings so closely, and let us run with perseverance the race that is set before us, looking to Jesus, the pioneer and perfecter of faith, who for the sake of the joy that was set before him endured the cross, disregarding its shame, and has taken his seat at the right hand of the throne of God. (Heb. 12:1-2)

Psalm

Psalm 72

Prayers for the king

Additional Reading

Joshua 1:1-9

Be strong

Hymn: Go Tell It on the Mountain, ELW 290/TFF 52

Holy God, our beginning and ending, thank you for the witnesses who have shown us your way. Teach us to run the race with eyes fixed on Jesus, that, seeing him clearly, we might be drawn to be like him.

Blessing for a Home at Epiphany

Matthew writes that when the magi saw the shining star stop overhead, they were filled with joy. "On entering the house, they saw the child with Mary his mother" (Matt. 2:10-11). In the home, Christ is met in family and friends, in visitors and strangers. In the home, faith is shared, nurtured, and put into action.

Twelfth Night (January 5), Epiphany of Our Lord (January 6), or another day during the time after Epiphany offers an occasion for gathering with friends and family members for a blessing for the home. Someone may lead the greeting and blessing, while another person may read the scripture passage. Following an eastern European tradition, a visual blessing may be inscribed with white chalk above the main door; for example, 20 + CMB + 26. The numbers change with each new year. The three letters stand for either the ancient Latin blessing *Christe mansionem benedicat*, which means, "Christ, bless this house," or the legendary names of the magi (Caspar, Melchior, and Balthasar).

Greeting

Peace to this house and to all who enter here.
By wisdom a house is built,
and through understanding it is established;
through knowledge its rooms are filled
with rare and beautiful treasures. *(Prov. 24:3-4)*

Reading

As we prepare to ask God's blessing on this household,
let us listen to the words of scripture.
In the beginning was the Word,
and the Word was with God, and the Word was God.

He was in the beginning with God.
All things came into being through him,
and without him not one thing came into being.
What has come into being in him was life,
and the life was the light of all people.
The Word became flesh and lived among us, and we have seen his glory,
the glory as of a father's only son, full of grace and truth.
From his fullness we have all received, grace upon grace.
(John 1:1-4, 14, 16)

Inscription

This inscription may be made with chalk above the entrance:

20 + C M B + 26

Write the appropriate character (left) while speaking the text (right).

The magi of old, known as
C Caspar,
M Melchior, and
B Balthasar
followed the star of God's Son who came to dwell among us
20 two thousand
26 and twenty-six years ago.
\+ Christ, bless this house,
\+ and remain with us throughout the new year.

Prayer of Blessing

you revealed your Son to all people by the shining light of a star.
We pray that you bless this home and all who live here
with your gracious presence.
May your love be our inspiration, your wisdom our guide,
your truth our light, and your peace our benediction;
through Christ our Lord. Amen.

Then everyone may walk from room to room, blessing the house with incense or by sprinkling with water, perhaps using a branch from the Christmas tree.

Tuesday, January 6, 2026

Epiphany of Our Lord

Matthew 2:1-12

Christ revealed to the nations

Then Herod secretly called for the magi and learned from them the exact time when the star had appeared. Then he sent them to Bethlehem, saying, "Go and search diligently for the child, and when you have found him, bring me word so that I may also go and pay him homage." When they had heard the king, they set out, and there, ahead of them, went the star that they had seen in the east, until it stopped over the place where the child was. When they saw that the star had stopped, they were overwhelmed with joy. On entering the house, they saw the child with Mary his mother, and they knelt down and paid him homage. Then, opening their treasure chests, they offered him gifts of gold, frankincense, and myrrh. (Matt. 2:7-11)

Psalm

Psalm 72:1-7, 10-14
All shall bow down

Additional Readings

Isaiah 60:1-6
Nations come to the light

Ephesians 3:1-12
The gospel's promise for all

Hymn: As with Gladness Men of Old, ELW 302

O God, on this day you revealed your Son to the nations by the leading of a star. Lead us now by faith to know your presence in our lives, and bring us at last to the full vision of your glory, through your Son, Jesus Christ our Lord, who lives and reigns with you and the Holy Spirit, one God, now and forever.

Time after Epiphany

The season of Christmas rejoiced in Emmanuel, God is with us. In the time after Epiphany, the story moves from Mary's arms into the world, where Jesus teaches, heals, and feeds those he meets, manifesting the good news of heaven in daily life. On the Epiphany of Our Lord (January 6), hearts and homes join the whole church in recognizing God revealed in Jesus. The time after Epiphany invites us to consider: How might our faith in Christ shine in our lives, shared for the sake of friends and family, neighbors near and far?

Table Prayer for Epiphany and the Time after Epiphany (January 6– February 17)

Generous God,
your delight for creation is revealed in Jesus,
who sets wide tables and feeds multitudes,
who breaks and becomes bread for the whole world.
May this meal strengthen our bodies and illuminate our spirits
so that our whole lives shine with love from heaven.
Grant this through Christ our Lord.
Amen.

Wednesday, January 7, 2026

Time after Epiphany

1 Kings 10:1-13

Gifts to Solomon from Sheba

When the queen of Sheba heard of the fame of Solomon (fame due to the name of the LORD), she came to test him with riddles. She came to Jerusalem with a very great retinue, with camels bearing spices and very much gold and precious stones, and when she came to Solomon, she told him all that was on her mind. Solomon answered all her questions; there was nothing hidden from the king that he could not explain to her. When the queen of Sheba had observed all the wisdom of Solomon, the house that he had built, the food of his table, the seating of his officials, and the attendance of his servants, their clothing, his valets, and his burnt offerings that he offered at the house of the LORD, it took her breath away. (1 Kings 10:1-5)

Psalm

Psalm 72

Prayers for the king

Additional Reading

Ephesians 3:14-21

Knowing the love of Christ

Hymn: Ask the Complicated Questions, ACS 1005

God of the nations, you draw all people to the marvels you have wrought. Let us approach your handiwork with questions, wonder, and awe, honoring you fully even as your beauty takes our breath away.

Thursday, January 8, 2026

Time after Epiphany

Ephesians 4:7, 11-16

Gifts according to Christ

But each of us was given grace according to the measure of Christ's gift. . . .

He himself granted that some are apostles, prophets, evangelists, pastors and teachers to equip the saints for the work of ministry, for building up the body of Christ, until all of us come to the unity of the faith and of the knowledge of the Son of God, to maturity, to the measure of the full stature of Christ. (Eph. 4:7, 11-13)

Psalm

Psalm 72

Prayers for the king

Additional Reading

1 Kings 10:14-25

Solomon's splendor

Hymn: Let us Talents and Tongues Employ, ELW 674/TFF 232

God of every blessing, you give us diverse gifts, that together we might reflect your complexity. Inspire in us appreciation of those whose talents differ from our own, and generosity in offering to others what you have bestowed upon us.

Friday, January 9, 2026

Time After Epiphany

Micah 5:2-9

One who is to rule Israel

But you, O Bethlehem of Ephrathah,
who are one of the little clans of Judah,
from you shall come forth for me
one who is to rule in Israel,
whose origin is from of old,
from ancient days.
Therefore he shall give them up until the time
when she who is in labor has brought forth;
then the rest of his kindred shall return
to the people of Israel. (Mic. 5:2-3)

Psalm

Psalm 72

Prayers for the king

Additional Reading

Luke 13:31-35

Jerusalem that kills the prophets

Hymn: When the Poor Ones, ELW 725

God of great surprises, from the overlooked peoples of the world you raise up hope. May we learn to respect our siblings whom others disrespect, and approach all people with honor and the expectation that you may appear.

Saturday, January 10, 2026

Time after Epiphany

Psalm 29

The voice of God upon the waters

Ascribe to the LORD, O heavenly beings,
ascribe to the LORD glory and strength.
Ascribe to the LORD the glory of his name;
worship the LORD in holy splendor.

The voice of the LORD is over the waters;
the God of glory thunders,
the LORD, over mighty waters.
The voice of the LORD is powerful;
the voice of the LORD is full of majesty. (Ps. 29:1-4)

Additional Readings

1 Samuel 7:3-17
Samuel guides Israel to peace

Acts 9:19b-31
Barnabas introduces Saul/Paul in Jerusalem

Hymn: God of Tempest, God of Whirlwind, ELW 400

God of thunder and raging oceans, you hold all the vast cosmos in your hands, and yet you attend also to us. Teach us to know you as you are and to announce your goodness in word and deed.

Sunday, January 11, 2026

Baptism of Our Lord

Matthew 3:13-17

Christ revealed as God's servant

Then Jesus came from Galilee to John at the Jordan, to be baptized by him. John would have prevented him, saying, "I need to be baptized by you, and do you come to me?" But Jesus answered him, "Let it be so now, for it is proper for us in this way to fulfill all righteousness." Then he consented. And when Jesus had been baptized, just as he came up from the water, suddenly the heavens were opened to him and he saw God's Spirit descending like a dove and alighting on him. And a voice from the heavens said, "This is my Son, the Beloved, with whom I am well pleased." (Matt. 3:13-17)

Psalm

Psalm 29
The voice of God is upon the waters

Additional Readings

Isaiah 42:1-9
The servant of God brings justice

Acts 10:34-43
Jesus' ministry after his baptism

Hymn: When Jesus Came to Jordan, ELW 305

O God our Father, at the baptism of Jesus you proclaimed him your beloved Son and anointed him with the Holy Spirit. Make all who are baptized into Christ faithful to their calling to be your daughters and sons, and empower us all with your Spirit, through Jesus Christ, our Savior and Lord, who lives and reigns with you and the Holy Spirit, one God, now and forever.

Monday, January 12, 2026

Time after Epiphany

Psalm 89:5-37

God anoints David to be a son

Then you spoke in a vision to your faithful one and said,
    "I have set the crown on one who is mighty;
    I have exalted one chosen from the people.
I have found my servant David;
    with my holy oil I have anointed him;
my hand shall always remain with him;
    my arm also shall strengthen him.
The enemy shall not outwit him;
    the wicked shall not humble him.
I will crush his foes before him
    and strike down those who hate him.
My faithfulness and steadfast love shall be with him,
    and in my name his horn shall be exalted. (Ps. 89:19-24)

Additional Readings

Genesis 35:1-15

God calls and blesses Jacob

Acts 10:44-48

Through Peter, God calls gentiles to be baptized

Hymn: Lord, Keep Us Steadfast in Your Word, ELW 517

Faithful God, you raised up David to serve your people, anointing him as your own. Through his mix of faithfulness and waywardness, you sought to keep him on your just pathway. Thank you for taking our hand as our steadfast companion.

Tuesday, January 13, 2026

Time after Epiphany

Acts 8:4-13

Philip preaches and baptizes

Now a certain man named Simon had previously practiced magic in the city and amazed the people of Samaria, saying that he was someone great. All of them, from the least to the greatest, listened to him eagerly, saying, "This man is the power of God that is called Great." And they listened eagerly to him because for a long time he had amazed them with his magic. But when they believed Philip, who was proclaiming the good news about the kingdom of God and the name of Jesus Christ, they were baptized, both men and women. Even Simon himself believed. After being baptized, he stayed constantly with Philip and was amazed when he saw the signs and great miracles that took place. (Acts 8:9-13)

Psalm

Psalm 89:5-37

God anoints David to be a son

Additional Reading

Jeremiah 1:4-10

God calls Jeremiah

Hymn: Making Their Way, ACS 979

God of the gospel, we become enchanted by magical thinking and by unexplainable tricks that entertain us. Do not let us lose sight of the truth that we know in your Son, Jesus. In him alone is our true salvation.

Wednesday, January 14, 2026

Time after Epiphany

Isaiah 51:1-16

Through water God's people cross over

Look to Abraham your father
and to Sarah, who bore you,
for he was but one when I called him,
but I blessed him and made him many.
For the LORD will comfort Zion;
he will comfort all her waste places
and will make her wilderness like Eden,
her desert like the garden of the LORD;
joy and gladness will be found in her,
thanksgiving and the voice of song. (Isa. 51:2-3)

Psalm

Psalm 89:5-37

God anoints David to be a son

Additional Reading

Matthew 12:15-21

The words of Isaiah applied to Jesus

Hymn: O God, to You I Cry in Pain, ACS 1021

God of comfort, you meet us in the waste places and wilderness through which we stumble. Let the hope we long for blossom in the presence of your generosity. May we be known as a joyful people.

Thursday, January 15, 2026

Time after Epiphany

Martin Luther King Jr., renewer of society, martyr, died 1968

Psalm 40:1-11

Doing the will of God

I waited patiently for the LORD;
he inclined to me and heard my cry.
He drew me up from the desolate pit,
out of the miry bog,
and set my feet upon a rock,
making my steps secure.
He put a new song in my mouth,
a song of praise to our God.
Many will see and fear
and put their trust in the LORD. (Ps. 40:1-3)

Additional Readings

Isaiah 22:15-25
God replaces disobedient leaders

Galatians 1:6-12
Paul's calling through a revelation of Christ

Hymn: Don't Be Afraid, ACS 1027

Listening God, you incline your ear to us, and in your compassion we again find our voice. May the bogs under our feet become solid ground, that we might walk with confidence in your love.

Friday, January 16, 2026

Time after Epiphany

Acts 1:1-5

The promise of the Holy Spirit

In the first book, Theophilus, I wrote about all that Jesus began to do and teach until the day when he was taken up to heaven, after giving instructions through the Holy Spirit to the apostles whom he had chosen. After his suffering he presented himself alive to them by many convincing proofs, appearing to them during forty days and speaking about the kingdom of God. While staying with them, he ordered them not to leave Jerusalem but to wait there for the promise of the Father. "This," he said, "is what you have heard from me; for John baptized with water, but you will be baptized with the Holy Spirit not many days from now." (Acts 1:1-5)

Psalm

Psalm 40:1-11

Doing the will of God

Additional Reading

Genesis 27:30-38

Isaac and Esau discover Jacob's deceit

Hymn: I Love to Tell the Story, ELW 661/TFF 228

Promising God, you have raised up witnesses, that we might know the power of your salvation. We thank you for all those whom you inspire to announce your loving story. May your Spirit move us to join them.

Saturday, January 17, 2026

Time after Epiphany

Antony of Egypt, renewer of the church, died around 356
Pachomius, renewer of the church, died 346

1 Kings 19:19-21

Elijah calls Elisha to follow him

So he set out from there and found Elisha son of Shaphat, who was plowing. There were twelve yoke of oxen ahead of him, and he was with the twelfth. Elijah passed by him and threw his mantle over him. He left the oxen, ran after Elijah, and said, "Let me kiss my father and my mother, and then I will follow you." Then Elijah said to him, "Go back again, for what have I done to you?" He returned from following him, took the yoke of oxen, and slaughtered them; using the equipment from the oxen, he boiled their flesh and gave it to the people, and they ate. Then he set out and followed Elijah and became his servant. (1 Kings 19:19-21)

Psalm

Psalm 40:1-11
Doing the will of God

Additional Reading

Luke 5:1-11
Jesus calls the first disciples

Hymn: Guide My Feet, ACS 987/TFF 153

God of the journey, you give us space to say our goodbyes as we set out to follow your call. Forgive us when we take our own sweet time and, distracted, delay walking in the way you set before us.

Sunday, January 18, 2026

Second Sunday after Epiphany

Confession of Peter transferred to January 19

Week of Prayer for Christian Unity begins

John 1:29-42

Christ revealed as the Lamb of God

The next day he saw Jesus coming toward him and declared, "Here is the Lamb of God who takes away the sin of the world! This is he of whom I said, 'After me comes a man who ranks ahead of me because he was before me.' I myself did not know him, but I came baptizing with water for this reason, that he might be revealed to Israel." And John testified, "I saw the Spirit descending from heaven like a dove, and it remained on him. I myself did not know him, but the one who sent me to baptize with water said to me, 'He on whom you see the Spirit descend and remain is the one who baptizes with the Holy Spirit.' And I myself have seen and have testified that this is the Chosen One." (John 1:29-34)

Psalm

Psalm 40:1-11

Doing the will of God

Additional Readings

Isaiah 49:1-7

The servant brings light to the nations

1 Corinthians 1:1-9

Paul's greeting to the church at Corinth

Hymn: Lamb of God Most Holy, ACS 932

Holy God, our strength and our redeemer, by your Spirit hold us forever, that through your grace we may worship you and faithfully serve you, follow you and joyfully find you, through Jesus Christ, our Savior and Lord.

Monday, January 19, 2026

Confession of Peter (transferred)

Henry, Bishop of Uppsala, martyr, died 1156

Matthew 16:13-19

Peter confesses: You are the Messiah

He said to them, "But who do you say that I am?" Simon Peter answered, "You are the Messiah, the Son of the living God." And Jesus answered him, "Blessed are you, Simon son of Jonah! For flesh and blood has not revealed this to you but my Father in heaven. And I tell you, you are Peter, and on this rock I will build my church, and the gates of Hades will not prevail against it. I will give you the keys of the kingdom of heaven, and whatever you bind on earth will be bound in heaven, and whatever you loose on earth will be loosed in heaven." (Matt. 16:15-19)

Psalm

Psalm 18:1-6, 16-19
My God, my rock, worthy of praise

Additional Readings

Acts 4:8-13
Salvation is in no one other than Jesus

1 Corinthians 10:1-5
Drinking from the spiritual rock of Christ

Hymn: Christ Is Made the Sure Foundation, ELW 645

Almighty God, you inspired Simon Peter to confess Jesus as the Messiah and Son of the living God. Keep your church firm on the rock of this faith, that in unity and peace it may proclaim one truth and follow one Lord, your Son, Jesus Christ our Savior, who lives and reigns with you and the Holy Spirit, one God, now and forever.

Tuesday, January 20, 2026

Time after Epiphany

Psalm 40:6-17

Not sacrifice, but divine mercy

"I delight to do your will, O my God;
your law is within my heart."

I have told the glad news of deliverance
in the great congregation;
see, I have not restrained my lips,
as you know, O LORD.
I have not hidden your saving help within my heart;
I have spoken of your faithfulness and your salvation;
I have not concealed your steadfast love and your faithfulness
from the great congregation. (Ps. 40:8-10)

Additional Readings

Isaiah 53:1-12
The one like a lamb

Hebrews 10:1-4
Animal sacrifices cannot take away sins

Hymn: Come, Thou Fount of Every Blessing, ELW 807/TFF 108

Exuberant God, may the delight you shower upon us so fully deliver us that we cannot help but share your goodness with the world. Let your story of salvation be ever found in our mouths.

Wednesday, January 21, 2026

Time after Epiphany

Agnes, martyr, died around 304

Isaiah 48:12-21

God saves the people through water

Thus says the LORD,
    your Redeemer, the Holy One of Israel:
I am the LORD your God,
    who teaches you how to succeed,
    who leads you in the way you should go.
O that you had paid attention to my commandments!
    Then your prosperity would have been like a river
    and your success like the waves of the sea;
your offspring would have been like the sand
    and your descendants like its grains;
their name would never be cut off
    or destroyed from before me. (Isa. 48:17-19)

Psalm

Psalm 40:6-17
Not sacrifice, but divine mercy

Additional Reading

Matthew 9:14-17
Christ, the bridegroom, the new wine

Hymn: Come, My Way, My Truth, My Life, ELW 816

God, you open before us the way that we should go and ask us to walk forward in faith. You promise us success unlike that which the world gives. Help us to love you and our neighbor as Jesus did.

Thursday, January 22, 2026

Time after Epiphany

Psalm 27:1-6

God is light and salvation

One thing I asked of the LORD;
this I seek:
to live in the house of the LORD
all the days of my life,
to behold the beauty of the LORD,
and to inquire in his temple.

For he will hide me in his shelter
in the day of trouble;
he will conceal me under the cover of his tent;
he will set me high on a rock. (Ps. 27:4-5)

Additional Readings

1 Samuel 1:1-20
The birth of Samuel

Galatians 1:11-24
The divine origin of Paul's gospel

Hymn: All Are Welcome, ELW 641

Sheltering God, as your Son Jesus abided with us in this place called Earth, you promise us a dwelling place where we may abide with you forever. Help us to understand the protection, freedom, and security that come with this assurance.

Friday, January 23, 2026

Time after Epiphany

1 Samuel 9:27—10:8

Saul anointed by Samuel as king

As they were going down to the outskirts of the town, Samuel said to Saul, "Tell the young man to go on before us, and when he has passed on, stop here yourself for a while, that I may make known to you the word of God." Samuel took a vial of oil and poured it on his head and kissed him; he said, "The LORD has anointed you ruler over his people Israel. You shall reign over the people of the LORD, and you will save them from the hand of their enemies all around." (1 Sam. 9:27—10:1a)

Psalm

Psalm 27:1-6

God is light and salvation

Additional Reading

Galatians 2:1-10

Paul's authority in the growing church

Hymn: Anointing Fall on Me, ACS 1013

Anointing God, as you once claimed Saul with a vial of oil, you have sealed us by the Holy Spirit and marked us with the cross forever. May we live ever aware of this powerful gift.

Saturday, January 24, 2026

Time after Epiphany

Luke 5:27-32

The call of Levi

After this he went out and saw a tax collector named Levi sitting at the tax-collection station, and he said to him, "Follow me." And he got up, left everything, and followed him.

Then Levi gave a great banquet for him in his house, and there was a large crowd of tax collectors and others reclining at the table with them. The Pharisees and their scribes were complaining to his disciples, saying, "Why do you eat and drink with tax collectors and sinners?" Jesus answered them, "Those who are well have no need of a physician but those who are sick; I have not come to call the righteous but sinners to repentance." (Luke 5:27-32)

Psalm

Psalm 27:1-6

God is light and salvation

Additional Reading

1 Samuel 15:34—16:13

God leads Gideon to victory

Hymn: What a Friend We Have in Jesus, ELW 742

Astonishing God, we use many names to proclaim your greatness. How strange and wonderful that the title you hold dear is "friend of sinners." We sinners thank you for your amazing grace and hospitality.

Sunday, January 25, 2026

Third Sunday after Epiphany

Conversion of Paul transferred to January 26

Week of Prayer for Christian Unity ends

Matthew 4:12-23

Christ revealed as a prophet

Now when Jesus heard that John had been arrested, he withdrew to Galilee. He left Nazareth and made his home in Capernaum by the sea, in the territory of Zebulun and Naphtali, so that what had been spoken through the prophet Isaiah might be fulfilled:

"Land of Zebulun, land of Naphtali,
on the road by the sea, across the Jordan, Galilee of the gentiles—
the people who sat in darkness
have seen a great light,
and for those who sat in the region and shadow of death
light has dawned." (Matt. 4:12-16)

Psalm

Psalm 27:1, 4-9
God is light and salvation

Additional Readings

Isaiah 9:1-4
Light shines for those in darkness

1 Corinthians 1:10-18
An appeal for unity in the gospel

Hymn: Christ, Be Our Light, ELW 715

Lord God, your loving kindness always goes before us and follows after us. Summon us into your light, and direct our steps in the ways of goodness that come through the cross of your Son, Jesus Christ, our Savior and Lord.

Monday, January 26, 2026
Conversion of Paul (transferred)

Timothy, Titus, and Silas, missionaries

Galatians 1:11-24

Paul receives a revelation of Christ

You have heard, no doubt, of my earlier life in Judaism. I was violently persecuting the church of God and was trying to destroy it. I advanced in Judaism beyond many among my people of the same age, for I was far more zealous for the traditions of my ancestors. But when the one who had set me apart before I was born and called me through his grace was pleased to reveal his Son to me, so that I might proclaim him among the gentiles, I did not confer with any human, nor did I go up to Jerusalem to those who were already apostles before me, but I went away at once into Arabia, and afterward I returned to Damascus. (Gal. 1:13-17)

Psalm

Psalm 67
Let all the peoples praise you, O God

Additional Readings

Acts 9:1-22
Saul is converted to Christ

Luke 21:10-19
The end times will require endurance

Hymn: How Clear Is Our Vocation, Lord, ELW 580

O God, by the preaching of your apostle Paul you have caused the light of the gospel to shine throughout the world. Grant that we may follow his example and be witnesses to the truth of your Son, Jesus Christ, our Savior and Lord, who lives and reigns with you and the Holy Spirit, one God, now and forever.

Tuesday, January 27, 2026

Time after Epiphany

Lydia, Dorcas, and Phoebe, witnesses to the faith

Psalm 27:7-14

Take courage in God

Hear, O Lord, when I cry aloud;
be gracious to me and answer me!
"Come," my heart says, "seek his face!"
Your face, Lord, do I seek.
Do not hide your face from me.

Do not turn your servant away in anger,
you who have been my help.
Do not cast me off; do not forsake me,
O God of my salvation! (Ps. 27:7-9)

Additional Readings

Judges 7:12-22
God leads Gideon to victory

Philippians 2:12-18
The call to shine like stars

Hymn: In the Midst of Earthly Life, ACS 1026

At times, O Lord, we seek your face and cannot find it. Life sends us hardships; we know our own failings; bad things unexpectedly happen. May the clouds part so that your presence might shine upon us.

Wednesday, January 28, 2026

Time after Epiphany

Thomas Aquinas, teacher, died 1274

Luke 1:67-79

Christ, the light dawning

Then his father Zechariah was filled with the Holy Spirit and prophesied:

"Blessed be the Lord God of Israel,
    for he has looked favorably on his people and redeemed them.
He has raised up a mighty savior for us
    in the house of his child David,
as he spoke through the mouth of his holy prophets from of old,
    that we would be saved from our enemies and from the hand of all
        who hate us." (Luke 1:67-71)

Psalm

Psalm 27:7-14

Take courage in God

Additional Reading

Genesis 49:1-2, 8-13, 21-26

Judah, Zebulun, Naphtali, and Joseph blessed

Hymn: Blessed Be the God of Israel, ELW 250

God of the prophets, for generations you promised to send us one who would redeem us from our sin. In Jesus, this mighty savior has arrived. May his name and yours be blessed.

Thursday, January 29, 2026

Time after Epiphany

Psalm 15

Abiding on God's holy hill

O Lord, who may abide in your tent?
    Who may dwell on your holy hill?

Those who walk blamelessly and do what is right
    and speak the truth from their heart;
who do not slander with their tongue
    and do no evil to their friends
    nor heap shame upon their neighbors;
in whose eyes the wicked are despised
    but who honor those who fear the Lord;
who stand by their oath even to their hurt;
who do not lend money at interest
    and do not take a bribe against the innocent. (Ps. 15:1-5a)

Additional Readings

Deuteronomy 16:18-20
Pursue only justice

1 Peter 3:8-12
Repay evil with a blessing

Hymn: Just As I Am, without One Plea, ELW 592

Righteous God, by ourselves there is nothing that would permit us to enter your presence, but you have met us with an everlasting love in Jesus. You embrace us, that our shame might cease.

Friday, January 30, 2026

Time after Epiphany

Deuteronomy 24:17—25:4

Do not deprive others of justice

"You shall not deprive a resident alien or an orphan of justice; you shall not take a widow's garment in pledge. Remember that you were a slave in Egypt and the LORD your God redeemed you from there; therefore I command you to do this.

"When you reap your harvest in your field and forget a sheaf in the field, you shall not go back to get it; it shall be left for the alien, the orphan, and the widow, so that the LORD your God may bless you in all your undertakings. When you beat your olive trees, do not strip what is left; it shall be for the alien, the orphan, and the widow." (Deut. 24:17-20)

Psalm

Psalm 15

Abiding on God's holy hill

Additional Reading

1 Timothy 5:17-24

Good works are conspicuous

Hymn: What Is the World Like, ACS 1047

Lover of strangers, teach us to share your love with refugees and immigrants seeking a secure and peaceful life. Motivate us to feed and care for them. Help us to celebrate the gift they are in our communities.

Saturday, January 31, 2026

Time after Epiphany

John 13:31-35

The new commandment

When he had gone out, Jesus said, "Now the Son of Man has been glorified, and God has been glorified in him. If God has been glorified in him, God will also glorify him in himself and will glorify him at once. Little children, I am with you only a little longer. You will look for me, and as I said to the Jews so now I say to you, 'Where I am going, you cannot come.' I give you a new commandment, that you love one another. Just as I have loved you, you also should love one another. By this everyone will know that you are my disciples, if you have love for one another." (John 13:31-35)

Psalm

Psalm 15
Abiding on God's holy hill

Additional Reading

Ruth 2:1-16
Ruth, one of the hungry

Hymn: Lord, Whose Love in Humble Service, ELW 712

Gracious God, sometimes the most basic thing is the most difficult for us to do. Guide your children until we learn to love others as Jesus first loved us. In this love we glimpse your glory.

Prayer List for February

Sunday, February 1, 2026

Fourth Sunday after Epiphany

Matthew 5:1-12

The teaching of Christ: Beatitudes

When Jesus saw the crowds, he went up the mountain, and after he sat down, his disciples came to him. And he began to speak and taught them, saying: . . .

"Blessed are those who are persecuted for the sake of righteousness, for theirs is the kingdom of heaven.

"Blessed are you when people revile you and persecute you and utter all kinds of evil against you falsely on my account. Rejoice and be glad, for your reward is great in heaven, for in the same way they persecuted the prophets who were before you." (Matt. 5:1-2, 10-12)

Psalm

Psalm 15
Abiding on God's holy hill

Additional Readings

Micah 6:1-8
The offering of justice, kindness, humility

1 Corinthians 1:18-31
Christ crucified, the wisdom and power of God

Hymn: Abide with Me, ELW 629

Holy God, you confound the world's wisdom in giving your kingdom to the lowly and the pure in heart. Give us such a hunger and thirst for justice, and perseverance in striving for peace, that in our words and deeds the world may see the life of your Son, Jesus Christ, our Savior and Lord.

Monday, February 2, 2026

Presentation of Our Lord

Luke 2:22-40

The child is brought to the temple

Simeon took him in his arms and praised God, saying,
 "Master, now you are dismissing your servant in peace,
  according to your word,
 for my eyes have seen your salvation,
  which you have prepared in the presence of all peoples,
 a light for revelation to the gentiles
  and for glory to your people Israel." (Luke 2:28-32)

Psalm

Psalm 84
How dear to me is your dwelling, O LORD

Additional Readings

Malachi 3:1-4
My messenger, a refiner and purifier

Hebrews 2:14-18
Jesus shares human flesh and sufferings

Hymn: This Is the Spirit's Entry Now, ELW 448

Almighty and ever-living God, your only-begotten Son was presented this day in the temple. May we be presented to you with clean and pure hearts by the same Jesus Christ our great high priest, who lives and reigns with you and the Holy Spirit, one God, now and forever.

Tuesday, February 3, 2026

Time after Epiphany

Ansgar, Bishop of Hamburg, missionary to Denmark and Sweden, died 865

Psalm 37:1-17

God will bless the righteous

The wicked draw the sword and bend their bows
  to bring down the poor and needy,
  to kill those who walk uprightly;
their sword shall enter their own heart,
  and their bows shall be broken.

Better is a little that the righteous person has
  than the abundance of many wicked.
For the arms of the wicked shall be broken,
  but the LORD upholds the righteous. (Ps. 37:14-17)

Additional Readings

Ruth 2:1-16
Ruth, one of the hungry

James 5:1-6
A warning to the ungenerous

Hymn: Take My Life, That I May Be, ELW 583/685

God of grace, you look with favor on those who are hungry, hurting, or lonely. Guide us in the way of your love as we strive to care for our neighbors, our communities, and each other.

Wednesday, February 4, 2026

Time after Epiphany

Luke 6:17-26

The beatitudes in Luke's gospel

[Jesus] came down with them and stood on a level place with a great crowd of his disciples and a great multitude of people from all Judea, Jerusalem, and the coast of Tyre and Sidon. They had come to hear him and to be healed of their diseases, and those who were troubled with unclean spirits were cured. And everyone in the crowd was trying to touch him, for power came out from him and healed all of them. (Luke 6:17-19)

Psalm

Psalm 37:1-17

God will bless the righteous

Additional Reading

Ruth 3:1-13; 4:13-22

Ruth, one of the blessed

Hymn: Lord, Listen to Your Children Praying, ELW 752/TFF 247

Merciful God, we come to you in times of grief and times of uncertainty. Restore our spirits. Wrap all who mourn in your compassion, strengthen communities of care, and remind us always of your love.

Thursday, February 5, 2026

Time after Epiphany

The Martyrs of Japan, died 1597

Psalm 112:1-9 [10]

Light shines in the darkness

Praise the LORD!
    Happy are those who fear the LORD,
    who greatly delight in his commandments.
Their descendants will be mighty in the land;
    the generation of the upright will be blessed.
Wealth and riches are in their houses,
    and their righteousness endures forever.
They rise in the darkness as a light for the upright;
    they are gracious, merciful, and righteous. (Ps. 112:1-4)

Additional Readings

Deuteronomy 4:1-14
The discipline of faith

1 John 5:1-5
God's children obey God's commandments

Hymn: The Word of God Is Source and Seed, ELW 506

Holy God, you created the stars, the soil, and each of us, your stewards of the lands we call home. Kindle in us a renewed desire to pay attention to the beauty of the earth, from sidewalk cracks to redwoods.

Friday, February 6, 2026

Time after Epiphany

James 3:13-18

A gentle life born of wisdom

Who is wise and knowledgeable among you? Show by your good life that your works are done with gentleness born of wisdom. But if you have bitter envy and selfish ambition in your hearts, do not be arrogant and lie about the truth. This is not wisdom that comes down from above but is earthly, unspiritual, devilish. For where there is envy and selfish ambition, there will also be disorder and wickedness of every kind. But the wisdom from above is first pure, then peaceable, gentle, willing to yield, full of mercy and good fruits, without a trace of partiality or hypocrisy. And the fruit of righteousness is sown in peace by those who make peace. (James 3:13-18)

Psalm

Psalm 112:1-9 [10]

Light shines in the darkness

Additional Reading

Isaiah 29:1-12

Hunger that goes unsatisfied

Hymn: Let Us Enter In, ACS 985

God of justice, sometimes peace seems far away, and in the midst of war, family conflict, or the busyness of life we can feel overwhelmed. Be with us as we try to live out your love in our lives.

Saturday, February 7, 2026

Time after Epiphany

Isaiah 29:13-16

Hearts far from God

The LORD said:
Because these people draw near with their mouths
  and honor me with their lips,
  while their hearts are far from me
and their worship of me is a human commandment learned by rote,
    so I will again do
  amazing things with this people,
  shocking and amazing.
The wisdom of their wise shall perish,
  and the discernment of the discerning shall be hidden.
(Isa. 29:13-14)

Psalm

Psalm 112:1-9 [10]
Light shines in the darkness

Additional Reading

Mark 7:1-8
The hypocrisy of lip service

Hymn: Lord, Let My Heart Be Good Soil, ELW 512/TFF 131

Glorious God, there is mystery and wonder all around us. Open our hearts to the new things you are doing in our lives and in the world, as we also honor those who have gone before us.

Sunday, February 8, 2026

Fifth Sunday after Epiphany

Matthew 5:13-20

The teaching of Christ: salt and light

[Jesus said:] "You are the salt of the earth, but if salt has lost its taste, how can its saltiness be restored? It is no longer good for anything but is thrown out and trampled under foot.

"You are the light of the world. A city built on a hill cannot be hid. People do not light a lamp and put it under the bushel basket; rather, they put it on the lampstand, and it gives light to all in the house. In the same way, let your light shine before others, so that they may see your good works and give glory to your Father in heaven." (Matt. 5:13-16)

Psalm

Psalm 112:1-9 [10]
Light shines in the darkness

Additional Readings

Isaiah 58:1-9a [9b-12]
The fast that God chooses

1 Corinthians 2:1-12 [13-16]
God's wisdom revealed through the Spirit

Hymn: Christ, Be Our Light, ELW 715

Lord God, with endless mercy you receive the prayers of all who call upon you. By your Spirit show us the things we ought to do, and give us the grace and power to do them, through Jesus Christ, our Savior and Lord.

Monday, February 9, 2026

Time after Epiphany

Psalm 119:105-112

The law is light

Accept my offerings of praise, O LORD,
    and teach me your ordinances.
I hold my life in my hand continually,
    but I do not forget your law.
The wicked have laid a snare for me,
    but I do not stray from your precepts.
Your decrees are my heritage forever;
    they are the joy of my heart.
I incline my heart to perform your statutes
    forever, to the end. (Ps. 119:108-112)

Additional Readings

2 Kings 22:3-20
Huldah urges Josiah to keep the law

Romans 11:2-10
A remnant remains faithful

Hymn: Neither Death nor Life, ELW 622

Loving God, protect us from all the forces in the world that would pull us away from you. Renew our spirits and our songs. When we feel far from you, wrap us in your compassion, mercy, and care.

Tuesday, February 10, 2026

Time after Epiphany

2 Corinthians 4:1-12

Christ, the light

Therefore, since it is by God's mercy that we are engaged in this ministry, we do not lose heart. We have renounced the shameful, underhanded ways; we refuse to practice cunning or to falsify God's word, but by the open statement of the truth we commend ourselves to the conscience of everyone in the sight of God. And even if our gospel is veiled, it is veiled to those who are perishing. In their case the god of this world has blinded the minds of the unbelievers, to keep them from seeing clearly the light of the gospel of the glory of Christ, who is the image of God. For we do not proclaim ourselves; we proclaim Jesus Christ as Lord and ourselves as your slaves for Jesus's sake. For it is the God who said, "Light will shine out of darkness," who has shone in our hearts to give the light of the knowledge of the glory of God in the face of Christ. (2 Cor. 4:1-6)

Psalm

Psalm 119:105-112

The law is light

Additional Reading

2 Kings 23:1-8, 21-25

King Josiah keeps the law

Hymn: Light Dawns on a Weary World, ELW 726

Abundant God, we proclaim Christ again and again—at the dinner table, in our hearts, and in our communities. Empower us to be reflections of your grace and love, and to renounce anything that distracts us from you.

Wednesday, February 11, 2026

Time after Epiphany

John 8:12-30

Christ the light of the world

Again Jesus spoke to them, saying, "I am the light of the world. Whoever follows me will never walk in darkness but will have the light of life." Then the Pharisees said to him, "You are testifying on your own behalf; your testimony is not valid." Jesus answered, "Even if I testify on my own behalf, my testimony is valid because I know where I have come from and where I am going, but you do not know where I come from or where I am going." (John 8:12-14)

Psalm

Psalm 119:105-112

The law is light

Additional Reading

Proverbs 6:6-23

The law is a lamp

Hymn: Faith Begins by Letting Go, ACS 1004

God of shelter, you know our going out and our coming in. May we confidently trust in you. Allow that trust to spark generosity and curiosity toward our neighbors and all of your creation.

Thursday, February 12, 2026
Time after Epiphany

Psalm 2

The one begotten of God

I will tell of the decree of the LORD:
He said to me, "You are my son;
today I have begotten you.
Ask of me, and I will make the nations your heritage
and the ends of the earth your possession.
You shall break them with a rod of iron
and dash them in pieces like a potter's vessel."

Now therefore, O kings, be wise;
be warned, O rulers of the earth.
Serve the LORD with fear;
with trembling kiss his feet,
or he will be angry, and you will perish in the way,
for his wrath is quickly kindled.
Happy are all who take refuge in him. (Ps. 2:7-12)

Additional Readings

Exodus 6:2-9
God promises deliverance through Moses

Hebrews 8:1-7
Christ, the mediator

Hymn: There's a Wideness in God's Mercy, ELW 587/588

Creator God, you are our refuge and our strength. Comfort and restore all who mourn, all who are living through times of turmoil and uncertainty, and all who are experiencing illness. Help us be Christ for one another.

Friday, February 13, 2026

Time after Epiphany

Hebrews 11:23-28

The faith of Moses

By faith Moses was hidden by his parents for three months after his birth, because they saw that the child was beautiful, and they were not afraid of the king's edict. By faith Moses, when he was grown up, refused to be called a son of Pharaoh's daughter, choosing rather to share ill-treatment with the people of God than to enjoy the fleeting pleasures of sin. He considered abuse suffered for the Christ to be greater wealth than the treasures of Egypt, for he was looking ahead to the reward. By faith he left Egypt, unafraid of the king's anger, for he persevered as though he saw him who is invisible. By faith he kept the Passover and the sprinkling of blood, so that the destroyer of the firstborn would not touch the firstborn of Israel. (Heb. 11:23-28)

Psalm

Psalm 2

The one begotten of God

Additional Reading

Exodus 19:9b-25

Israel consecrated at Sinai

Hymn: Goodness Is Stronger Than Evil, ELW 721

God of mercy, you are present with people from every time and place. Connect us with our siblings in faith from all walks of life, and from all countries and backgrounds, as we joyfully live out your love.

Saturday, February 14, 2026

Time after Epiphany

Cyril, monk, died 869; Methodius, bishop, died 885; missionaries to the Slavs

Mark 9:9-13

The coming of Elijah

As they were coming down the mountain, he ordered them to tell no one about what they had seen, until after the Son of Man had risen from the dead. So they kept the matter to themselves, questioning what this rising from the dead could mean. Then they asked him, "Why do the scribes say that Elijah must come first?" He said to them, "Elijah is indeed coming first to restore all things. How then is it written about the Son of Man, that he is to go through many sufferings and be treated with contempt? But I tell you that Elijah has come, and they did to him whatever they pleased, as it is written about him." (Mark 9:9-13)

Psalm

Psalm 2

The one begotten of God

Additional Reading

1 Kings 21:20-29

Elijah pronounces God's sentence

Hymn: O Living Breath of God, ELW 407

Eternal God, as we read and listen to your word, remind us that we are connected to all the faithful people who came before us, and to all who will come after us. Thank you for weaving us into your story of salvation.

Sunday, February 15, 2026

Transfiguration of Our Lord

Matthew 17:1-9

Christ revealed as God's beloved Son

Six days later, Jesus took with him Peter and James and his brother John and led them up a high mountain, by themselves. And he was transfigured before them, and his face shone like the sun, and his clothes became bright as light. Suddenly there appeared to them Moses and Elijah, talking with him. Then Peter said to Jesus, "Lord, it is good for us to be here; if you wish, I will set up three tents here, one for you, one for Moses, and one for Elijah." While he was still speaking, suddenly a bright cloud overshadowed them, and a voice from the cloud said, "This is my Son, the Beloved; with him I am well pleased; listen to him!" (Matt. 17:1-5)

Psalm

Psalm 2
The one begotten of God

Additional Readings

Exodus 24:12-18
Moses enters the cloud of God's glory

2 Peter 1:16-21
Shining with the glory of God

Hymn: O Christ, What Can It Mean for Us, ELW 431

O God, in the transfiguration of your Son you confirmed the mysteries of the faith by the witness of Moses and Elijah, and in the voice from the bright cloud declaring Jesus your beloved Son, you foreshadowed our adoption as your children. Make us heirs with Christ of your glory, and bring us to enjoy its fullness, through Jesus Christ, our Savior and Lord, who lives and reigns with you and the Holy Spirit, one God, now and forever.

Monday, February 16, 2026

Time after Epiphany

Psalm 78:17-20, 52-55

Israel led to God's holy mountain

Then he led out his people like sheep
    and guided them in the wilderness like a flock.
He led them in safety so that they were not afraid,
    but the sea overwhelmed their enemies.
And he brought them to his holy hill,
    to the mountain that his right hand had won.
He drove out nations before them;
    he apportioned them for a possession
    and settled the tribes of Israel in their tents. (Ps. 78:52-55)

Additional Readings

Exodus 33:7-23
Moses asks to see God's glory

Acts 7:30-34
Moses on holy ground

Hymn: When the Poor Ones, ELW 725

God, you are a shepherd to your people. Shelter us when we need your care, and strengthen us so that we have the ability to care for others. Reveal yourself to us in each person we meet.

Tuesday, February 17, 2026

Time after Epiphany

Romans 11:1-6

A remnant chosen by grace

I ask, then, has God rejected his people? By no means! I myself am an Israelite, a descendant of Abraham, a member of the tribe of Benjamin. God has not rejected his people whom he foreknew. Do you not know what the scripture says of Elijah, how he pleads with God against Israel? "Lord, they have killed your prophets, they have demolished your altars; I alone am left, and they are seeking my life." But what is the divine reply to him? "I have kept for myself seven thousand who have not bowed the knee to Baal." So, too, at the present time there is a remnant chosen by grace. (Rom. 11:1-5)

Psalm

Psalm 78:17-20, 52-55

Israel led to God's holy mountain

Additional Reading

1 Kings 19:9-18

Elijah hears God

Hymn: My Hope Is Built on Nothing Less, ELW 596/TFF 192

Holy God, you draw all people to yourself. Whether we are in a season of abundance or scarcity, hope or despair, wellness or illness, you are with us. Bring us ever nearer to you and to our neighbors, through your grace.

Lent

Lent is a forty-day journey from Ash Wednesday to Easter. Christians enter into this time of discernment with Noah's family, sheltered by God in the ark for forty days; with the Israelites whom God freed from slavery, who journeyed through the desert for forty years; and with Moses, Elijah, and Jesus, who fasted for forty days in order to prepare for lives of faithfulness..

During Lent Christians journey with those who are preparing for baptism at Easter. With them we all reflect on our responses to the baptismal questions: Do you renounce the forces and powers that defy and rebel against God? Do you believe in God the Father, the Son, and the Holy Spirit? (*ELW*, p. 229)

We renew our promise to live among God's people, to hear God's word and receive the Lord's supper, to proclaim in word and deed the good news, to serve others following Jesus' example, and to strive for justice and peace in all the earth (*ELW*, p. 236). In preparation for this renewal many Christians take up the traditional Lenten practices of prayer, fasting, and giving to people in need.

Table Prayer for the Season of Lent

Blessed are you, O God, giver of all.
You send us daily bread
and invite us to accompany you
in the transformation of the world.
Be present with us as we eat this meal
and share our joys and sorrows.
Send us out to be bread for others in a world hungry for your mercy.
In Jesus' name we pray. Amen.

Wednesday, February 18, 2026

Ash Wednesday

Martin Luther, renewer of the church, died 1546

Matthew 6:1-6, 16-21

The practice of faith

[Jesus said,] "Do not store up for yourselves treasures on earth, where moth and rust consume and where thieves break in and steal, but store up for yourselves treasures in heaven, where neither moth nor rust consumes and where thieves do not break in and steal. For where your treasure is, there your heart will be also." (Matt. 6:19-21)

Psalm

Psalm 51:1-17
Plea for mercy

Additional Readings

Joel 2:1-2, 12-17
Return to God

2 Corinthians 5:20b—6:10
Now is the day of salvation

Hymn: What Is the World Like, ACS 1047

Gracious God, out of your love and mercy you breathed into dust the breath of life, creating us to serve you and our neighbors. Call forth our prayers and acts of kindness, and strengthen us to face our mortality with confidence in the mercy of your Son, Jesus Christ, our Savior and Lord, who lives and reigns with you and the Holy Spirit, one God, now and forever.

Thursday, February 19, 2026

Week before Lent 1

Psalm 51

Create in me a clean heart

Have mercy on me, O God,
according to your steadfast love;
according to your abundant mercy,
blot out my transgressions.
Wash me thoroughly from my iniquity,
and cleanse me from my sin.

For I know my transgressions,
and my sin is ever before me.
Against you, you alone, have I sinned
and done what is evil in your sight,
so that you are justified in your sentence
and blameless when you pass judgment.
Indeed, I was born guilty,
a sinner when my mother conceived me. (Ps. 51:1-5)

Additional Readings

Jonah 3:1-10
Nineveh hears Jonah's preaching and repents

Romans 1:1-7
Appointed to preach the good news of Christ

Hymn: God, When Human Bonds Are Broken, ELW 603

Loving God, we are human. We fall short of being the people you call us to be. We sin; we harm one another and the earth. Forgive us, and help us forgive each other, as we return to your mercy and care.

Friday, February 20, 2026

Week before Lent 1

Jonah 4:1-11

God mercifully reproves Jonah

But this was very displeasing to Jonah, and he became angry. He prayed to the LORD and said, "O LORD! Is not this what I said while I was still in my own country? That is why I fled to Tarshish at the beginning, for I knew that you are a gracious and merciful God, slow to anger, abounding in steadfast love, and relenting from punishment. And now, O LORD, please take my life from me, for it is better for me to die than to live." And the LORD said, "Is it right for you to be angry?" Then Jonah went out of the city and sat down east of the city and made a booth for himself there. He sat under it in the shade, waiting to see what would become of the city. (Jonah 4:1-5)

Psalm

Psalm 51

Create in me a clean heart

Additional Reading

Romans 1:8-17

Live by faith

Hymn: Healer of Our Every Ill, ELW 612

Compassionate God, you created us with both free will and the ability to listen for your voice. Guide us as we make decisions, and remind us that you pour out abundant grace as we learn and grow.

Saturday, February 21, 2026

Week before Lent 1

Isaiah 58:1-12

The fast that God chooses

Is not this the fast that I choose:
to loose the bonds of injustice,
to undo the straps of the yoke,
to let the oppressed go free,
and to break every yoke?
Is it not to share your bread with the hungry
and bring the homeless poor into your house;
when you see the naked, to cover them
and not to hide yourself from your own kin?
Then your light shall break forth like the dawn,
and your healing shall spring up quickly;
your vindicator shall go before you;
the glory of the LORD shall be your rear guard.
Then you shall call, and the LORD will answer;
you shall cry for help, and he will say, "Here I am." (Isa. 58:6-9a)

Psalm

Psalm 51

Create in me a clean heart

Additional Reading

Matthew 18:1-7

The humble one is the greatest

Hymn: Here I Am, Lord, ELW 574/TFF 230

God of the margins, transform us in response to your love. Help us be attentive to the way we are bound up in harmful systems, and show us a new way of compassion and grace through Christ.

Sunday, February 22, 2026

First Sunday in Lent

Matthew 4:1-11

The temptation of Jesus

Then Jesus was led up by the Spirit into the wilderness to be tested by the devil. He fasted forty days and forty nights, and afterward he was famished. The tempter came and said to him, "If you are the Son of God, command these stones to become loaves of bread." But he answered, "It is written,

'One does not live by bread alone,
but by every word that comes from the mouth of God.'"

(Matt. 4:1-4)

Psalm

Psalm 32
Mercy embraces us

Additional Readings

Genesis 2:15-17; 3:1-7
Eating of the tree of knowledge

Romans 5:12-19
Death came, life comes

Hymn: Loaves Were Broken, Words Were Spoken, ACS 966

Lord God, our strength, the struggle between good and evil rages within and around us, and the devil and all the forces that defy you tempt us with empty promises. Keep us steadfast in your word, and when we fall, raise us again and restore us through your Son, Jesus Christ, our Savior and Lord, who lives and reigns with you and the Holy Spirit, one God, now and forever.

Monday, February 23, 2026

Week of Lent 1

Polycarp, Bishop of Smyrna, martyr, died 156

Psalm 32

Mercy embraces us

Then I acknowledged my sin to you,
    and I did not hide my iniquity;
I said, "I will confess my transgressions to the LORD,"
    and you forgave the guilt of my sin.

Therefore let all who are faithful
    offer prayer to you;
at a time of distress, the rush of mighty waters
    shall not reach them.
You are a hiding place for me;
    you preserve me from trouble;
    you surround me with glad cries of deliverance. (Ps. 32:5-7)

Additional Readings

1 Kings 19:1-8
An angel feeds Elijah in the wilderness

Hebrews 2:10-18
Christ goes before us in suffering

Hymn: O God, We Call, ACS 1075

O Lord Jesus, make us instruments of your peace, that where there is hatred, we may sow love, where there is injury, pardon, and where there is despair, hope. Grant, O divine master, that we may seek to console, to understand, and to love in your name, for you live and reign with the Father and the Holy Spirit, one God, now and forever.

Tuesday, February 24, 2026

Week of Lent 1

Hebrews 4:14—5:10

Christ was tempted as we are

Since, then, we have a great high priest who has passed through the heavens, Jesus, the Son of God, let us hold fast to our confession. For we do not have a high priest who is unable to sympathize with our weaknesses, but we have one who in every respect has been tested as we are, yet without sin. Let us therefore approach the throne of grace with boldness, so that we may receive mercy and find grace to help in time of need. (Heb. 4:14-16)

Psalm

Psalm 32

Mercy embraces us

Additional Reading

Genesis 4:1-16

God protects Cain

Hymn: Build Us Up, Lord, ELW 670

God of grace, you encourage us to come to you with all that weighs on our minds and hearts. Receive our prayers, and remind us that you name and claim us as beloved children.

Wednesday, February 25, 2026

Week of Lent 1

Elizabeth Fedde, deaconess, died 1921

Matthew 18:10-14

Not one of these little ones should be lost

[Jesus said,] "Take care that you do not despise one of these little ones, for I tell you, in heaven their angels continually see the face of my Father in heaven. What do you think? If a shepherd has a hundred sheep and one of them has gone astray, does he not leave the ninety-nine on the mountains and go in search of the one that went astray? And if he finds it, truly I tell you, he rejoices over it more than over the ninety-nine that never went astray. So it is not the will of your Father in heaven that one of these little ones should be lost." (Matt. 18:10-14)

Psalm

Psalm 32

Mercy embraces us

Additional Reading

Exodus 34:1-9, 27-28

God's revelation of mercy

Hymn: Will You Let Me Be Your Servant, ELW 659

Creator God, sometimes we lose our way and stray from your love. Call us back to you. Call us back to ourselves. Help us be reminders of your love in a world desperately crying out for healing and restoration.

Thursday, February 26, 2026

Week of Lent 1

Psalm 121

The LORD watches over you

The LORD is your keeper;
the LORD is your shade at your right hand.
The sun shall not strike you by day
nor the moon by night.

The LORD will keep you from all evil;
he will keep your life.
The LORD will keep
your going out and your coming in
from this time on and forevermore. (Ps. 121:5-8)

Additional Readings

Isaiah 51:1-3
Look to Abraham and Sarah

2 Timothy 1:3-7
Faith handed down from faithful mothers

Hymn: Kneeling in the Dust to Form Us, ACS 1099

Steadfast God, you care for your people and for all of creation. May we trust in your promise passed down through generations, that death is not the end, and that your love is abundant and everlasting.

Friday, February 27, 2026

Week of Lent 1

Micah 7:18-20

God's faithfulness

Who is a God like you, pardoning iniquity
    and passing over the transgression
    of the remnant of his possession?
He does not retain his anger forever
    because he delights in showing steadfast love.
He will again have compassion upon us;
    he will tread our iniquities under foot.
You will cast all our sins
    into the depths of the sea.
You will show faithfulness to Jacob
    and steadfast love to Abraham,
as you have sworn to our ancestors
    from the days of old. (Micah 7:18-20)

Psalm

Psalm 121

The LORD watches over you

Additional Reading

Acts 3:11-16

Abraham, Isaac, and Jacob's God glorifies Jesus

Hymn: You Have Come Down to the Lakeshore, ELW 817/TFF 154

God, we sing out to you! You are a God of compassion, forgiveness, and grace. Thank you for enfolding us in your care. Enable us to follow where you lead.

Saturday, February 28, 2026

Week of Lent 1

Isaiah 51:4-8

God's word means justice for all

Listen to me, my people,
    and give heed to me, my nation,
for a teaching will go out from me
    and my justice for a light to the peoples.
I will bring near my deliverance swiftly;
    my salvation has gone out,
    and my arms will rule the peoples;
the coastlands wait for me,
    and for my arm they hope. (Isa. 51:4-5)

Psalm

Psalm 121

The LORD watches over you

Additional Reading

Luke 7:1-10

Room at the table of Abraham

Hymn: Build a Longer Table, ACS 1062

Triune God, we lift our prayers to you because we know you hear us when we call. Guide us to walk closer to you and your reign here on earth, trusting that our lives are always in your keeping.

Prayer List for March

Sunday, March 1, 2026

Second Sunday in Lent

George Herbert, hymnwriter, died 1633

John 3:1-17

The mission of Christ: saving the world

[Jesus answered Nicodemus:] "And just as Moses lifted up the serpent in the wilderness, so must the Son of Man be lifted up, that whoever believes in him may have eternal life.

"For God so loved the world that he gave his only Son, so that everyone who believes in him may not perish but may have eternal life. "Indeed, God did not send the Son into the world to condemn the world but in order that the world might be saved through him." (John 3:14-17)

Psalm

Psalm 121
The Lord watches over you

Additional Readings

Genesis 12:1-4a
The blessing of God upon Abram

Romans 4:1-5, 13-17
The promise to those of Abraham's faith

Hymn: What Wondrous Love Is This, ELW 666

O God, our leader and guide, in the waters of baptism you bring us to new birth to live as your children. Strengthen our faith in your promises, that by your Spirit we may lift up your life to all the world through your Son, Jesus Christ, our Savior and Lord, who lives and reigns with you and the Holy Spirit, one God, now and forever.

Monday, March 2, 2026

Week of Lent 2

John Wesley, died 1791; Charles Wesley, died 1788; renewers of the church

Psalm 128

God promises life

Happy is everyone who fears the LORD,
 who walks in his ways.
You shall eat the fruit of the labor of your hands;
 you shall be happy, and it shall go well with you.

Your wife will be like a fruitful vine
 within your house;
your children will be like olive shoots
 around your table.
Thus shall the man be blessed
 who fears the LORD. (Ps. 128:1-4)

Additional Readings

Numbers 21:4-9
Moses lifts up the serpent

Hebrews 3:1-6
Moses the servant, Christ the son

Hymn: Guide My Feet, ACS 987/TFF 153

God of abundance and delight, you are the morning dew and the afternoon shade, the evening star and the promise of dawn. Show us the life that shines through cracks of brokenness. Guide us to be your people.

Tuesday, March 3, 2026

Week of Lent 2

Isaiah 65:17-25

God promises a new creation

For I am about to create new heavens
and a new earth;
the former things shall not be remembered
or come to mind.
But be glad and rejoice forever
in what I am creating,
for I am about to create Jerusalem as a joy
and its people as a delight.
I will rejoice in Jerusalem
and delight in my people;
no more shall the sound of weeping be heard in it
or the cry of distress. (Isa. 65:17-19)

Psalm

Psalm 128
God promises life

Additional Reading

Romans 4:6-13
Abraham saved through faith

Hymn: God the Sculptor of the Mountains, ELW 736/TFF 222

God who makes and makes again, you are the holy Sculptor, Tinkerer, Imaginer. Teach us to see possibilities around us and cultivate our creativity. Guide us to be co-artists with you, that we might usher in your new creation.

Wednesday, March 4, 2026

Week of Lent 2

John 7:53—8:11

Jesus does not condemn the sinner

The scribes and the Pharisees brought a woman who had been caught in adultery, and, making her stand before all of them, they said to him, "Teacher, this woman was caught in the very act of committing adultery. Now in the law Moses commanded us to stone such women. Now what do you say?" They said this to test him, so that they might have some charge to bring against him. Jesus bent down and wrote with his finger on the ground. When they kept on questioning him, he straightened up and said to them, "Let anyone among you who is without sin be the first to throw a stone at her." (John 8:3-7)

Psalm

Psalm 128

God promises life

Additional Reading

Ezekiel 36:22-32

God will renew the people

Hymn: There's a Wideness in God's Mercy, ELW 587/588

God of boundless mercy, what message did you trace in the dust? Your grace arrives in life-giving mystery. How can we live in response? Teach us humility and self-examination. Your word begins the world again.

Thursday, March 5, 2026

Week of Lent 2

Psalm 95

The rock of our salvation

O come, let us sing to the LORD;
    let us make a joyful noise to the rock of our salvation!
Let us come into his presence with thanksgiving;
    let us make a joyful noise to him with songs of praise!
For the LORD is a great God
    and a great King above all gods.
In his hand are the depths of the earth;
    the heights of the mountains are his also.
The sea is his, for he made it,
    and the dry land, which his hands have formed. (Ps. 95:1-5)

Additional Readings

Exodus 16:1-8
Israel complains of hunger in the wilderness

Colossians 1:15-23
Christ, the reconciliation of all things

Hymn: Love Divine, All Loves Excelling, ELW 631

O God of sea and dry land, God of mountains and depths, how expansive and beyond our comprehension is your glory! Join our hearts to the song of creation, that we might praise you with all our being.

Friday, March 6, 2026

Week of Lent 2

Ephesians 2:11-22

Christ, the reconciliation of Jew and gentile

So then, remember that at one time you gentiles by birth, called "the uncircumcision" by those who are called "the circumcision"—a circumcision made in the flesh by human hands—remember that you were at that time without Christ, being aliens from the commonwealth of Israel and strangers to the covenants of promise, having no hope and without God in the world. But now in Christ Jesus you who once were far off have been brought near by the blood of Christ. For he is our peace; in his flesh he has made both into one and has broken down the dividing wall, that is, the hostility between us. (Eph. 2:11-14)

Psalm

Psalm 95

The rock of our salvation

Additional Reading

Exodus 16:9-21

God gives manna and quail

Hymn: I Want Jesus to Walk with Me, ELW 325/TFF 66

God of peace eternal, you gather your children across division and hatred to make one people in the body of Christ. Teach us to love and respect our neighbors. Guide our hearts to yearn for unity.

Saturday, March 7, 2026
Week of Lent 2

Perpetua and Felicity and companions, martyrs at Carthage, died 202

Exodus 16:27-35

Manna and the sabbath

On the seventh day some of the people went out to gather [manna], and they found none. The LORD said to Moses, "How long will you refuse to keep my commandments and instructions? See! The LORD has given you the Sabbath; therefore on the sixth day he gives you food for two days; each of you stay where you are; do not leave your place on the seventh day." So the people rested on the seventh day. (Exod. 16:27-30)

Psalm

Psalm 95

The rock of our salvation

Additional Reading

John 4:1-6

Jesus travels to Jacob's well in Samaria

Hymn: Deep Peace, ACS 1018

God of Sabbath, at the heart of your law is rest for all. In these Lenten days, when the journey of faith feels wearisome, bring us again into your loving arms, and help us to trust in the abundance you have promised.

Sunday, March 8, 2026

Third Sunday in Lent

John 4:5-42

The woman at the well

Jesus said to [the Samaritan woman], "Everyone who drinks of this water will be thirsty again, but those who drink of the water that I will give them will never be thirsty. The water that I will give will become in them a spring of water gushing up to eternal life." The woman said to him, "Sir, give me this water, so that I may never be thirsty or have to keep coming here to draw water." (John 4:13-15)

Psalm

Psalm 95

The rock of our salvation

Additional Readings

Exodus 17:1-7

Water from the rock

Romans 5:1-11

Reconciled to God by Christ's death

Hymn: My Life Flows On in Endless Song, ELW 763

Merciful God, the fountain of living water, you quench our thirst and wash away our sin. Give us this water always. Bring us to drink from the well that flows with the beauty of your truth through Jesus Christ, our Savior and Lord, who lives and reigns with you and the Holy Spirit, one God, now and forever.

Monday, March 9, 2026

Week of Lent 3

Psalm 81

We drink from the rock

"But my people did not listen to my voice;
    Israel would not submit to me.
So I gave them over to their stubborn hearts,
    to follow their own counsels.
O that my people would listen to me,
    that Israel would walk in my ways!
Then I would quickly subdue their enemies
    and turn my hand against their foes.
Those who hate the LORD would cringe before him,
    and their doom would last forever.
I would feed you with the finest of the wheat,
    and with honey from the rock I would satisfy you." (Ps. 81:11-16)

Additional Readings

Genesis 24:1-27
Rebekah at the well

2 John 1-13
A woman reminded to abide in Christ

Hymn: Lord Jesus, You Shall Be My Song, ELW 808

God of honey and wheat, you desire deeply for your people to listen and trust. When we stray from you, you do not give up on us. Open our ears and guide our feet, that we might return to life.

Tuesday, March 10, 2026
Week of Lent 3

Harriet Tubman, died 1913; Sojourner Truth, died 1883; renewers of society

1 Corinthians 10:1-4

Drinking from Christ, the spiritual rock

I do not want you to be ignorant, brothers and sisters, that our ancestors were all under the cloud, and all passed through the sea, and all were baptized into Moses in the cloud and in the sea, and all ate the same spiritual food, and all drank the same spiritual drink. For they drank from the spiritual rock that followed them, and the rock was Christ. (1 Cor. 10:1-4)

Psalm

Psalm 81
We drink from the rock

Additional Reading

Genesis 29:1-14
Rachel at the well

Hymn: Come to the Water of Life, ACS 955

O God our rock who flows with water, you claim us in baptism, and through water you nourish our lives. Teach us to be good stewards of water in our homes and homelands, that all your children may know its gift.

Wednesday, March 11, 2026

Week of Lent 3

John 7:14-31, 37-39

Drink of Jesus, the Messiah

On the last day of the festival, the great day, while Jesus was standing there, he cried out, "Let anyone who is thirsty come to me, and let the one who believes in me drink. As the scripture has said, 'Out of the believer's heart shall flow rivers of living water.'" Now he said this about the Spirit, which believers in him were to receive, for as yet there was no Spirit because Jesus was not yet glorified. (John 7:37-39)

Psalm

Psalm 81

We drink from the rock

Additional Reading

Jeremiah 2:4-13

God, the living water

Hymn: All Who Are Thirsty, ACS 981

God of living water, your Spirit flows through our hearts. Help us to listen and notice the ways you move in our lives, and to trust in the loving presence of your Son, Jesus Christ.

Thursday, March 12, 2026

Week of Lent 3

Gregory the Great, Bishop of Rome, died 604

Psalm 23

My head anointed with oil

Even though I walk through the darkest valley,
 I fear no evil,
for you are with me;
 your rod and your staff,
 they comfort me.

You prepare a table before me
 in the presence of my enemies;
you anoint my head with oil;
 my cup overflows.
Surely goodness and mercy shall follow me
 all the days of my life,
and I shall dwell in the house of the LORD
 my whole life long. (Ps. 23:4-6)

Additional Readings

1 Samuel 15:10-21
The prophet Samuel confronts the king

Ephesians 4:25-32
Called to honesty and forbearance

Hymn: Softly and Tenderly Jesus Is Calling, ELW 608/TFF 155

God our shepherd and comforter, you know our darkest valley and promise never to leave our side. Grant us the vision of your cup overflowing, that even in shadowy times we might be nourished in your love.

Friday, March 13, 2026
Week of Lent 3

Ephesians 5:1-9
Now in the Lord you are light

Let no one deceive you with empty words, for because of these things the wrath of God comes on those who are disobedient. Therefore do not be associated with them, for once you were darkness, but now in the Lord you are light. Walk as children of light, for the fruit of the light is found in all that is good and right and true. (Eph. 5:6-9)

Psalm
Psalm 23
My head anointed with oil

Additional Reading
1 Samuel 15:22-31
The king confesses his sinful disobedience

Hymn: This Little Light of Mine, ELW 677/TFF 65

God of revelation, you have called us your children. Shine brilliantly in our lives, that we might see clearly what is true, and in the shadows your light casts, let us dance and find rest in you.

Saturday, March 14, 2026

Week of Lent 3

1 Samuel 15:32-34

Samuel grieves over Saul

Then Samuel said, "Bring Agag king of the Amalekites here to me." And Agag came to him haltingly. Agag said, "Surely death is bitter." Samuel said,

> "As your sword has made women childless,
> so your mother shall be childless among women."

And Samuel hewed Agag in pieces before the LORD in Gilgal.

Then Samuel went to Ramah, and Saul went up to his house in Gibeah of Saul. (1 Sam. 15:32-34)

Psalm

Psalm 23

My head anointed with oil

Additional Reading

John 1:1-9

Christ comes with light and life

Hymn: All Things of Dust to Dust Return, ACS 920

O God, you know the bitterness of grief and the brokenness of human hearts. The depth of pain we carry and inflict on one another, only you can know. Carry our burdens and correct our paths.

Sunday, March 15, 2026

Fourth Sunday in Lent

John 9:1-41

The man born blind

Jesus heard that [the Pharisees] had driven him out, and when he found him he said, "Do you believe in the Son of Man?" He answered, "And who is he, sir? Tell me, so that I may believe in him." Jesus said to him, "You have seen him, and the one speaking with you is he." He said, "Lord, I believe." And he worshiped him. Jesus said, "I came into this world for judgment, so that those who do not see may see and those who do see may become blind." (John 9:35-39)

Psalm

Psalm 23

My head anointed with oil

Additional Readings

1 Samuel 16:1-13

David is chosen and anointed

Ephesians 5:8-14

Live as children of light

Hymn: Total Praise, ACS 1080

Bend your ear to our prayers, Lord Christ, and come among us. By your gracious life and death for us, bring light into the darkness of our hearts, and anoint us with your Spirit, for you live and reign with the Father and the Holy Spirit, one God, now and forever.

Monday, March 16, 2026

Week of Lent 4

Psalm 146

God opens the eyes of the blind

Happy are those whose help is the God of Jacob,
    whose hope is in the Lord their God,
who made heaven and earth,
    the sea, and all that is in them;
who keeps faith forever;
    who executes justice for the oppressed;
    who gives food to the hungry. (Ps. 146:5-7)

Additional Readings

Isaiah 59:9-19
The blindness of injustice

Acts 9:1-20
Saul is baptized, his sight restored

Hymn: Give Me Jesus, ELW 770/TFF165

O God, you hold creation from beginning to end. You know the arc of justice. You meet us in our hunger, despair, and need. Plant hope in our hearts, nourished by trust in you.

Tuesday, March 17, 2026

Week of Lent 4

Patrick, bishop, missionary to Ireland, died 461

Isaiah 42:14-21

God will heal the blind

For a long time I have held my peace;
    I have kept still and restrained myself;
now I will cry out like a woman in labor;
    I will gasp and pant.
I will lay waste mountains and hills
    and dry up all their herbage;
I will turn the rivers into islands
    and dry up the pools.
I will lead the blind
    by a road they do not know;
by paths they have not known
    I will guide them.
I will turn the darkness before them into light,
    the rough places into level ground.
These are the things I will do,
    and I will not forsake them. (Isa. 42:14-16)

Psalm

Psalm 146

God opens the eyes of the blind

Additional Reading

Colossians 1:9-14

The inheritance of the saints in light

Hymn: Mothering God, You Gave Me Birth, ELW 735

O God, our mother who labors, you protect us fiercely, like a parent watching over her child. Fill us with gratitude for all that you provide. Guide us toward love. Protect us from despair.

Wednesday, March 18, 2026

Week of Lent 4

Matthew 9:27-34

Jesus heals the blind

As Jesus went on from there, two blind men followed him, crying loudly, "Have mercy on us, Son of David!" When he entered the house, the blind men came to him, and Jesus said to them, "Do you have faith that I can do this?" They said to him, "Yes, Lord." Then he touched their eyes and said, "According to your faith, let it be done to you." And their eyes were opened. Then Jesus sternly ordered them, "See that no one knows of this." But they went away and spread the news about him through all of that district. (Matt. 9:27-31)

Psalm

Psalm 146

God opens the eyes of the blind

Additional Reading

Isaiah 60:17-22

God our light

Hymn: When Peace like a River, ELW 785/TFF 194

God of opening and insight, you reveal yourself in our lives of faith. Hear our cries for mercy, touch us, and restore us to wholeness. Spark in us the desire to share all that we have seen of your love.

Thursday, March 19, 2026

Joseph, Guardian of Jesus

Matthew 1:16, 18-21, 24a

The Lord appears to Joseph in a dream

Now the birth of Jesus the Messiah took place in this way. When his mother Mary had been engaged to Joseph, but before they lived together, she was found to be pregnant from the Holy Spirit. Her husband Joseph, being a righteous man and unwilling to expose her to public disgrace, planned to divorce her quietly. But just when he had resolved to do this, an angel of the Lord appeared to him in a dream and said, "Joseph, son of David, do not be afraid to take Mary as your wife, for the child conceived in her is from the Holy Spirit. She will bear a son, and you are to name him Jesus, for he will save his people from their sins." (Matt. 1:18-21)

Psalm

Psalm 89:1-29

The LORD's steadfast love is established forever

Additional Readings

2 Samuel 7:4, 8-16

God makes a covenant with David

Romans 4:13-18

The promise to those who share Abraham's faith

Hymn: Bind Us Together, TFF 217

O God, from the family of your servant David you raised up Joseph to be the guardian of your incarnate Son and the husband of his blessed mother. Give us grace to imitate his uprightness of life and his obedience to your commands, through Jesus Christ, our Savior and Lord, who lives and reigns with you and the Holy Spirit, one God, now and forever.

Friday, March 20, 2026

Week of Lent 4

Revelation 11:15-19

The word of God: thanksgiving and singing

Then the twenty-four elders who sit on their thrones before God fell on their faces and worshiped God, singing,

"We give you thanks, Lord God Almighty,
who are and who were,
for you have taken your great power
and begun to reign.
The nations raged,
but your wrath has come,
and the time for judging the dead,
for rewarding your servants, the prophets
and saints and all who fear your name,
both small and great,
and for destroying those who destroy the earth."

Then God's temple in heaven was opened, and the ark of his covenant was seen within his temple, and there were flashes of lightning, rumblings, peals of thunder, an earthquake, and heavy hail. (Rev. 11:16-19)

Psalm

Psalm 130

Mercy and redemption

Additional Reading

Ezekiel 33:10-16

The word of God: repent and live

Hymn: Crashing Waters at Creation, ELW 455

God of thunder and hail, you are mighty, and your justice is beyond our knowing. Humble us in worship and show us refuge from the storms of life. Teach us to trust in your power and grace.

Saturday, March 21, 2026

Week of Lent 4

Thomas Cranmer, Bishop of Canterbury, martyr, died 1556

Ezekiel 36:8-15

Blessings upon Israel

But you, O mountains of Israel, shall shoot out your branches and yield your fruit to my people Israel, for they shall soon come home. See now, I am for you; I will turn to you, and you shall be tilled and sown, and I will multiply your population, the whole house of Israel, all of it; the towns shall be inhabited and the waste places rebuilt, and I will multiply humans and animals upon you. They shall increase and be fruitful, and I will cause you to be inhabited as in your former times and will do more good to you than ever before. Then you shall know that I am the LORD. I will lead people upon you—my people Israel—and they shall possess you, and you shall be their inheritance. No longer shall you bereave them of children. (Ezek. 36:8-12)

Psalm

Psalm 130

Mercy and redemption

Additional Reading

Luke 24:44-53

Jesus blesses the disciples

Hymn: My Song Is Love Unknown, ELW 343

God of the mountains, you are our rock and our foundation, the steady one to whom we return. Help us to trust in the promises you have made. Show our feet the path home to you.

Sunday, March 22, 2026

Fifth Sunday in Lent

Jonathan Edwards, teacher, missionary to American Indians, died 1758

John 11:1-45

The raising of Lazarus

So they took away the stone. And Jesus looked upward and said, "Father, I thank you for having heard me. I knew that you always hear me, but I have said this for the sake of the crowd standing here, so that they may believe that you sent me." When he had said this, he cried with a loud voice, "Lazarus, come out!" The dead man came out, his hands and feet bound with strips of cloth and his face wrapped in a cloth. Jesus said to them, "Unbind him, and let him go."

Many of the Jews, therefore, who had come with Mary and had seen what Jesus did believed in him. (John 11:41-45)

Psalm

Psalm 130
Mercy and redemption

Additional Readings

Ezekiel 37:1-14
The dry bones of Israel

Romans 8:6-11
Life in the Spirit

Hymn: Send Me, Lord, ELW 809/TFF 244

Almighty God, your Son came into the world to free us all from sin and death. Breathe upon us the power of your Spirit, that we may be raised to new life in Christ and serve you in righteousness all our days, through Jesus Christ, our Savior and Lord, who lives and reigns with you and the Holy Spirit, one God, now and forever.

Monday, March 23, 2026

Week of Lent 5

Psalm 143

Save me from death

Save me, O LORD, from my enemies;
  I have fled to you for refuge.
Teach me to do your will,
  for you are my God.
Let your good spirit lead me
  on a level path.

For your name's sake, O LORD, preserve my life.
  In your righteousness bring me out of trouble.
In your steadfast love cut off my enemies,
  and destroy all my adversaries,
  for I am your servant. (Ps. 143:9-12)

Additional Readings

1 Kings 17:17-24
Elijah raises the widow's son

Acts 20:7-12
Paul raises a young man

Hymn: Take, Oh, Take Me As I Am, ELW 814

Steadfast God, when the journey before us is rocky, you make an even path. In the midst of our enemies, you grant salvation and renew our spirits. Teach us your ways. Make us, your servants, dwell in peace.

Tuesday, March 24, 2026

Week of Lent 5

Oscar Arnulfo Romero, Bishop of El Salvador, martyr, died 1980

2 Kings 4:18-37

Elisha raises a child from death

When Elisha came into the house, he saw the child lying dead on his bed. So he went in and closed the door on the two of them and prayed to the LORD. Then he got up on the bed and lay upon the child, putting his mouth upon his mouth, his eyes upon his eyes, and his hands upon his hands, and while he lay bent over him, the flesh of the child became warm. He got down, walked once to and fro in the room, then got up again and bent over him; the child sneezed seven times, and the child opened his eyes. Elisha summoned Gehazi and said, "Call the Shunammite woman." So he called her. When she came to him, he said, "Take your son." She came and fell at his feet, bowing to the ground; then she took her son and left. (2 Kings 4:32-37)

Psalm

Psalm 143

Save me from death

Additional Reading

Ephesians 2:1-10

Alive in Christ

Hymn: Come, Bring Your Burdens to God, ACS 1009

God of hope and wonder, you work miracles in the midst of tragedy. When we tremble in despair, come by our side and give us enough breath for each day. Help us to trust in the promise of new life.

Wednesday, March 25, 2026

Annunciation of Our Lord

Luke 1:26-38

The angel greets Mary

In the sixth month the angel Gabriel was sent by God to a town in Galilee called Nazareth, to a virgin engaged to a man whose name was Joseph, of the house of David. The virgin's name was Mary. And he came to her and said, "Greetings, favored one! The Lord is with you." But she was much perplexed by his words and pondered what sort of greeting this might be. The angel said to her, "Do not be afraid, Mary, for you have found favor with God. And now, you will conceive in your womb and bear a son, and you will name him Jesus." (Luke 1:26-31)

Psalm

Psalm 45
Your name will be remembered

Additional Readings

Isaiah 7:10-14
A young woman will bear a son

Hebrews 10:4-10
The offering of Jesus' body sanctifies us

Hymn: Freedom Is Coming, ACS 903/TFF 46

Pour your grace into our hearts, O God, that we who have known the incarnation of your Son, Jesus Christ, announced by an angel, may by his cross and passion be brought to the glory of his resurrection; for he lives and reigns with you, in the unity of the Holy Spirit, one God, now and forever.

Thursday, March 26, 2026

Week of Lent 5

Psalm 31:9-16

I commend my spirit

Be gracious to me, O Lord, for I am in distress;
my eye wastes away from grief,
my soul and body also.
For my life is spent with sorrow
and my years with sighing;
my strength fails because of my misery,
and my bones waste away. . . .

But I trust in you, O Lord;
I say, "You are my God."
My times are in your hand;
deliver me from the hand of my enemies and persecutors.
Let your face shine upon your servant;
save me in your steadfast love. (Ps. 31:9-10, 14-16)

Additional Readings

1 Samuel 16:11-13
Samuel anoints David

Philippians 1:1-11
Encouraged to follow Christ's righteousness

Hymn: Come, Holy Spirit, ACS 940

God who suffers with us, you know what it is to be human. When we sigh, you sigh with us. When we cry out, you cry with us. Wrap us in your loving presence, that we may know your spirit.

Friday, March 27, 2026

Week of Lent 5

Philippians 1:21-30

Seeing Christ in this life

Only, live your life in a manner worthy of the gospel of Christ, so that, whether I come and see you or am absent and hear about you, I will know that you are standing firm in one spirit, striving side by side with one mind for the faith of the gospel and in no way frightened by those opposing you. For them, this is evidence of their destruction but of your salvation. And this is God's doing. For he has graciously granted you the privilege not only of believing in Christ but of suffering for him as well, since you are having the same struggle that you saw I had and now hear that I still have. (Phil. 1:27-30)

Psalm

Psalm 31:9-16

I commend my spirit

Additional Reading

Job 13:13-19

A servant keeps silence

Hymn: When the Storms of Life Are Raging, TFF 198

God our strength, you know our human struggle, and your gift to us is community. In the face of fear, teach us to gather. In the midst of suffering, make us one people as your family.

Saturday, March 28, 2026

Week of Lent 5

Mark 10:32-34

Going up to Jerusalem

They were on the road, going up to Jerusalem, and Jesus was walking ahead of them; they were amazed, and those who followed were afraid. He took the twelve aside again and began to tell them what was to happen to him, saying, "Look, we are going up to Jerusalem, and the Son of Man will be handed over to the chief priests and the scribes, and they will condemn him to death; then they will hand him over to the gentiles; they will mock him and spit upon him and flog him and kill him, and after three days he will rise again." (Mark 10:32-34)

Psalm

Psalm 31:9-16

I commend my spirit

Additional Reading

Lamentations 3:55-66

A cry for help

Hymn: Many and Great, O God, ELW 837

God of the cross, you know the end of life's earthly journey, and yet you do not fear. Although we abandon you in fear, you do not abandon us. Grant us patience and hope for the days ahead.

Holy Week

On the Sunday of the Passion, Christians enter into Holy Week. This day opens before the Christian community the final period of preparation before the celebration of the Three Days of the Lord's passion, death, and resurrection.

In many churches, palm branches will be given to worshipers for the procession into the worship space. Following an ancient custom, many Christians bring their palms home and place them in the household prayer center, behind a cross or sacred image, or above the indoor lintel of the entryway.

At sunset on Maundy Thursday, Lent comes to an end as the church begins the celebration of the events through which Christ has become the life and the resurrection for all who believe.

Prayer for Placing Palms in the Home

Use this blessing when placing palms in the home after the Palm Sunday liturgy. t

Blessed is the One who comes in the name of the Lord!
May we who place these palms receive Christ into our midst
with the joy that marked the entrance to Jerusalem.
May we hold no betrayal in our hearts,
but peacefully welcome Christ
who lives and reigns with you and the Holy Spirit,
one God, now and forever. Amen.

Sunday, March 29, 2026

Sunday of the Passion/Palm Sunday

Hans Nielsen Hauge, renewer of the church, died 1824

Matthew 26:14—27:66

The passion and death of Jesus

Then Jesus cried again with a loud voice and breathed his last. At that moment the curtain of the temple was torn in two, from top to bottom. The earth shook, and the rocks were split. The tombs also were opened, and many bodies of the saints who had fallen asleep were raised. After his resurrection they came out of the tombs and entered the holy city and appeared to many. Now when the centurion and those with him, who were keeping watch over Jesus, saw the earthquake and what took place, they were terrified and said, "Truly this man was God's Son!" (Matt. 27:50-54)

Psalm

Psalm 31:9-16
I commend my spirit

Additional Readings

Isaiah 50:4-9a
The servant submits to suffering

Philippians 2:5-11
Death on a cross

Hymn: Open My Heart, ACS 1079

Sovereign God, you have established your rule in the human heart through the servanthood of Jesus Christ. By your Spirit, keep us in the joyful procession of those who with their tongues confess Jesus as Lord and with their lives praise him as Savior, who lives and reigns with you and the Holy Spirit, one God, now and forever.

Monday, March 30, 2026

Monday in Holy Week

Psalm 36:5-11

Refuge under the shadow of your wings

Your steadfast love, O Lord, extends to the heavens,
your faithfulness to the clouds.
Your righteousness is like the mighty mountains;
your judgments are like the great deep;
you save humans and animals alike, O Lord.

How precious is your steadfast love, O God!
All people may take refuge in the shadow of your wings.
They feast on the abundance of your house,
and you give them drink from the river of your delights.
For with you is the fountain of life;
in your light we see light. (Ps. 36:5-9)

Additional Readings

Isaiah 42:1-9
The servant brings forth justice

Hebrews 9:11-15
The blood of Christ redeems for eternal life

John 12:1-11
Mary of Bethany anoints Jesus

Hymn: Nothing Can Trouble, ACS 1033

O God, your Son chose the path that led to pain before joy and the cross before glory. Plant his cross in our hearts, so that in its power and love we may come at last to joy and glory, through Jesus Christ, our Savior and Lord, who lives and reigns with you and the Holy Spirit, one God, now and forever.

Tuesday, March 31, 2026

Tuesday in Holy Week

John Donne, poet, died 1631

1 Corinthians 1:18-31

The cross of Christ reveals God's power and wisdom

Where is the one who is wise? Where is the scholar? Where is the debater of this age? Has not God made foolish the wisdom of the world? For since, in the wisdom of God, the world did not know God through wisdom, God decided, through the foolishness of the proclamation, to save those who believe. For Jews ask for signs and Greeks desire wisdom, but we proclaim Christ crucified, a stumbling block to Jews and foolishness to gentiles, but to those who are the called, both Jews and Greeks, Christ the power of God and the wisdom of God. For God's foolishness is wiser than human wisdom, and God's weakness is stronger than human strength. (1 Cor. 1:20-25)

Psalm

Psalm 71:1-14
From my mother's womb you have been my strength

Additional Readings

Isaiah 49:1-7
The servant brings salvation to earth's ends

John 12:20-36
Jesus speaks of his death

Hymn: Come and Fill Our Hearts, ELW 528

Lord Jesus, you have called us to follow you. Grant that our love may not grow cold in your service, and that we may not fail or deny you in the time of trial, for you live and reign with the Father and the Holy Spirit, one God, now and forever.

Prayer List for April

Wednesday, April 1, 2026

Wednesday in Holy Week

Isaiah 50:4-9a

The servant is vindicated by God

The Lord God has opened my ear,
    and I was not rebellious;
    I did not turn backward.
I gave my back to those who struck me
    and my cheeks to those who pulled out the beard;
I did not hide my face
    from insult and spitting.

The Lord God helps me;
    therefore I have not been disgraced;
therefore I have set my face like flint,
    and I know that I shall not be put to shame;
    he who vindicates me is near. (Isa. 50:5-8a)

Psalm

Psalm 70

Be pleased, O God, to deliver me

Additional Readings

Hebrews 12:1-3

Look to Jesus, who endured the cross

John 13:21-32

Jesus foretells his betrayal

Hymn: Ah, Holy Jesus, ELW 349

Almighty God, your Son our Savior suffered at human hands and endured the shame of the cross. Grant that we may walk in the way of his cross and find it the way of life and peace, through Jesus Christ, our Savior and Lord, who lives and reigns with you and the Holy Spirit, one God, now and forever.

The Three Days

The Three Days begin at sunset on Maundy Thursday and end at sunset on Easter Day. For seventy-two hours, Christians prepare for and celebrate new life and love that lasts forever. Scripture proclaimed during the Three Days moves toward the baptismal font where new siblings in Christ are born of water and the Spirit, and where the baptized renew their own baptismal promises.

There are many ways to practice the Three Days at home and in the worshiping community. Forms of prayer, fasting, service, and silent reflection invite Christians to focus on the salvation story. Preparations can be made for the celebration of Easter: cleaning, coloring eggs, baking Easter breads, gathering greens or flowers to adorn crosses and sacred images. In those communities where baptisms will be celebrated, prayers may be offered for those to be received into the church.

Table Prayer for the Three Days

Blessed are you, O Lord our God.
You take away the sin of the world.
Nourish us with your promises
and strengthen us with this food,
so that we are sustained by your grace
for the journey from death to life,
through Jesus Christ our Lord. Amen.

Thursday, April 2, 2026

Maundy Thursday

John 13:1-17, 31b-35

The service of Christ: footwashing and meal

After [Jesus] had washed their feet, had put on his robe, and had reclined again, he said to them, "Do you know what I have done to you? You call me Teacher and Lord, and you are right, for that is what I am. So if I, your Lord and Teacher, have washed your feet, you also ought to wash one another's feet. For I have set you an example, that you also should do as I have done to you." (John 13:12-15)

Psalm

Psalm 116:1-2, 12-19
The cup of salvation

Additional Readings

Exodus 12:1-4 [5-10] 11-14
The passover of the Lord

1 Corinthians 11:23-26
Proclaim the Lord's death

Hymn: Three Holy Days Enfold Us Now, ACS 930

Eternal God, in the sharing of a meal your Son established a new covenant for all people, and in the washing of feet he showed us the dignity of service. Grant that by the power of your Holy Spirit these signs of our life in faith may speak again to our hearts, feed our spirits, and refresh our bodies, through Jesus Christ, our Savior and Lord, who lives and reigns with you and the Holy Spirit, one God, now and forever.

Friday, April 3, 2026

Good Friday

John 18:1—19:42

The passion and death of Jesus

When Jesus saw his mother and the disciple whom he loved standing beside her, he said to his mother, "Woman, here is your son." Then he said to the disciple, "Here is your mother." And from that hour the disciple took her into his own home.

After this, when Jesus knew that all was now finished, he said (in order to fulfill the scripture), "I am thirsty." A jar full of sour wine was standing there. So they put a sponge full of the wine on a branch of hyssop and held it to his mouth. When Jesus had received the wine, he said, "It is finished." Then he bowed his head and gave up his spirit. (John 19:26-30)

Psalm

Psalm 22
Why have you forsaken me?

Additional Readings

Isaiah 52:13—53:12
The suffering servant

Hebrews 10:16-25
The way to God is opened

Hymn: Were You There, ELW 353/TFF 81

Merciful God, your Son was lifted up on the cross to draw all people to himself. Grant that we who have been born out of his wounded side may at all times find mercy in him, Jesus Christ, our Savior and Lord, who lives and reigns with you and the Holy Spirit, one God, now and forever.

Saturday, April 4, 2026

Resurrection of Our Lord
Vigil of Easter

Benedict the African, confessor, died 1589

Romans 6:3-11

Dying and rising with Christ

Do you not know that all of us who were baptized into Christ Jesus were baptized into his death? Therefore we were buried with him by baptism into death, so that, just as Christ was raised from the dead by the glory of the Father, so we also might walk in newness of life.

For if we have been united with him in a death like his, we will certainly be united with him in a resurrection like his. (Rom. 6:3-5)

Psalm

Psalm 46
The God of Jacob is our stronghold

Additional Readings

Genesis 7:1-5, 11-18; 8:6-18; 9:8-13
Flood

John 20:1-18
Seeing the risen Christ

Hymn: Where Charity and Love Are Shown, ACS 931

O God, you are the creator of the world, the liberator of your people, and the wisdom of the earth. By the resurrection of your Son free us from our fears, restore us in your image, and ignite us with your light, through Jesus Christ, our Savior and Lord, who lives and reigns with you and the Holy Spirit, one God, now and forever.

Sunday, April 5, 2026

Resurrection of Our Lord

Easter Day

Matthew 28:1-10

Proclaim the resurrection

But the angel said to the women, "Do not be afraid, for I know that you are looking for Jesus who was crucified. He is not here, for he has been raised, as he said. Come, see the place where he lay. Then go quickly and tell his disciples, 'He has been raised from the dead, and indeed he is going ahead of you to Galilee; there you will see him.' This is my message for you." So they left the tomb quickly with fear and great joy and ran to tell his disciples. (Matt. 28:5-8)

Psalm

Psalm 118:1-2, 14-24
On this day God has acted

Additional Readings

Acts 10:34-43
God raised Jesus on the third day

Colossians 3:1-4
Raised with Christ

Hymn: Alleluia! Jesus Is Risen! ELW 377/TFF 91

God of mercy, we no longer look for Jesus among the dead, for he is alive and has become the Lord of life. Increase in our minds and hearts the risen life we share with Christ, and help us to grow as your people toward the fullness of eternal life with you, through Jesus Christ, our Savior and Lord, who lives and reigns with you and the Holy Spirit, one God, now and forever.

Easter

In the Christian church, Easter is not one day but a season of fifty days. During this time we explore the many ways God raises us up to new life. In a world where death threatens people on all sides, we declare that God is the God of life who has conquered death in Jesus Christ. We are invited to participate in Christ's death and resurrection, and to lean into our hope that one day, by God's grace, we will stand among God's resurrected people and see God face to face.

The fifty days were once called *Pentecost*, Greek for "fifty." We end this sacred time caught up in God's transforming Spirit that breaks down divisions and sends us out to accompany Jesus in tending and mending the world..

Table Prayer for the Season of Easter

O God, you raised Jesus to new life
by the power of your Holy Spirit.
Wherever we encounter pain or death,
send your Spirit with signs of your liberating life.
May this food we share
strengthen us to be Christ's body alive in the world.
In Jesus' name we pray. Amen.

Monday, April 6, 2026

Week of Easter 1

Albrecht Dürer, died 1528; Matthias Grünewald, died 1529;
Lucas Cranach, died 1553; artists

Psalm 118:1-2, 14-24

On this day God has acted

The stone that the builders rejected
    has become the chief cornerstone.
This is the LORD's doing;
    it is marvelous in our eyes.
This is the day that the LORD has made;
    let us rejoice and be glad in it. (Ps. 118:22-24)

Additional Readings

Exodus 14:10-31; 15:20-21
Israel crosses over the sea

Colossians 3:5-11
The new life in Christ

Hymn: Day of Delight and Beauty Unbounded, ACS 933

Creator God, we greet each new day basking in the goodness of your creation. We see you in the early morning light and in the midst of our daily conversations. Encourage us to celebrate and embrace all you have made.

Tuesday, April 7, 2026

Week of Easter 1

Colossians 3:12-17

The new life in Christ

Therefore, as God's chosen ones, holy and beloved, clothe yourselves with compassion, kindness, humility, meekness, and patience. Bear with one another and, if anyone has a complaint against another, forgive each other; just as the Lord has forgiven you, so you also must forgive. Above all, clothe yourselves with love, which binds everything together in perfect harmony. And let the peace of Christ rule in your hearts, to which indeed you were called in one body. And be thankful. (Col. 3:12-15)

Psalm

Psalm 118:1-2, 14-24
On this day God has acted

Additional Reading

Exodus 15:1-18
Song at the sea

Hymn: Beloved, God's Chosen, ELW 648

Creative God, you made a world filled with delightful diversity. Your face meets us as we look into the eyes of our neighbor. Your voice speaks to us as we listen to one another. Open our hearts to recognize you in all people.

Wednesday, April 8, 2026

Week of Easter 1

Joshua 3:1-17

Israel crosses into the promised land

When the people set out from their tents to cross over the Jordan, the priests bearing the ark of the covenant were in front of the people. Now the Jordan overflows all its banks throughout the time of harvest. So when those who bore the ark had come to the Jordan and the feet of the priests bearing the ark were dipped in the edge of the water, the waters flowing from above stood still, rising up in a single heap far off at Adam, the city that is beside Zarethan, while those flowing toward the sea of the Arabah, the Dead Sea, were wholly cut off. Then the people crossed over opposite Jericho. While all Israel were crossing over on dry ground, the priests who bore the ark of the covenant of the LORD stood firmly on dry ground in the middle of the Jordan, until the entire nation finished crossing over the Jordan. (Josh. 3:14-17)

Psalm

Psalm 118:1-2, 14-24

On this day God has acted

Additional Reading

Matthew 28:1-10

Proclaim the resurrection

Hymn: I'm a-Goin'-a Eat at the Welcome Table, TFF 263

God who journeys with us each new day, you have led your people through barren lands and stormy seas. Your arms carried us when we grew weary. Help us feel your presence in the midst of daily life.

Thursday, April 9, 2026

Week of Easter 1

Dietrich Bonhoeffer, theologian, died 1945

Psalm 16

Fullness of joy

I bless the LORD, who gives me counsel;
in the night also my heart instructs me.
I keep the LORD always before me;
because he is at my right hand, I shall not be moved.

Therefore my heart is glad, and my soul rejoices;
my body also rests secure.
For you do not give me up to Sheol
or let your faithful one see the Pit.

You show me the path of life.
In your presence there is fullness of joy;
in your right hand are pleasures forevermore. (Ps. 16:7-11)

Additional Readings

Song of Songs 2:8-15
Arise, for the winter is past

Colossians 4:2-5
The new life in Christ

Hymn: Joyful Is the Dark, ACS 1096

Joy-filled God, your hands shaped our world. We marvel at all you have made. We see you in the stars and in the desert sands. Open our hearts to feel the joy you have in creating all things.

Friday, April 10, 2026
Week of Easter 1

Mikael Agricola, Bishop of Turku, died 1557

1 Corinthians 15:1-11

Witnesses to the risen Christ

For I handed on to you as of first importance what I in turn had received: that Christ died for our sins in accordance with the scriptures and that he was buried and that he was raised on the third day in accordance with the scriptures and that he appeared to Cephas, then to the twelve. Then he appeared to more than five hundred brothers and sisters at one time, most of whom are still alive, though some have died. Then he appeared to James, then to all the apostles. Last of all, as to one untimely born, he appeared also to me. (1 Cor. 15:3-8)

Psalm

Psalm 16

Fullness of joy

Additional Reading

Song of Songs 5:9—6:3

The beloved in the garden

Hymn: Christ Has Arisen, Alleluia, ELW 364/TFF 96

God of past, present, and future, you have sustained your people in every generation. You continue to call us to be who you created us to be. May your holy presence inspire and give shape to the human community.

Saturday, April 11, 2026

Week of Easter 1

Song of Songs 8:6-7

Love is strong as death

Set me as a seal upon your heart,
    as a seal upon your arm,
for love is strong as death,
    passion fierce as the grave.
Its flashes are flashes of fire,
    a raging flame.
Many waters cannot quench love,
    neither can floods drown it.
If one offered for love
    all the wealth of one's house,
    it would be utterly scorned. (Song 8:6-7)

Psalm

Psalm 16
Fullness of joy

Additional Reading

John 20:11-20
The witness of Mary Magdalene

Hymn: Let Us Enter In, ACS 985

Loving God, you created each of us out of divine love and in your own image. You invite us to share this holy, deep love with all the world. May we know and share your transforming goodness.

Sunday, April 12, 2026

Second Sunday of Easter

John 20:19-31

Beholding the wounds of the risen Christ

A week later [Jesus'] disciples were again in the house, and Thomas was with them. Although the doors were shut, Jesus came and stood among them and said, "Peace be with you." Then he said to Thomas, "Put your finger here and see my hands. Reach out your hand and put it in my side. Do not doubt but believe." Thomas answered him, "My Lord and my God!" Jesus said to him, "Have you believed because you have seen me? Blessed are those who have not seen and yet have come to believe." (John 20:26-29)

Psalm

Psalm 16
Fullness of joy

Additional Readings

Acts 2:14a, 22-32
God fulfills the promise to David

1 Peter 1:3-9
New birth to a living hope

Hymn: Touch That Soothes and Heals, ACS 939

Almighty and eternal God, the strength of those who believe and the hope of those who doubt, may we, who have not seen, have faith in you and receive the fullness of Christ's blessing, who lives and reigns with you and the Holy Spirit, one God, now and forever.

Monday, April 13, 2026

Week of Easter 2

Psalm 114

God saves through water

Why is it, O sea, that you flee?
    O Jordan, that you turn back?
O mountains, that you skip like rams?
    O hills, like lambs?

Tremble, O earth, at the presence of the LORD,
    at the presence of the God of Jacob,
who turns the rock into a pool of water,
    the flint into a spring of water. (Ps. 114:5-8)

Additional Readings

Judges 6:36-40
Gideon and the fleece

1 Corinthians 15:12-20
Paul teaches the resurrection

Hymn: Come to the Water of Life, ACS 955

All-powerful God, you created the waters and dry land. We bask in the beauty of all you have made. In still waters and barren hills, we feel your presence. Awaken a sense of awe within us for this gift.

Tuesday, April 14, 2026

Week of Easter 2

1 Corinthians 15:19-28

Paul teaches the resurrection

For since death came through a human, the resurrection of the dead has also come through a human, for as all die in Adam, so all will be made alive in Christ. But each in its own order: Christ the first fruits, then at his coming those who belong to Christ. Then comes the end, when he hands over the kingdom to God the Father, after he has destroyed every ruler and every authority and power. For he must reign until he has put all his enemies under his feet. (1 Cor. 15:21-25)

Psalm

Psalm 114

God saves through water

Additional Reading

Jonah 1:1-17

Jonah saved from the sea

Hymn: Some Glad Morning When This Life Is O'er, TFF 176

God of abundance, you yearn for the world to be united in a holy and lasting peace. You sent Jesus to model a loving and just way of life. Help us build bridges of understanding and cooperation.

Wednesday, April 15, 2026

Week of Easter 2

Matthew 12:38-42

Jesus speaks of the sign of Jonah

Then some of the scribes and Pharisees said to [Jesus], "Teacher, we wish to see a sign from you." But he answered them, "An evil and adulterous generation asks for a sign, but no sign will be given to it except the sign of the prophet Jonah. For just as Jonah was three days and three nights in the belly of the sea monster, so for three days and three nights the Son of Man will be in the heart of the earth. The people of Nineveh will rise up at the judgment with this generation and condemn it, because they repented at the proclamation of Jonah, and indeed something greater than Jonah is here! The queen of the South will rise up at the judgment with this generation and condemn it, because she came from the ends of the earth to listen to the wisdom of Solomon, and indeed something greater than Solomon is here!" (Matt. 12:38-42)

Psalm

Psalm 114

God saves through water

Additional Reading

Jonah 2:1-10

Jonah's praise for deliverance

Hymn: Christ Is Living, ACS 934

Patient God, your people are often slow to hear and understand who you are calling us to be. Help us live each day grounded in your holy stories and steeped in the promise that you are present in every moment.

Thursday, April 16, 2026

Week of Easter 2

Psalm 116:1-4, 12-19

I will call upon God

I love the LORD because he has heard
    my voice and my supplications.
Because he inclined his ear to me,
    therefore I will call on him as long as I live.
The snares of death encompassed me;
    the pangs of Sheol laid hold on me;
    I suffered distress and anguish.
Then I called on the name of the LORD,
    "O LORD, I pray, save my life!" (Ps. 116:1-4)

Additional Readings

Isaiah 25:1-5
Praise for deliverance

1 Peter 1:8b-12
The promised salvation comes

Hymn: There Is a Longing in Our Hearts, ACS 1078

Ever-present God, we find comfort knowing that we live each day in your arms of mercy. In life and in death we belong to you. Open our hearts to receive your sustaining love.

Friday, April 17, 2026

Week of Easter 2

Isaiah 26:1-4

God sets up victory like bulwarks

On that day this song will be sung in the land of Judah:
We have a strong city;
    he sets up walls and bulwarks as a safeguard.
Open the gates,
    so that the righteous nation that maintains faithfulness
    may enter in.
Those of steadfast mind you keep in peace,
    in peace because they trust in you.
Trust in the LORD forever,
    for in the LORD GOD
    you have an everlasting rock. (Isa. 26:1-4)

Psalm

Psalm 116:1-4, 12-19
I will call upon God

Additional Reading

1 Peter 1:13-16
A holy life

Hymn: Why Should I Feel Discouraged, TFF 252

Peace-filled God, your heart grieves for our suffering. You desire all people and nations to love and care for one another. Fill our hearts and minds with your holy comfort and love. Use our lives to build lasting peace.

Saturday, April 18, 2026

Week of Easter 2

Luke 14:12-14

Welcome those in need to your table

[Jesus] said also to the one who had invited him, "When you give a luncheon or a dinner, do not invite your friends or your brothers and sisters or your relatives or rich neighbors, in case they may invite you in return, and you would be repaid. But when you give a banquet, invite the poor, the crippled, the lame, and the blind. And you will be blessed because they cannot repay you, for you will be repaid at the resurrection of the righteous." (Luke 14:12-14)

Psalm

Psalm 116:1-4, 12-19

I will call upon God

Additional Reading

Isaiah 25:6-9

The feast for all peoples

Hymn: Spirit, Open My Heart, ACS 1043

Welcoming God, you invite us to your table. You provide a bountiful banquet, where strangers become friends and all are welcome. Open our hearts to imagine and create a place where everyone has a seat of honor.

Sunday, April 19, 2026

Third Sunday of Easter

Olavus Petri, priest, died 1552; Laurentius Petri, Bishop of Uppsala, died 1573; renewers of the church

Luke 24:13-35

Eating with the risen Christ

As [the two disciples] came near the village to which they were going, he walked ahead as if he were going on. But they urged him strongly, saying, "Stay with us, because it is almost evening and the day is now nearly over." So he went in to stay with them. When he was at the table with them, he took bread, blessed and broke it, and gave it to them. Then their eyes were opened, and they recognized him, and he vanished from their sight. They said to each other, "Were not our hearts burning within us while he was talking to us on the road, while he was opening the scriptures to us?" (Luke 24:28-32)

Psalm

Psalm 116:1-4, 12-19
I will call upon God

Additional Readings

Acts 2:14a, 36-41
Receiving God's promise through baptism

1 Peter 1:17-23
Born anew

Hymn: Day of Arising, ELW 374

O God, your Son makes himself known to all his disciples in the breaking of bread. Open the eyes of our faith, that we may see him in his redeeming work, who lives and reigns with you and the Holy Spirit, one God, now and forever.

Monday, April 20, 2026

Week of Easter 3

Psalm 134

Praise God day and night

Come, bless the LORD, all you servants of the LORD,
 who stand by night in the house of the LORD!
Lift up your hands to the holy place,
 and bless the LORD.

May the LORD, maker of heaven and earth,
 bless you from Zion. (Ps. 134:1-3)

Additional Readings

Genesis 18:1-14
Abraham and Sarah eat with God

1 Peter 1:23-25
The word of God endures

Hymn: Oh, Sing to the Lord, ELW 822/TFF 274

Blessed are you, Creator of the universe. We marvel at all your works. We stand beneath the sparkling stars and beside the rolling ocean waves and feel your creative presence. Help us be caretakers of all that you have made.

Tuesday, April 21, 2026

Week of Easter 3

Anselm, Bishop of Canterbury, died 1109

Proverbs 8:32—9:6

Wisdom serves a meal

Wisdom has built her house;
    she has hewn her seven pillars.
She has slaughtered her animals; she has mixed her wine;
    she has also set her table.
She has sent out her female servants; she calls
    from the highest places in the town,
"You who are simple, turn in here!"
    To those without sense she says,
"Come, eat of my bread
    and drink of the wine I have mixed.
Lay aside immaturity and live,
    and walk in the way of insight." (Prov. 9:1-6)

Psalm

Psalm 134

Praise God day and night

Additional Reading

1 Peter 2:1-3

Long for the pure spiritual milk

Hymn: Come and Seek the Ways of Wisdom, ACS 971

God of wisdom and welcome, remind us daily of your invitation to abundant life. Give us joy in your word and courage to live your teaching in our lives, that we may be wise and blessed.

Wednesday, April 22, 2026

Week of Easter 3

Exodus 24:1-11

Moses and the elders eat with God

Then Moses and Aaron, Nadab and Abihu, and seventy of the elders of Israel went up, and they saw the God of Israel. Under his feet there was something like a pavement of sapphire stone, like the very heaven for clearness. God did not lay his hand on the chief men of the Israelites; they beheld God, and they ate and drank. (Exod. 24:9-11)

Psalm

Psalm 134

Praise God day and night

Additional Reading

John 21:1-14

The risen Christ eats with the disciples

Hymn: All Glory Be to God on High, ELW 410

Mysterious and awesome God, your holiness breaks into the world and makes all things new again. Your Spirit renews hope, clears vision, and opens space for creativity. Rekindle in us an awareness of your presence in our midst.

Thursday, April 23, 2026
Week of Easter 3

Toyohiko Kagawa, renewer of society, died 1960

Psalm 23

God our shepherd

You prepare a table before me
    in the presence of my enemies;
you anoint my head with oil;
    my cup overflows.
Surely goodness and mercy shall follow me
    all the days of my life,
and I shall dwell in the house of the LORD
    my whole life long. (Ps. 23:5-6)

Additional Readings

Exodus 2:15b-25
Moses the shepherd

1 Peter 2:9-12
Living as God's people

Hymn: We Come Now to Your Table, ACS 970

God of goodness and mercy, you promise to walk beside us always. You set a table of abundance, welcoming all. We have been called your holy ones. Remind us of this sacred anointing and send us forth in hope.

Friday, April 24, 2026

Week of Easter 4

1 Peter 2:13-17

Living honorably in the world

For the Lord's sake be subject to every human authority, whether to the emperor as supreme or to governors as sent by him to punish those who do wrong and to praise those who do right. For it is God's will that by doing right you should silence the ignorance of the foolish. As servants of God, live as free people, yet do not use your freedom as a pretext for evil. Honor everyone. Love the family of believers. Fear God. Honor the emperor. (1 Peter 2:13-17)

Psalm

Psalm 23
God our shepherd

Additional Reading

Exodus 3:16-22; 4:18-20
Moses the shepherd of Israel

Hymn: Have Thine Own Way, Lord, TFF 152

Builder of community, you have created us to live alongside our neighbors. You have a vision of one global family in which all live in peace and with justice. Shape our hearts to embrace the good news of your reign.

Saturday, April 25, 2026

Mark, Evangelist

Mark 1:1-15

The beginning of the gospel of Jesus Christ

The beginning of the good news of Jesus Christ.
As it is written in the prophet Isaiah,
"See, I am sending my messenger ahead of you,
who will prepare your way,
the voice of one crying out in the wilderness:
'Prepare the way of the Lord;
make his paths straight,' "
so John the baptizer appeared in the wilderness, proclaiming a baptism of repentance for the forgiveness of sins. And the whole Judean region and all the people of Jerusalem were going out to him and were baptized by him in the River Jordan, confessing their sins. (Mark 1:1-5)

Psalm

Psalm 57
Be merciful to me, O God

Additional Readings

Isaiah 52:7-10
The messenger announces salvation

2 Timothy 4:6-11, 18
The good fight of faith

Hymn: All Earth Is Hopeful, ELW 266/TFF 47

Almighty God, you have enriched your church with Mark's proclamation of the gospel. Give us grace to believe firmly in the good news of salvation and to walk daily in accord with it, through Jesus Christ, our Savior and Lord, who lives and reigns with you and the Holy Spirit, one God, now and forever.

Sunday, April 26, 2026

Fourth Sunday of Easter

John 10:1-10

Christ the shepherd

So again Jesus said to them, "Very truly, I tell you, I am the gate for the sheep. All who came before me are thieves and bandits, but the sheep did not listen to them. I am the gate. Whoever enters by me will be saved and will come in and go out and find pasture. The thief comes only to steal and kill and destroy. I came that they may have life and have it abundantly." (John 10:7-10)

Psalm

Psalm 23
God our shepherd

Additional Readings

Acts 2:42-47
The believers' common life

1 Peter 2:19-25
Follow the shepherd, even in suffering

Hymn: Lift Up Your Heads, ACS 1032

O God our shepherd, you know your sheep by name and lead us to safety through the valleys of death. Guide us by your voice, that we may walk in certainty and security to the joyous feast prepared in your house, through Jesus Christ, our Savior and Lord, who lives and reigns with you and the Holy Spirit, one God, now and forever.

Monday, April 27, 2026

Week of Easter 4

Psalm 100

We are the sheep of God's pasture

Make a joyful noise to the LORD, all the earth.
Serve the LORD with gladness;
come into his presence with singing.

Know that the LORD is God.
It is he who made us, and we are his;
we are his people and the sheep of his pasture.

Enter his gates with thanksgiving
and his courts with praise.
Give thanks to him; bless his name.

For the LORD is good;
his steadfast love endures forever
and his faithfulness to all generations. (Ps. 100)

Additional Readings

Ezekiel 34:17-23
God the true shepherd

1 Peter 5:1-5
Tend the flock of God

Hymn: The Earth Adorned in Verdant Robe, ACS 1068

Joy-filled God, the whole earth proclaims the goodness of all you have made. You created each person, and we belong to you. May we live our days basking in your goodness and steadfast love.

Tuesday, April 28, 2026

Week of Easter 4

Hebrews 13:20-21

God's blessing through Christ the shepherd

Now may the God of peace, who brought back from the dead our Lord Jesus, the great shepherd of the sheep, by the blood of the eternal covenant, make you complete in everything good so that you may do his will, as he works among us that which is pleasing in his sight, through Jesus Christ, to whom be the glory forever. Amen. (Heb. 13:20-21)

Psalm

Psalm 100

We are the sheep of God's pasture

Additional Reading

Ezekiel 34:23-31

God provides perfect pasture

Hymn: O Christ the Same, ELW 760

God our shepherd, through the life, death, and resurrection of your Son Jesus, you know our joys and sorrows. Strengthen our trust that what is written most deeply on our hearts is already held in your care.

Wednesday, April 29, 2026

Week of Easter 4

Catherine of Siena, theologian, died 1380

Jeremiah 23:1-8

God will gather the flock

Woe to the shepherds who destroy and scatter the sheep of my pasture! says the LORD. Therefore thus says the LORD, the God of Israel, concerning the shepherds who shepherd my people: It is you who have scattered my flock and have driven them away, and you have not attended to them. So I will attend to you for your evil doings, says the LORD. Then I myself will gather the remnant of my flock out of all the lands where I have driven them, and I will bring them back to their fold, and they shall be fruitful and multiply. I will raise up shepherds over them who will shepherd them, and they shall no longer fear or be dismayed, nor shall any be missing, says the LORD. (Jer. 23:1-4)

Psalm

Psalm 100

We are the sheep of God's pasture

Additional Reading

Matthew 20:17-28

Jesus came to serve

Hymn: Savior, like a Shepherd Lead Us, ELW 789/TFF 254

Holy Shepherd, you yearn for your people to live in peace. Let all feel the comfort of your protective presence. Help us to trust that you are leading us and encouraging us in our daily lives.

Thursday, April 30, 2026

Week of Easter 4

Psalm 31:1-5, 15-16

I commend my spirit

In you, O Lord, I seek refuge;
  do not let me ever be put to shame;
  in your righteousness deliver me.
Incline your ear to me;
  rescue me speedily.
Be a rock of refuge for me,
  a strong fortress to save me.

You are indeed my rock and my fortress;
  for your name's sake lead me and guide me;
take me out of the net that is hidden for me,
  for you are my refuge.
Into your hand I commit my spirit;
  you have redeemed me, O Lord, faithful God. (Ps. 31:1-5)

Additional Readings

Genesis 12:1-3
The call of Abram

Acts 6:8-15
Stephen is arrested

Hymn: Gracious Spirit, Heed Our Pleading, ELW 401/TFF 103

Rock of Ages, you have been our solid foundation from one generation to the next. You have been a refuge and a fortress. May we find continual assurance as your Holy Spirit encourages and lifts us up.

Prayer List for May

Friday, May 1, 2026

Philip and James, Apostles

John 14:8-14

The Son and the Father are one

Philip said to him, "Lord, show us the Father, and we will be satisfied." Jesus said to him, "Have I been with you all this time, Philip, and you still do not know me? Whoever has seen me has seen the Father. How can you say, 'Show us the Father'? Do you not believe that I am in the Father and the Father is in me? The words that I say to you I do not speak on my own, but the Father who dwells in me does his works." (John 14:8-10)

Psalm

Psalm 44:1-3, 20-26
Save us for the sake of your love

Additional Readings

Isaiah 30:18-21
God's mercy and justice

2 Corinthians 4:1-6
Proclaiming Jesus Christ as Lord

Hymn: When We Are Living, ELW 639

Almighty God, you gave to your apostles Philip and James grace and strength to bear witness to your Son. Grant that we, remembering their victory of faith, may glorify in life and death the name of our Lord Jesus Christ, who lives and reigns and you and the Holy Spirit, one God, now and forever.

Saturday, May 2, 2026

Week of Easter 4

Athanasius, Bishop of Alexandria, died 373

Jeremiah 26:20-24

A prophet of the Lord persecuted

There was another man prophesying in the name of the Lord, Uriah son of Shemaiah from Kiriath-jearim. He prophesied against this city and against this land in words exactly like those of Jeremiah. And when King Jehoiakim, with all his warriors and all the officials, heard his words, the king sought to put him to death, but when Uriah heard of it, he was afraid and fled and escaped to Egypt. Then King Jehoiakim sent Elnathan son of Achbor and men with him to Egypt, and they took Uriah from Egypt and brought him to King Jehoiakim, who struck him down with the sword and threw his dead body into the burial place of the common people.

But the hand of Ahikam son of Shaphan was with Jeremiah so that he was not given over into the hands of the people to be put to death. (Jer. 26:20-24)

Psalm

Psalm 31:1-5, 15-16
I commend my spirit

Additional Reading

John 8:48-59
John 8:48-59

Hymn: If We Live, We Live to the Lord, ACS 1025

God of the prophets, through action and word, in thought and deed, many have followed your ways, even to untimely death. Give us courage both in our living and in our dying to follow your message of hope and peace.

Sunday, May 3, 2026

Fifth Sunday of Easter

John 14:1-14

Christ the way, truth, life

Thomas said to him, “Lord, we do not know where you are going. How can we know the way?” Jesus said to him, “I am the way and the truth and the life. No one comes to the Father except through me. If you know me, you will know i my Father also. From now on you do know him and have seen him.” (John 14:5-7)

Psalm

Psalm 31:1-5, 15-16
I commend my spirit

Additional Readings

Acts 7:55-60
Martyrdom of Stephen

1 Peter 2:2-10
God’s chosen people

Hymn: You Are the Way, ELW 758

Almighty God, your Son Jesus Christ is the way, the truth, and the life. Give us grace to love one another, to follow in the way of his commandments, and to share his risen life with all the world, for he lives and reigns with you and the Holy Spirit, one God, now and forever.

Monday, May 4, 2026

Week of Easter 5

Monica, mother of Augustine, died 387

Psalm 102:1-17

Prayer for deliverance

But you, O LORD, are enthroned forever;
your name endures to all generations.
You will rise up and have compassion on Zion,
for it is time to favor it;
the appointed time has come.
For your servants hold its stones dear
and have pity on its dust.
The nations will fear the name of the LORD
and all the kings of the earth your glory.
For the LORD will build up Zion;
he will appear in his glory. (Ps. 102:12-16)

Additional Readings

Exodus 13:17-22
God leads the way

Acts 7:17-40
Stephen addresses the council

Hymn: Lead Me, Guide Me, ELW 768/TFF 70

God of appointed times and endless compassion, you hold the fullness of each moment in your merciful hands, and we wait upon your presence. Give us the patience of stones, that we may weather the hardships of this day.

Tuesday, May 5, 2026
Week of Easter 5

Proverbs 3:5-12
God, the truth and life

Trust in the LORD with all your heart,
    and do not rely on your own insight.
In all your ways acknowledge him,
    and he will make straight your paths.
Do not be wise in your own eyes;
    fear the LORD and turn away from evil.
It will be a healing for your flesh
    and a refreshment for your body. (Prov. 3:5-8)

Psalm
Psalm 102:1-17
Prayer for deliverance

Additional Reading
Acts 7:44-56
Stephen confronts the council

Hymn: Come and Seek the Ways of Wisdom, ACS 971

You are the healer of wounds, O God, and the refresher of bodies. Set tired feet on steady paths of wholeness. Guide us in your ways of wisdom and insight, so that our lives may follow in your grace.

Wednesday, May 6, 2026

Week of Easter 5

John 8:31-38

Jesus, the truth of God

Jesus answered [the Jews who had believed in him], "Very truly, I tell you, everyone who commits sin is a slave to sin. The slave does not have a permanent place in the household; the son has a place there forever. So if the Son makes you free, you will be free indeed. I know that you are descendants of Abraham, yet you look for an opportunity to kill me because there is no place in you for my word. I declare what I have seen in the Father's presence; as for you, you should do what you have heard from the Father." (John 8:34-38)

Psalm

Psalm 102:1-17

Prayer for deliverance

Additional Reading

Proverbs 3:13-18

God, the truth and life

Hymn: Let My Spirit Always Sing, ACS 1020

Liberating God, from all that would enslave, you set us free! Unshackle hardened hearts, and open minds imprisoned by fear, so that your forgiveness might carry us to new life and new love for your sake.

Thursday, May 7, 2026

Week of Easter 5

Psalm 66:8-20

Be joyful in God, all you lands

Bless our God, O peoples;
    let the sound of his praise be heard,
who has kept us among the living
    and has not let our feet slip.
For you, O God, have tested us;
    you have tried us as silver is tried.
You brought us into the net;
    you laid burdens on our backs;
you let people ride over our heads;
    we went through fire and through water;
yet you have brought us out to a spacious place. (Ps. 66:8-12)

Additional Readings

Genesis 6:5-22
God's command to Noah

Acts 27:1-12
Paul sails for Rome

Hymn: I've Got Peace Like a River, TFF 258

With every breath our bodies take, we praise and bless you, O God. Guide us on your tried-and-true path, and carry us into your spacious embrace, that we might praise and bless you anew.

Friday, May 8, 2026

Week of Easter 5

Julian of Norwich, renewer of the church, died around 1416

Genesis 7:1-24

The great flood

Then the LORD said to Noah, "Go into the ark, you and all your household, for I have seen that you alone are righteous before me in this generation. Take with you seven pairs of all clean animals, the male and its mate; and a pair of the animals that are not clean, the male and its mate; and seven pairs of the birds of the air also, male and female, to keep their kind alive on the face of all the earth. For in seven days I will send rain on the earth for forty days and forty nights, and every living thing that I have made I will blot out from the face of the ground." And Noah did all that the LORD had commanded him. (Gen. 7:1-5)

Psalm

Psalm 66:8-20

Be joyful in God, all you lands

Additional Reading

Acts 27:13-38

Paul survives shipwreck

Hymn: God, Who Stretched the Spangled Heavens, ELW 771

God of the rain and the ark, both floodwaters and our protection are found in you. Sustain all your children overwhelmed by ecological tumult, and reveal your resilient grace, that it would carry your creation when waters rise.

Saturday, May 9, 2026

Week of Easter 5

Nicolaus Ludwig von Zinzendorf, renewer of the church, hymnwriter, died 1760

John 14:27-29

Peace I leave with you

[Jesus said,] "Peace I leave with you; my peace I give to you. I do not give to you as the world gives. Do not let your hearts be troubled, and do not let them be afraid. You heard me say to you, 'I am going away, and I am coming to you.' If you loved me, you would rejoice that I am going to the Father, because the Father is greater than I. And now I have told you this before it occurs, so that when it does occur you may believe." (John 14:27-29)

Psalm

Psalm 66:8-20

Be joyful in God, all you lands

Additional Reading

Genesis 8:13-19

The flood waters subside

Hymn: Deep Peace, ACS 1018

Gracious God, you grant us your peace even when we feel your absence. Calm our troubled hearts and ease the fear felt by bodies, so that in your settling grace, we might become instruments for your peace and presence.

Sunday, May 10, 2026

Sixth Sunday of Easter

John 14:15-21

Christ our advocate

[Jesus said,] "If you love me, you will keep my commandments. And I will ask the Father, and he will give you another Advocate, to be with you forever. This is the Spirit of truth, whom the world cannot receive because it neither sees him nor knows him. You know him because he abides with you, and he will be in you." (John 14:15-17)

Psalm

Psalm 66:8-20

Be joyful in God, all you lands

Additional Readings

Acts 17:22-31

Paul's message to the Athenians

1 Peter 3:13-22

The days of Noah, a sign of baptism

Hymn: Abide with Me, ELW 629

Almighty and ever-living God, you hold together all things in heaven and on earth. In your great mercy receive the prayers of all your children, and give to all the world the Spirit of your truth and peace, through Jesus Christ, our Savior and Lord, who lives and reigns with you and the Holy Spirit, one God, now and forever.

Monday, May 11, 2026

Week of Easter 6

Psalm 93

God reigns above the floods

The LORD is king; he is robed in majesty;
 the LORD is robed; he is girded with strength.
He has established the world; it shall never be moved;
 your throne is established from of old;
 you are from everlasting. . . .
More majestic than the thunders of mighty waters,
 more majestic than the waves of the sea,
 majestic on high is the LORD!

Your decrees are very sure;
 holiness befits your house,
 O LORD, forevermore. (Ps. 93:1-2, 4-5)

Additional Readings

Genesis 9:8-17
Sign of the covenant

Acts 27:39-44
Paul and his companions come safely to land

Hymn: All Creatures, Worship God Most High, ELW 835

The waves crash and recede, but your love remains, O God. Shelter us in your strong compassion, and when we drift through uncertain waters, anchor us again to the promise of your protection.

Tuesday, May 12, 2026

Week of Easter 6

1 Peter 3:8-12

We are God's sheep

Finally, all of you, have unity of spirit, sympathy, love for one another, a tender heart, and a humble mind. Do not repay evil for evil or abuse for abuse, but, on the contrary, repay with a blessing. It is for this that you were called—that you might inherit a blessing. For

"Those who desire to love life
  and to see good days,
let them keep their tongues from evil
  and their lips from speaking deceit;
let them turn away from evil and do good;
  let them seek peace and pursue it.
For the eyes of the Lord are on the righteous,
  and his ears are open to their prayer.
But the face of the Lord is against those who do evil."

(1 Peter 3:8-12)

Psalm

Psalm 93

God reigns above the floods

Additional Reading

Deuteronomy 5:22-33

Moses delivers God's commandments

Hymn: Lord, Listen to Your Children Praying, ELW 752/TFF 247

Suffering One, you show us the way to swallow bitter insults and repay evil with forgiveness. By your grace, help us absorb and transform the treachery in our lives into seeds, which when buried break forth in blessing.

Wednesday, May 13, 2026

Week of Easter 6

John 16:16-24

A little while, and you shall see

[Jesus said,] "A little while, and you will no longer see me, and again a little while, and you will see me." Then some of his disciples said to one another, "What does he mean by saying to us, 'A little while, and you will no longer see me, and again a little while, and you will see me,' and 'because I am going to the Father'?" They said, "What does he mean by this 'a little while'? We do not know what he is talking about." Jesus knew that they wanted to ask him, so he said to them, "Are you discussing among yourselves what I meant when I said, 'A little while, and you will no longer see me, and again a little while, and you will see me'? Very truly, I tell you, you will weep and mourn, but the world will rejoice; you will have pain, but your pain will turn into joy. (John 16:16-20)

Psalm

Psalm 93

God reigns above the floods

Additional Reading

Deuteronomy 31:1-13

Moses promises God's presence

Hymn: Healer of Our Every Ill, ELW 612

God of joy and sorrow, presence and absence, reveal yourself today. May all who labor through loss or groan in grief find hope in your anticipated presence, just as expectant mothers wait for pain to turn into newborn joy.

Thursday, May 14, 2026

Ascension of Our Lord

Matthias, Apostle transferred to May 15

Luke 24:44-53

Christ present in all times and places

Then [Jesus] opened [the disciples'] minds to understand the scriptures, and he said to them, "Thus it is written, that the Messiah is to suffer and to rise from the dead on the third day and that repentance and forgiveness of sins is to be proclaimed in his name to all nations, beginning from Jerusalem. You are witnesses of these things. And see, I am sending upon you what my Father promised, so stay here in the city until you have been clothed with power from on high." (Luke 24:45-49)

Psalm

Psalm 47

God has gone up with a shout

Additional Readings

Acts 1:1-11

Jesus sends the apostles

Ephesians 1:15-23

Seeing the risen and ascended Christ

Hymn: Hail Thee, Festival Day! ELW 394

Almighty God, your blessed Son, our Savior Jesus Christ, ascended far above all heavens that he might fill all things. Mercifully give us faith to trust that, as he promised, he abides with us on earth to the end of time, who lives and reigns with you and the Holy Spirit, one God, now and forever.

Friday, May 15, 2026

Matthias, Apostle (transferred)

Luke 6:12-16

Jesus calls the Twelve

Now during those days [Jesus] went out to the mountain to pray, and he spent the night in prayer to God. And when day came, he called his disciples and chose twelve of them, whom he also named apostles: Simon, whom he named Peter, and his brother Andrew, and James, and John, and Philip, and Bartholomew, and Matthew, and Thomas, and James son of Alphaeus, and Simon, who was called the Zealot, and Judas son of James, and Judas Iscariot, who became a traitor. (Luke 6:12-16)

Psalm

Psalm 56
I am bound by the vow I made to you

Additional Readings

Isaiah 66:1-2
Heaven is God's throne, earth is God's footstool

Acts 1:15-26
The apostles cast lots for Matthias

Hymn: I Come with Joy, ELW 482

Almighty God, you chose your faithful servant Matthias to be numbered among the twelve. Grant that your church may always be taught and guided by faithful and true pastors, through Jesus Christ our shepherd, who lives and reigns with you and the Holy Spirit, one God, now and forever.

Saturday, May 16, 2026

Week of Easter 6

2 Kings 2:13-15

The spirit rests on Elisha

[Elisha] picked up the mantle of Elijah that had fallen from him and went back and stood on the bank of the Jordan. He took the mantle of Elijah that had fallen from him and struck the water. He said, "Where is the LORD, the God of Elijah? Where is he?" He struck the water again, and the water was parted to the one side and to the other, and Elisha crossed over.

When the company of prophets who were at Jericho saw him at a distance, they declared, "The spirit of Elijah rests on Elisha." They came to meet him and bowed to the ground before him.
(2 Kings 2:13-15)

Psalm

Psalm 93

Praise to God who reigns

Additional Reading

John 8:21-30

Jesus speaks of going to the Father

Hymn: Swing Low, Sweet Chariot, TFF 171

God, you part the water and lead us to future shores. As your spirit rested on Elisha, so bring your presence to rest on your servants now. Carry your prophets through crisis, and confirm their call as you pass it to new generations.

Sunday, May 17, 2026

Seventh Sunday of Easter

John 17:1-11

Christ's prayer for his disciples

[Jesus prayed,] "I have made your name known to those whom you gave me from the world. They were yours, and you gave them to me, and they have kept your word. Now they know that everything you have given me is from you, for the words that you gave to me I have given to them, and they have received them and know in truth that I came from you, and they have believed that you sent me. I am asking on their behalf; I am not asking on behalf of the world but on behalf of those whom you gave me, because they are yours. All mine are yours, and yours are mine, and I have been glorified in them. And now I am no longer in the world, but they are in the world, and I am coming to you. Holy Father, protect them in your name that you have given me, so that they may be one, as we are one." (John 17:6-11)

Psalm

Psalm 68:1-10, 32-35
Sing to God

Additional Readings

Acts 1:6-14
Jesus' companions at prayer

1 Peter 4:12-14; 5:6-11
God sustains those who suffer

Hymn: We Are All One in Christ, ELW 643/TFF 221

O God of glory, your Son Jesus Christ suffered for us and ascended to your right hand. Unite us with Christ and each other in suffering and in joy, that all the world may be drawn into your bountiful presence, through Jesus Christ, our Savior and Lord, who lives and reigns with you and the Holy Spirit, one God, now and forever.

Monday, May 18, 2026

Week of Easter 7

Erik, King of Sweden, martyr, died 1160

Psalm 99

Priests and people praise God

The LORD is king; let the peoples tremble!
He sits enthroned upon the cherubim; let the earth quake!
The LORD is great in Zion;
he is exalted over all the peoples.
Let them praise your great and awesome name.
Holy is he!
Mighty King, lover of justice,
you have established equity;
you have executed justice
and righteousness in Jacob.
Extol the LORD our God;
worship at his footstool.
Holy is he! (Ps. 99:1-5)

Additional Readings

Leviticus 9:1-11, 22-24
The high priest Aaron offers sacrifice

1 Peter 4:1-6
Live by the will of God

Hymn: O Beauty Ever Ancient, ACS 1100

Lover of justice, your mercy is revealed through spring blossoms, and your righteousness falls like rain. Make our hearts a garden of holy desire so that your peace may be revealed in our work and our ways.

Tuesday, May 19, 2026

Week of Easter 7

1 Peter 4:7-11

Be good stewards of grace

The end of all things is near; therefore be serious and discipline yourselves for the sake of your prayers. Above all, maintain constant love for one another, for love covers a multitude of sins. Be hospitable to one another without complaining. Like good stewards of the manifold grace of God, serve one another with whatever gift each of you has received. Whoever speaks must do so as one speaking the very words of God; whoever serves must do so with the strength that God supplies, so that God may be glorified in all things through Jesus Christ. To him belong the glory and the power forever and ever. Amen. (1 Peter 4:7-11)

Psalm

Psalm 99

Priests and people praise God

Additional Reading

Numbers 16:41-50

The high priest Aaron makes atonement

Hymn: Let Streams of Living Justice, ELW 710

Your love covers all creation, O God. Weave all that we say and do into a blanket of your compassion, so that with Jesus, your servant and Son, we might serve you in strength and speak your words in love.

Wednesday, May 20, 2026

Week of Easter 7

1 Kings 8:54-65

Solomon offers sacrifice

Then the king and all Israel with him offered sacrifice before the LORD. Solomon offered as sacrifices of well-being to the LORD twenty-two thousand oxen and one hundred twenty thousand sheep. So the king and all the people of Israel dedicated the house of the LORD. The same day the king consecrated the middle of the court that was in front of the house of the Lord, for there he offered the burnt offerings and the grain offerings and the fat pieces of the sacrifices of well-being, because the bronze altar that was before the LORD was too small to receive the burnt offerings and the grain offerings and the fat pieces of the sacrifices of well-being.

So Solomon held the festival at that time and all Israel with him—a great assembly, people from Lebo-hamath to the Wadi of Egypt—before the LORD our God, seven days. (1 Kings 8:62-65)

Psalm

Psalm 99

Priests and people praise God

Additional Reading

John 3:31-36

The Son and the Father

Hymn: O Christ, Your Heart, Compassionate, ELW 722

Living God, no sanctuary or sacrifice is worthy of your grace, but you offer it as freely as each breath. Receive our meager prayers, that by your blessing, our very lives may become an offering of authentic worship and praise.

Thursday, May 21, 2026

Week of Easter 7

Helena, mother of Constantine, died around 330

Psalm 33:12-22

Our help and our shield

Truly the eye of the LORD is on those who fear him,
on those who hope in his steadfast love,
to deliver their soul from death
and to keep them alive in famine.

Our soul waits for the LORD;
he is our help and shield.
Our heart is glad in him
because we trust in his holy name.
Let your steadfast love, O LORD, be upon us,
even as we hope in you. (Ps. 33:18-22)

Psalm

Exodus 19:1-9a

The covenant at Sinai

Additional Reading

Acts 2:1-11

The giving of the Spirit

Hymn: For the Troubles and the Sufferings, ACS 1051

Mighty God and helper of souls, you fill those hungry for hope, and you shield the vulnerable with steadfast love. Turn us again toward your tender gaze, that we might be found and fed by your unending mercy.

Friday, May 22, 2026

Week of Easter 7

Romans 8:14-17

Led by the Spirit of God

For all who are led by the Spirit of God are children of God. For you did not receive a spirit of slavery to fall back into fear, but you received a spirit of adoption. When we cry, "Abba! Father!" it is that very Spirit bearing witness with our spirit that we are children of God, and if children, then heirs: heirs of God and joint heirs with Christ, if we in fact suffer with him so that we may also be glorified with him. (Rom. 8:14-17)

Psalm

Psalm 33:12-22

Our help and our shield

Additional Reading

Exodus 19:16-25

Moses and Aaron meet the LORD

Hymn: Go, My Children, with My Blessing, ELW 543/TFF 161

Loving God, from out of suffering you adopt us as children, and with joy you make us heirs. Be present to those who yearn for family's embrace. Hold us when we feel frightened and like a motherless child.

Saturday, May 23, 2026

Vigil of Pentecost

John 7:37-39

Jesus, the true living water

On the last day of the festival, the great day, while Jesus was standing there, he cried out, "Let anyone who is thirsty come to me, and let the one who believes in me drink. As the scripture has said, 'Out of the believer's heart shall flow rivers of living water.'" Now he said this about the Spirit, which believers in him were to receive, for as yet there was no Spirit because Jesus was not yet glorified. (John 7:37-39)

Psalm

Psalm 33:12-22
The LORD is our helper and our shield.

Additional Readings

Exodus 19:1-9a
The covenant at Sinai

Romans 8:14-17, 22-27
Praying with the Spirit

Hymn: Come to Me, All Pilgrims Thirsty, ELW 777

Almighty and ever-living God, you fulfilled the promise of Easter by sending the gift of your Holy Spirit. Look upon your people gathered in prayer, open to receive the Spirit's flame. May it come to rest in our hearts and heal the divisions of word and tongue, that with one voice and one song we may praise your name in joy and thanksgiving; through Jesus Christ, our Savior and Lord, who lives and reigns with you and the Holy Spirit, one God, now and forever.

Pentecost

The festival of Pentecost celebrates the Spirit poured out on the people, the breath of God offering strength, peace, and the power to forgive sins. Christians trust that the Spirit is present wherever two or more are gathered in Jesus' name. The Spirit intercedes on our behalf, stirs in hearts and whole communities, and understands sighs too deep for words. This season we remember that God is still present and working through our human experiences. We pray for the Spirit to guide us in faith, hope, and love. And we ask the Spirit to show us patience and wisdom to live in peace with each other and our neighbors.

Table Prayer for Pentecost

Blessed are you, O Lord our God.
We give you thanks for this meal
and ask for the courage and compassion
to live like your abundance has the first and last word on our lives
until all who hunger have daily bread,
and all who have their fill are hungry for justice,
through Jesus Christ our Lord. Amen.

Thanksgiving for the Holy Spirit

Use this prayer during the week following Pentecost Sunday.

O Spirit of God, seek us;
Good Spirit, pray with us;
Spirit of counsel, inform us;
Spirit of might, free us;
Spirit of truth, enlighten us;
Spirit of Christ, raise us;
O Holy Spirit, dwell in us. Amen.

Sunday, May 24, 2026

Day of Pentecost

Nicolaus Copernicus, died 1543; Leonhard Euler, died 1783; scientists

John 20:19-23

The Spirit poured out

When it was evening on that day, the first day of the week, and the doors were locked where the disciples were, for fear of the Jews, Jesus came and stood among them and said, "Peace be with you." After he said this, he showed them his hands and his side. Then the disciples rejoiced when they saw the Lord. Jesus said to them again, "Peace be with you. As the Father has sent me, so I send you." When he had said this, he breathed on them and said to them, "Receive the Holy Spirit. If you forgive the sins of any, they are forgiven them; if you retain the sins of any, they are retained." (John 20:19-23)

Psalm

Psalm 104:24-34, 35b
Renewing the face of the earth

Additional Readings

Acts 2:1-21
Filled with the Spirit

1 Corinthians 12:3b-13
Varieties of gifts, the same Spirit

Hymn: Gracious Spirit, Heed Our Pleading, ELW 401/TFF 103

O God, on this day you open the hearts of your faithful people by sending into us your Holy Spirit. Direct us by the light of that Spirit, that we may have a right judgment in all things and rejoice at all times in your peace, through Jesus Christ, your Son and our Lord, who lives and reigns with you and the Holy Spirit, one God, now and forever.

Monday, May 25, 2026

Time after Pentecost

Psalm 104:24-34, 35b

Renewing the face of the earth

O Lord, how manifold are your works!
In wisdom you have made them all;
the earth is full of your creatures. . . .

These all look to you
to give them their food in due season;
when you give to them, they gather it up;
when you open your hand, they are filled with good things.
When you hide your face, they are dismayed;
when you take away their breath, they die
and return to their dust.
When you send forth your spirit, they are created,
and you renew the face of the ground. (Ps. 104:24, 27-30)

Additional Readings

Joel 2:18-29
The promised spirit of God

Romans 8:18-24
We have the first fruits of the Spirit

Hymn: When You Send Forth Your Spirit, ACS 945

God of soil and air, your Spirit renews the face of the earth. Bring your refreshing breeze to lungs choked by poisoned air, and extend your restful grace to lands exhausted or depleted, that all creation might flourish and breathe.

Tuesday, May 26, 2026

Time after Pentecost

Romans 8:26-27

Praying in the Spirit

Likewise the Spirit helps us in our weakness, for we do not know how to pray as we ought, but that very Spirit intercedes with groanings too deep for words. And God, who searches hearts, knows what is the mind of the Spirit, because the Spirit intercedes for the saints according to the will of God. (Rom. 8:26-27)

Psalm

Psalm 104:24-34, 35b

The spirit of God on Amasai

Additional Reading

Ezekiel 39:7-8, 21-29

The promised spirit of God

Hymn: Every Time I Feel the Spirit, ACS 942/TFF 241

Interceding Spirit, you search all hearts and you know all minds. Ease the groans of anguish too deep for words, and strengthen our weakened hearts, so that your healing hope springs from the depths of our being.

Wednesday, May 27, 2026

Time after Pentecost

John Calvin, renewer of the church, died 1564

Numbers 11:24-30

The spirit rests on Israel's elders

Two men remained in the camp, one named Eldad and the other named Medad, and the spirit rested on them; they were among those registered, but they had not gone out to the tent, so they prophesied in the camp. And a young man ran and told Moses, "Eldad and Medad are prophesying in the camp." And Joshua son of Nun, the assistant of Moses, one of his chosen men, said, "My lord Moses, stop them!" But Moses said to him, "Are you jealous for my sake? Would that all the Lord's people were prophets and that the Lord would put his spirit on them!" And Moses and the elders of Israel returned to the camp. (Num. 11:26-30)

Psalm

Psalm 104:24-34, 35b

Renewing the face of the earth

Additional Reading

John 7:37-39

Jesus, the true living water

Hymn: How Clear Is Our Vocation, Lord, ELW 580

God, you speak through unexpected people and reveal yourself in places we dare not go. Expose our jealousy wherever your mercy crosses our petty borders, so that your prophets might again lead us to lands where your compassion flows.

Thursday, May 28, 2026

Time after Pentecost

Psalm 8

How exalted is your name

O LORD, our Sovereign,
 how majestic is your name in all the earth!

You have set your glory above the heavens.
 Out of the mouths of babes and infants
you have founded a bulwark because of your foes,
 to silence the enemy and the avenger.

When I look at your heavens, the work of your fingers,
 the moon and the stars that you have established;
what are humans that you are mindful of them,
 mortals that you care for them?

Yet you have made them a little lower than God
 and crowned them with glory and honor. (Ps. 8:1-4)

Additional Readings

Job 38:1-11
Creation story from Job

2 Timothy 1:8-12a
Grace revealed in Christ

Hymn: For the Beauty of the Earth, ELW 879

Composer of our days and director of our lives, your wonder is engraved in the foundations of all creation. Tune our hearts to praise, and silence our crowded minds so we might sing the majesty of your love.

Friday, May 29, 2026

Time after Pentecost

Jiří Tranovský, hymnwriter, died 1637

2 Timothy 1:12b-14

The treasure of the triune God

But I am not ashamed, for I know the one in whom I have put my trust, and I am sure that he is able to guard until that day the deposit I have entrusted to him. Hold to the standard of sound teaching that you have heard from me, in the faith and love that are in Christ Jesus. Guard the good deposit entrusted to you, with the help of the Holy Spirit living in us. (2 Tim. 1:12b-14)

Psalm

Psalm 8

How exalted is your name

Additional Reading

Job 38:12-21

Creation story from Job

Hymn: God, Whose Giving Knows No Ending, ELW 678

Jesus, our great treasure, your faith and love are gifts beyond measure. As you entrust your teaching to fools and squander your grace unreservedly, may we love without shame and freely trust in your life, death, and resurrection.

Saturday, May 30, 2026

Time after Pentecost

John 14:15-17

Father, Son, Spirit

[Jesus said,] "If you love me, you will keep my commandments. And I will ask the Father, and he will give you another Advocate, to be with you forever. This is the Spirit of truth, whom the world cannot receive because it neither sees him nor knows him. You know him because he abides with you, and he will be in you." (John 14:15-17)

Psalm

Psalm 8

How exalted is your name

Additional Reading

Job 38:22-38

Creation story from Job

Hymn: Mercy, We Abide in You, ACS 1077

Great Three and abiding One, your truth is revealed through diversity and your compassion is received in unity. Open the eyes of our hearts to your Trinitarian love as it delights to dwell among and within us today.

Time after Pentecost

Summer

In worship during the time after Pentecost we listen to gospel stories about Jesus' teaching and healing ministry. This season is launched by the dramatic movement of the Spirit that unites young and old, people of all genders, and people who speak all the known languages of the world. The rest of the season involves learning to pay attention to the more subtle movements of God's creative Spirit in everyday life.

For those of us in the Northern Hemisphere, this season of spiritual growth corresponds to the time of planting and growing crops that feed all of us who are hungry. For many, the rhythms of life change during the summer and provide for a more restful way of being in the world. We pray that the re-creation of this season offers us a clearer focus on who God declares us to be and on how we should live as God's people.

Table Prayer for Summer

Holy God, you gave us your good creation
and invited us to be co-creators
and sustainers of its gifts with you.
Let this food grown from the earth nourish our bodies
so that we might be the body of your Son,
continuing in service to the world.
In Jesus' name we pray. Amen.

Sunday, May 31, 2026

The Holy Trinity

Visit of Mary to Elizabeth transferred to June 1

Matthew 28:16-20

Living in the community of the Trinity

Now the eleven disciples went to Galilee, to the mountain to which Jesus had directed them. When they saw him, they worshiped him, but they doubted. And Jesus came and said to them, "All authority in heaven and on earth has been given to me. Go therefore and make disciples of all nations, baptizing them in the name of the Father and of the Son and of the Holy Spirit and teaching them to obey everything that I have commanded you. And remember, I am with you always, to the end of the age." (Matt. 28:16-20)

Psalm

Psalm 8

How exalted is your name

Additional Readings

Genesis 1:1—2:4a

Creation of the heavens and the earth

2 Corinthians 13:11-13

Paul's farewell

Hymn: Come, Join the Dance of Trinity, ELW 412

God of heaven and earth, before the foundation of the universe and the beginning of time you are the triune God: Author of creation, eternal Word of salvation, life-giving Spirit of wisdom. Guide us to all truth by your Spirit, that we may proclaim all that Christ has revealed and rejoice in the glory he shares with us. Glory and praise to you, Father, Son, and Holy Spirit, now and forever.

Prayer List for June

Monday, June 1, 2026

Visit of Mary to Elizabeth (transferred)

Justin, martyr at Rome, died around 165

Luke 1:39-57

Mary greets Elizabeth

In those days Mary set out and went with haste to a Judean town in the hill country, where she entered the house of Zechariah and greeted Elizabeth. When Elizabeth heard Mary's greeting, the child leaped in her womb. And Elizabeth was filled with the Holy Spirit and exclaimed with a loud cry, "Blessed are you among women, and blessed is the fruit of your womb." (Luke 1:39-42)

Psalm

Psalm 113
God, the helper of the needy

Additional Readings

1 Samuel 2:1-10
Hannah's thanksgiving

Romans 12:9-16b
Rejoice with those who rejoice

Hymn: Praise to the Lord, ELW 844

Mighty God, by whose grace Elizabeth rejoiced with Mary and greeted her as the mother of the Lord: look with favor on your lowly servants that, with Mary, we may magnify your holy name and rejoice to acclaim her Son as our Savior, who lives and reigns with you and the Holy Spirit, one God, now and forever.

Tuesday, June 2, 2026

Time after Pentecost

Psalm 29

Praise the glory of God

Ascribe to the LORD, O heavenly beings,
ascribe to the LORD glory and strength.
Ascribe to the LORD the glory of his name;
worship the LORD in holy splendor. . . .

The LORD sits enthroned over the flood;
the LORD sits enthroned as king forever.
May the LORD give strength to his people!
May the LORD bless his people with peace! (Ps. 29:1-2, 10-11)

Additional Readings

Job 39:13-25
Creation story from Job

1 Corinthians 12:4-13
The Spirit in the community

Hymn: Lord, Thee I Love with All My Heart, ELW 750

Holy God, we give you thanks for your presence in our world and for the ways in which your Spirit intercedes for us, heeding the pleas of your people. Send your Spirit upon us, and journey with us.

Wednesday, June 3, 2026

Time after Pentecost

The Martyrs of Uganda, died 1886
John XXIII, Bishop of Rome, died 1963

John 14:25-26

Father, Son, Spirit

[Jesus said,] "I have said these things to you while I am still with you. But the Advocate, the Holy Spirit, whom the Father will send in my name, will teach you everything and remind you of all that I have said to you." (John 14:25-26)

Psalm

Psalm 29
Praise the glory of God

Additional Reading

Job 39:26—40:5
Creation story from Job; Job's response

Hymn: Lord, Keep Us Steadfast in Your Word, ELW 517

Gracious God, you keep us steadfast. Send your Spirit into this world and be our advocate. Open hearts and minds to every way your word speaks to us, that we may continue in the path Christ set before us.

Thursday, June 4, 2026

Time after Pentecost

Psalm 50:7-15

The salvation of God

"Hear, O my people, and I will speak,
O Israel, I will testify against you.
I am God, your God. . . .

"Offer to God a sacrifice of thanksgiving,
and pay your vows to the Most High.
Call on me in the day of trouble;
I will deliver you, and you shall glorify me." (Ps. 50:7, 14-15)

Additional Readings

Lamentations 1:7-11
Jerusalem becomes unclean

2 Peter 2:17-22
The world's entanglements

Hymn: We Praise You, O God, ELW 870

O God, we give you thanks for the myriad ways in which your word comes to us. Surround us in your grace, and strongly embrace us in days of trouble.

Friday, June 5, 2026

Time after Pentecost

Boniface, Bishop of Mainz, missionary to Germany, martyr, died 754

Acts 28:1-10

Paul in Malta heals Publius

Now in the vicinity of that place were lands belonging to the leading man of the island, named Publius, who received us and entertained us hospitably for three days. It so happened that the father of Publius lay sick in bed with fever and dysentery. Paul visited him and cured him by praying and putting his hands on him. After this happened, the rest of the people on the island who had diseases also came and were cured. They bestowed many honors on us, and when we were about to sail, they put on board all the provisions we needed. (Acts 28:7-10)

Psalm

Psalm 50:7-15
The salvation of God

Additional Reading

Lamentations 3:40-58
Let us return to God

Hymn: Golden Breaks the Dawn, ELW 852

Living God, you give us our daily bread and heal us with your unending mercy and comfort. Be with us throughout our lives, and reveal to us your love in unexpected ways.

Saturday, June 6, 2026

Time after Pentecost

Matthew 9:27-34

Jesus heals those who are blind or mute

As Jesus went on from there, two blind men followed him, crying loudly, "Have mercy on us, Son of David!" When he entered the house, the blind men came to him, and Jesus said to them, "Do you have faith that I can do this?" They said to him, "Yes, Lord." Then he touched their eyes and said, "According to your faith, let it be done to you." And their eyes were opened. Then Jesus sternly ordered them, "See that no one knows of this." But they went away and spread the news about him through all of that district. (Matt. 9:27-31)

Psalm

Psalm 50:7-15

The salvation of God

Additional Reading

Exodus 34:1-9

Moses makes new tablets

Hymn: Praise, Praise! You are my Rock, ELW 862

You are our rock and our salvation, O risen Christ. As you healed the blind man who came to you, bring your healing presence into our world and break down those divisions that seek to separate your people.

Sunday, June 7, 2026

Time after Pentecost

Seattle, chief of the Duwamish Confederacy, died 1866

Matthew 9:9-13, 18-26

Christ heals a woman and raises a girl

As Jesus was walking along, he saw a man called Matthew sitting at the tax-collection station, and he said to him, "Follow me." And he got up and followed him.

And as he sat at dinner in the house, many tax collectors and sinners came and were sitting with Jesus and his disciples. When the Pharisees saw this, they said to his disciples, "Why does your teacher eat with tax collectors and sinners?" But when he heard this, he said, "Those who are well have no need of a physician, but those who are sick. Go and learn what this means, 'I desire mercy, not sacrifice.' For I have not come to call the righteous but sinners." (Matt. 9:9-13)

Psalm

Psalm 50:7-15
The salvation of God

Additional Readings

Hosea 5:15—6:6
God desires steadfast love

Romans 4:13-25
The faith of Abraham

Hymn: Lord, Take My Hand and Lead Me, ELW 767

O God, you are the source of life and the ground of our being. By the power of your Spirit bring healing to this wounded world, and raise us to the new life of your Son, Jesus Christ, our Savior and Lord.

Monday, June 8, 2026

Time after Pentecost

Psalm 40:1-8

God's will, not sacrifice

Happy are those who make
    the Lord their trust,
who do not turn to the proud,
    to those who go astray after false gods.
You have multiplied, O Lord my God,
    your wondrous deeds and your thoughts toward us;
    none can compare with you.
Were I to proclaim and tell of them,
    they would be more than can be counted. (Ps. 40:4-5)

Additional Readings

Leviticus 15:25-31; 22:1-9
Purity regulations

2 Corinthians 6:14—7:2
We are the temple of God

Hymn: Built on a Rock, ELW 652

Almighty God, we give you thanks for your presence in our lives. As the church stands on Christ's firm foundation of living stone, help us to embody a call to strong discipleship built on trust in you.

Tuesday, June 9, 2026

Time after Pentecost

Columba, died 597; Aidan, died 651; Bede, died 735; renewers of the church

Hosea 8:11-14; 10:1-2

God rejects Israel's sacrifice

When Ephraim multiplied altars to expiate sin,
they became to him altars for sinning. . . .
Though they offer choice sacrifices,
though they eat flesh,
the LORD does not accept them.
Now he will remember their iniquity
and punish their sins;
they shall return to Egypt.
Israel has forgotten his Maker
and built palaces,
and Judah has multiplied fortified cities,
but I will send a fire upon his cities,
and it shall devour his strongholds. (Hosea 8:11, 13-14)

Psalm

Psalm 40:1-8

God's will, not sacrifice

Additional Reading

Hebrews 13:1-16

Sacrifices pleasing to God

Hymn: Commonwealth Is God's Commandment, ACS 1036

Holy One, your commandment is for us to love one another. We pray for a world where your grace can be found amid our broken humanity. Guide us, that we may make space for all to be welcomed.

Wednesday, June 10, 2026

Time after Pentecost

Hosea 14:1-9

God will be merciful to Israel

I will heal their disloyalty;
    I will love them freely,
    for my anger has turned from them.
I will be like the dew to Israel;
    he shall blossom like the lily;
    he shall strike root like the forests of Lebanon.
His shoots shall spread out;
    his beauty shall be like the olive tree
    and his fragrance like that of Lebanon.
They shall again live beneath my shadow;
    they shall flourish as a garden;
they shall blossom like the vine;
    their fragrance shall be like the wine of Lebanon. (Hosea 14:4-7)

Psalm

Psalm 40:1-8
God's will, not sacrifice

Additional Reading

Matthew 12:1-8
Mercy, not sacrifice

Hymn: Feed us with Hunger for Justice, ACS 968

Merciful God, you were with your people in the wilderness and desert. Heal divisions that separate us from you and from others. Wrap us in your love, grace, and peace, and open us to share those blessings with our neighbors.

Thursday, June 11, 2026

Barnabas, Apostle

Acts 11:19-30; 13:1-3

Barnabas and Saul are set apart

Now in the church at Antioch there were prophets and teachers: Barnabas, Simeon who was called Niger, Lucius of Cyrene, Manaen a childhood friend of Herod the ruler, and Saul. While they were worshiping the Lord and fasting, the Holy Spirit said, "Set apart for me Barnabas and Saul for the work to which I have called them." Then after fasting and praying they laid their hands on them and sent them off. (Acts 13:1-3)

Psalm

Psalm 112

Happy are the God-fearing

Additional Readings

Isaiah 42:5-12

The LORD calls us in righteousness

Matthew 10:7-16

Jesus sends out the Twelve

Hymn: O Christ, Your Heart, Compassionate, ELW 722

We praise you, O God, for the life of your faithful servant Barnabas, who, seeking not his own renown but the well-being of your church, gave generously of his life and possessions for the relief of the poor and the spread of the gospel. Grant that we may follow his example and by our actions give glory to you, Father, Son, and Holy Spirit, now and forever.

Friday, June 12, 2026

Time after Pentecost

Psalm 100

We are God's people

Make a joyful noise to the LORD, all the earth.
Serve the LORD with gladness;
come into his presence with singing.

Know that the LORD is God.
It is he who made us, and we are his;
we are his people and the sheep of his pasture.

Enter his gates with thanksgiving
and his courts with praise.
Give thanks to him; bless his name.

For the LORD is good;
his steadfast love endures forever
and his faithfulness to all generations. (Ps. 100)

Additional Readings

Exodus 4:27-31
Aaron called to Moses' side

Acts 7:35-43
Israel doubts Moses, prevails upon Aaron

Hymn: Open Now Thy Gates of Beauty, ELW 533

God, we give you thanks for the beauty of your creation. As we dwell in your word, we praise you for your steadfast love. Speak to us both in times of great joy and in times of our deepest need.

Saturday, June 13, 2026

Time after Pentecost

Mark 7:1-13

Moses' witness spurned by religious leaders

Then [Jesus] said to [the Pharisees], "You have a fine way of rejecting the commandment of God in order to keep your tradition! For Moses said, 'Honor your father and your mother,' and, 'Whoever speaks evil of father or mother must surely die.' But you say that if anyone tells father or mother, 'Whatever support you might have had from me is Corban' (that is, an offering to God), then you no longer permit doing anything for a father or mother, thus nullifying the word of God through your tradition that you have handed on. And you do many things like this." (Mark 7:9-13)

Psalm

Psalm 100

We are God's people

Additional Reading

Exodus 6:28—7:13

Moses and Aaron before Pharaoh

Hymn: All People That on Earth Do Dwell, ELW 883

Living God, we raise our voices in thanksgiving and praise for the freeing gift of grace you bestow. Help us to embody that grace and love of your Son, enabling us to share it with all we encounter.

Sunday, June 14, 2026

Time after Pentecost

Basil the Great, Bishop of Caesarea, died 379; Gregory, Bishop of Nyssa, died around 385; Gregory of Nazianzus, Bishop of Constantinople, died around 389; Macrina, teacher, died around 379

Matthew 9:35—10:8 [9-23]

The sending of the Twelve

These twelve [disciples] Jesus sent out with the following instructions: "Do not take a road leading to gentiles, and do not enter a Samaritan town, but go rather to the lost sheep of the house of Israel. As you go, proclaim the good news, 'The kingdom of heaven has come near.' Cure the sick; raise the dead; cleanse those with a skin disease; cast out demons. You received without payment; give without payment." (Matt. 10:5-8)

Psalm

Psalm 100
We are God's people

Additional Readings

Exodus 19:2-8a
The covenant with Israel at Sinai

Romans 5:1-8
While we were sinners, Christ died for us

Hymn: God's Work, Our Hands, ACS 1000

God of compassion, you have opened the way for us and brought us to yourself. Pour your love into our hearts, that, overflowing with joy, we may freely share the blessings of your realm and faithfully proclaim the good news of your Son, Jesus Christ, our Savior and Lord.

Monday, June 15, 2026

Time after Pentecost

Psalm 105:1-11, 37-45

God saves the chosen people

So he brought his people out with joy,
his chosen ones with singing.
He gave them the lands of the nations,
and they took possession of the wealth of the peoples,
that they might keep his statutes
and observe his laws.
Praise the LORD! (Ps. 105:43-45)

Additional Readings

Joshua 1:1-11
God calls Joshua

1 Thessalonians 3:1-5
Timothy is sent to Thessalonica

Hymn: When Memory Fades, ELW 792

Great Redeemer, you claim us as your own and we give thanks for the joy you bring to our lives. Unite us as your people and as one with your Spirit until this life's end—and beyond.

Tuesday, June 16, 2026

Time after Pentecost

2 Thessalonians 2:13—3:5

The life of those chosen by God

But we must always give thanks to God for you, brothers and sisters beloved by the Lord, because God chose you as the first fruits for salvation through sanctification by the Spirit and through belief in the truth. For this purpose he called you through our gospel, so that you may obtain the glory of our Lord Jesus Christ. So then, brothers and sisters, stand firm and hold fast to the traditions that you were taught by us, either by word of mouth or by our letter. (2 Thess. 2:13-15)

Psalm

Psalm 105:1-11, 37-45

God saves the chosen people

Additional Reading

1 Samuel 3:1-9

God calls Samuel

Hymn: Thankful Hearts and Voices Raise, ELW 204–207

God of all nations, you call us to yourself. We praise you for your presence in our lives. Walk with us as we proclaim the good news of your Son, and help us stand firm in our faith in you.

Wednesday, June 17, 2026

Time after Pentecost

Emanuel Nine, martyrs, died 2015

Proverbs 4:10-27

Choosing the way of wisdom

Hear, my child, and accept my words,
that the years of your life may be many.
I have taught you the way of wisdom;
I have led you in the paths of uprightness.
When you walk, your step will not be hampered,
and if you run, you will not stumble.
Keep hold of instruction; do not let go;
guard her, for she is your life. (Prov. 4:10-13)

Psalm

Psalm 105:1-11, 37-45
God saves the chosen people

Additional Reading

Luke 6:12-19
Jesus chooses the apostles

Hymn: The Church of Christ, in Every Age, ELW 729

Leading God, we are people called into renewal. Help the church in every age hold fast to your word and live in your love. Give us wisdom and courage to witness to the Spirit's movement in our ever-changing world.

Thursday, June 18, 2026

Time after Pentecost

Psalm 69:7-10 [11-15] 16-18

Draw near to me

Answer me, O LORD, for your steadfast love is good;
according to your abundant mercy, turn to me.
Do not hide your face from your servant,
for I am in distress—make haste to answer me.
Draw near to me; redeem me;
set me free because of my enemies. (Ps. 69:16-18)

Additional Readings

Jeremiah 18:12-17
Israel's stubborn idolatry

Hebrews 2:5-9
Exaltation through abasement

Hymn: What Wondrous Love Is This, ELW 666

Most holy God, your steadfast love is good and wondrous. Help us sing out the good news of your gospel message, and shape us in becoming the disciples you have called us to be.

Friday, June 19, 2026

Time after Pentecost

Acts 5:17-26

The apostles are persecuted

Then the high priest took action; he and all who were with him (that is, the sect of the Sadducees), being filled with jealousy, arrested the apostles and put them in the public prison. But during the night an angel of the Lord opened the prison doors, brought them out, and said, "Go, stand in the temple and tell the people the whole message about this life." When they heard this, they entered the temple at daybreak and went on with their teaching.

When the high priest and those with him arrived, they called together the council and the whole body of the elders of Israel and sent to the prison to have them brought. But when the temple police went there, they did not find them in the prison, so they returned and reported, "We found the prison securely locked and the guards standing at the doors, but when we opened them we found no one inside." Now when the captain of the temple and the chief priests heard these words, they were perplexed about them, wondering what might be going on. (Acts 5:17-24)

Psalm

Psalm 69:7-10 [11-15] 16-18

Draw near to me

Additional Reading

Jeremiah 18:18-23

A plot against Jeremiah

Hymn: Loving Spirit, ELW 397

God of all strength and comfort, send your loving Spirit upon us. Draw us closer not only to you but to one another. Remind us of your unending presence, and inspire us to bear that presence in a hurting world.

Saturday, June 20, 2026

Time after Pentecost

Jeremiah 20:1-6

Jeremiah persecuted by Pashhur

Now the priest Pashhur son of Immer, who was chief officer in the house of the LORD, heard Jeremiah prophesying these things. Then Pashhur struck the prophet Jeremiah and put him in the stocks that were in the upper Benjamin Gate of the house of the LORD. The next morning when Pashhur released Jeremiah from the stocks, Jeremiah said to him, "The LORD has named you not Pashhur but 'Terror-all-around.' For thus says the LORD: I am making you a terror to yourself and to all your friends, and they shall fall by the sword of their enemies while you look on. And I will give all Judah into the hand of the king of Babylon; he shall carry them captive to Babylon and shall kill them with the sword. I will give all the wealth of this city, all its gains, all its prized belongings, and all the treasures of the kings of Judah into the hand of their enemies, who shall plunder them and seize them and carry them to Babylon. And you, Pashhur, and all who live in your house, shall go into captivity, and to Babylon you shall go." (Jer. 20:1-6a)

Psalm

Psalm 69:7-10 [11-15] 16-18

Draw near to me

Additional Reading

Luke 11:53—12:3

What is secret will become known

Hymn: Lord Jesus, You Shall Be My Song, ELW 808

God, we give you thanks for your witness in our lives and for the ways you walk with us in our witness to you. Lead us and guide us along life's way. Take our hand in moments of struggle.

Sunday, June 21, 2026

Time after Pentecost

Onesimos Nesib, translator, evangelist, died 1931

Matthew 10:24-39

The cost of discipleship

[Jesus said,] "Whoever loves father or mother more than me is not worthy of me, and whoever loves son or daughter more than me is not worthy of me, and whoever does not take up the cross and follow me is not worthy of me. Those who find their life will lose it, and those who lose their life for my sake will find it." (Matt. 10:37-39)

Psalm

Psalm 69:7-10 [11-15] 16-18
Draw near to me

Additional Readings

Jeremiah 20:7-13
The prophet must speak

Romans 6:1b-11
Buried and raised with Christ in baptism

Hymn: How Firm a Foundation, ELW 796

Teach us, good Lord God, to serve you as you deserve, to give and not to count the cost, to fight and not to heed the wounds, to toil and not to seek for rest, to labor and not to ask for reward, except that of knowing that we do your will, through Jesus Christ, our Savior and Lord.

Monday, June 22, 2026

Time after Pentecost

Psalm 6

Prayer for deliverance

O LORD, do not rebuke me in your anger
  or discipline me in your wrath.
Be gracious to me, O LORD, for I am languishing;
  O LORD, heal me, for my bones are shaking with terror.
My soul also is struck with terror,
  while you, O LORD—how long?

Turn, O LORD, save my life;
  deliver me for the sake of your steadfast love.
For in death there is no remembrance of you;
  in Sheol who can give you praise? (Ps. 6:1-5)

Additional Readings

Micah 7:1-7
The corruption of the people

Revelation 2:1-7
Remember from what you have fallen

Hymn: Jesus, Remember Me, ELW 616

Creator God, you look upon all people as beloved in your eyes. In the brokenness of this world, remind us of your grace and help us to extend it to one another. Soften our hardened hearts to unite us in love.

Tuesday, June 23, 2026

Time after Pentecost

Revelation 2:8-11

The faithful receive the crown of life

"And to the angel of the church in Smyrna write: These are the words of the First and the Last, who was dead and came to life:

"I know your affliction and your poverty, even though you are rich. I know the slander on the part of those who say that they are Jews and are not but are a synagogue of Satan. Do not fear what you are about to suffer. Beware, the devil is about to throw some of you into prison so that you may be tested, and for ten days you will have affliction. Be faithful until death, and I will give you the crown of life. Let anyone who has an ear listen to what the Spirit is saying to the churches. Whoever conquers will not be harmed by the second death." (Rev. 2:8-11)

Psalm

Psalm 6

Prayer for deliverance

Additional Reading

Jeremiah 26:1-12

Prophesy against Jerusalem

Hymn: The King of Love My Shepherd Is, ELW 502

Nurturing Shepherd, you watch over your people, and your love surrounds us even in suffering. Expand our vision so that we may see the many wondrous ways your grace and mercy sustain us.

Wednesday, June 24, 2026

John the Baptist

Luke 1:57-67 [68-80]

The birth and naming of John

On the eighth day [Elizabeth and her neighbors and relatives] came to circumcise the child, and they were going to name him Zechariah after his father. But his mother said, "No; he is to be called John." They said to her, "None of your relatives has this name." Then they began motioning to his father to find out what name he wanted to give him. He asked for a writing tablet and wrote, "His name is John." And all of them were amazed. Immediately his mouth was opened and his tongue freed, and he began to speak, praising God. (Luke 1:59-64)

Psalm

Psalm 141
My eyes are turned to God

Additional Readings

Malachi 3:1-4
My messenger, a refiner and purifier

Acts 13:13-26
The gospel for the descendants of Abraham

Hymn: Blessed Be the God of Israel, ELW 552

Almighty God, by your gracious providence your servant John the Baptist was born to Elizabeth and Zechariah. Grant to your people the wisdom to see your purpose and the openness to hear your will, that the light of Christ may increase in us, through Jesus Christ, our Savior and Lord, who lives and reigns with you and the Holy Spirit, one God, now and forever.

Thursday, June 25, 2026

Time after Pentecost

Presentation of the Augsburg Confession, 1530
Philipp Melanchthon, renewer of the church, died 1560

Psalm 89:1-4, 15-18

I sing of your love

I will sing of your steadfast love, O Lord, forever;
with my mouth I will proclaim your faithfulness to all generations.
I declare that your steadfast love is established forever;
your faithfulness is as firm as the heavens.

You said, "I have made a covenant with my chosen one;
I have sworn to my servant David:
'I will establish your descendants forever
and build your throne for all generations.'" (Ps. 89:1-4)

Additional Readings

Jeremiah 25:8-14
Captivity of Israel foretold

Galatians 5:2-6
The nature of Christian freedom

Hymn: As Rivers Flow from a Distant Spring, ACS 1046

Creator, we sing of your steadfast love. We give thanks for all who have witnessed to your good news. Help your church be open to the Spirit's movement and celebrate the many and varied ways your word is expressed.

Friday, June 26, 2026

Time after Pentecost

Galatians 5:7-12

Beware of false teachers

You were running well; who prevented you from obeying the truth? Such persuasion does not come from the one who calls you. A little yeast leavens the whole batch of dough. I am confident about you in the Lord that you will not think otherwise. But whoever it is that is confusing you will pay the penalty. But my brothers and sisters, why am I still being persecuted if I am still preaching circumcision? In that case the offense of the cross has been removed. I wish those who unsettle you would castrate themselves! (Gal. 5:7-12)

Psalm

Psalm 89:1-4, 15-18
I sing of your love

Additional Reading

Jeremiah 25:8-14
Captivity of Israel foretold

Hymn: Rise, Shine, You People! ELW 665

God of mercy, help us to rise and shine as your people. As Christ has entered our human story, guide us to see your work in all the stories of the world, celebrating the good news of your grace.

Saturday, June 27, 2026

Time after Pentecost

Cyril, Bishop of Alexandria, died 444

Jeremiah 28:1-4

Hananiah prophesies falsely

In that same year, at the beginning of the reign of King Zedekiah of Judah, in the fifth month of the fourth year, the prophet Hananiah son of Azzur, from Gibeon, spoke to me in the house of the LORD, in the presence of the priests and all the people, saying, "Thus says the LORD of hosts, the God of Israel: I have broken the yoke of the king of Babylon. Within two years I will bring back to this place all the vessels of the LORD's house, which King Nebuchadnezzar of Babylon took away from this place and carried to Babylon. I will also bring back to this place King Jeconiah son of Jehoiakim of Judah and all the exiles from Judah who went to Babylon, says the LORD, for I will break the yoke of the king of Babylon." (Jer. 28:1-4)

Psalm

Psalm 89:1-4, 15-18
I sing of your love

Additional Reading

Luke 17:1-4
Causing little ones to stumble

Hymn: Forgive Our Sins as We Forgive, ELW 605

O God, you teach us to come to you in prayer for all that we need. Direct our steps in this life and help us trust in the forgiveness you provide. Then help us to extend it to others.

Sunday, June 28, 2026

Time after Pentecost

Irenaeus, Bishop of Lyons, died around 202

Matthew 10:40-42

Welcome Christ in those Christ sends

[Jesus said to his disciples,] "Whoever welcomes you welcomes me, and whoever welcomes me welcomes the one who sent me. Whoever welcomes a prophet in the name of a prophet will receive a prophet's reward, and whoever welcomes a righteous person in the name of a righteous person will receive the reward of the righteous, and whoever gives even a cup of cold water to one of these little ones in the name of a disciple—truly I tell you, none of these will lose their reward." (Matt. 10:40-42)

Psalm

Psalm 89:1-4, 15-18
I sing of your love

Additional Readings

Jeremiah 28:5-9
Test of a true prophet

Romans 6:12-23
No longer under law but under grace

Hymn: God, We Gather as Your People, ACS 1038

O God, you direct our lives by your grace, and your words of justice and mercy reshape the world. Mold us into a people who welcome your word and serve one another through Jesus Christ, our Savior and Lord.

Monday, June 29, 2026

Peter and Paul, Apostles

John 21:15-19

Jesus says to Peter: Tend my sheep

When [the disciples] had finished breakfast, Jesus said to Simon Peter, "Simon son of John, do you love me more than these?" He said to him, "Yes, Lord; you know that I love you." Jesus said to him, "Feed my lambs." A second time he said to him, "Simon son of John, do you love me?" He said to him, "Yes, Lord; you know that I love you." Jesus said to him, "Tend my sheep." He said to him the third time, "Simon son of John, do you love me?" Peter felt hurt because he said to him the third time, "Do you love me?" And he said to him, "Lord, you know everything; you know that I love you." Jesus said to him, "Feed my sheep." (John 21:15-17)

Psalm

Psalm 87:1-3, 5-7
Glorious things are spoken of you

Additional Readings

Acts 12:1-11
Peter released from prison

2 Timothy 4:6-8, 17-18
The good fight of faith

Hymn: In Christ Called to Baptize, ELW 575

Almighty God, we praise you that your blessed apostles Peter and Paul glorified you by their martyrdoms. Grant that your church throughout the world may always be instructed by their teaching and example, be knit together in unity by your Spirit, and ever stand firm upon the one foundation who is Jesus Christ our Lord, for he lives and reigns with you and the Holy Spirit, one God, now and forever.

Tuesday, June 30, 2026

Time after Pentecost

Psalm 119:161-168

Loving God's law

Princes persecute me without cause,
but my heart stands in awe of your words.
I rejoice at your word
like one who finds great spoil.
I hate and abhor falsehood,
but I love your law.
Seven times a day I praise you
for your righteous ordinances.
Great peace have those who love your law;
nothing can make them stumble.
I hope for your salvation, O LORD,
and I fulfill your commandments. (Ps. 119:161-166)

Additional Readings

1 Kings 21:17-29
Elijah confronts Ahab

1 John 4:1-6
Testing the spirits

Hymn: O God, to You I Cry in Pain, ACS 1021

God who sees, your people come to you in times of great joy and incredible sorrow. Provide the strength to face each day. Teach us to recognize and embody your peace, grace, mercy, and justice.

Prayer List for July

Wednesday, July 1, 2026

Time after Pentecost

Catherine Winkworth, died 1878; John Mason Neale, died 1866; hymn translators

Matthew 11:20-24

Jesus prophesies against the cities

Then [Jesus] began to reproach the cities in which most of his deeds of power had been done because they did not repent. "Woe to you, Chorazin! Woe to you, Bethsaida! For if the deeds of power done in you had been done in Tyre and Sidon, they would have repented long ago in sackcloth and ashes. But I tell you, on the day of judgment it will be more tolerable for Tyre and Sidon than for you. And you, Capernaum,

will you be exalted to heaven?
No, you will be brought down to Hades.

"For if the deeds of power done in you had been done in Sodom, it would have remained until this day. But I tell you that on the day of judgment it will be more tolerable for the land of Sodom than for you." (Matt. 11:20-24)

Psalm

Psalm 119:161-168

Loving God's law

Additional Reading

Jeremiah 18:1-11

Jeremiah at the potter's wheel

Hymn: My Lord, What a Morning, ELW 438/TFF 40

Ever-patient God, you implore us to return to you and live. Inspire us this day to confess all that blocks our pathway to you, and open our eyes to discover the road to your infinite goodness.

Thursday, July 2, 2026

Time after Pentecost

Psalm 145:8-14

God is full of compassion

The LORD is gracious and merciful,
    slow to anger and abounding in steadfast love.
The LORD is good to all,
    and his compassion is over all that he has made.

All your works shall give thanks to you, O LORD,
    and all your faithful shall bless you.
They shall speak of the glory of your kingdom
    and tell of your power,
to make known to all people your mighty deeds
    and the glorious splendor of your kingdom. (Ps. 145:8-12)

Additional Readings

Zechariah 1:1-6
Israel urged to repent

Romans 7:1-6
Dying to the law through Christ

Hymn: Great Is Thy Faithfulness, ELW 733/TFF 283

Loving God, your compassion is inexhaustible and your forbearance awakens us anew every morning. Enliven us to rejoice in your unfathomable mercy and to sing of your exquisite tenderness to our groaning world.

Friday, July 3, 2026

Thomas, Apostle

John 14:1-7

Jesus, the way, the truth, the life

Thomas said to [Jesus], "Lord, we do not know where you are going. How can we know the way?" Jesus said to him, "I am the way and the truth and the life. No one comes to the Father except through me. If you know me, you will know my Father also. From now on you do know him and have seen him." (John 14:5-7)

Psalm

Psalm 136:1-4, 23-26
God's mercy endures forever

Additional Readings

Judges 6:36-40
God affirms Gideon's calling

Ephesians 4:11-16
The body of Christ has various gifts

Hymn: Come, My Way, My Truth, My Life, ELW 816

Ever-living God, you strengthened your apostle Thomas with firm and certain faith in the resurrection of your Son. Grant that we too may confess our faith in Jesus Christ, our Lord and our God, who lives and reigns with you and the Holy Spirit, one God, now and forever.

Saturday, July 4, 2026

Time after Pentecost

Luke 10:21-24

Jesus rejoices in the Holy Spirit

At that very hour Jesus rejoiced in the Holy Spirit and said, "I thank you, Father, Lord of heaven and earth, because you have hidden these things from the wise and the intelligent and have revealed them to infants; yes, Father, for such was your gracious will. All things have been handed over to me by my Father, and no one knows who the Son is except the Father or who the Father is except the Son and anyone to whom the Son chooses to reveal him."

Then turning to the disciples, Jesus said to them privately, "Blessed are the eyes that see what you see! For I tell you that many prophets and kings desired to see what you see but did not see it and to hear what you hear but did not hear it." (Luke 10:21-24)

Psalm

Psalm 145:8-14

God is full of compassion

Additional Reading

Zechariah 4:1-7

By my Spirit, says God

Hymn: Children of the Heavenly Father, ELW 781

Surprising God of cross and manger and empty tomb, you reveal your glory in simple places and yet in majestic ways. Open our hearts, that we may constantly marvel at your wondrous presence in the ordinary places of our lives.

Sunday, July 5, 2026

Time after Pentecost

Matthew 11:16-19, 25-30

The yoke of discipleship

[Jesus said,] "Come to me, all you who are weary and are carrying heavy burdens, and I will give you rest. Take my yoke upon you, and learn from me, for I am gentle and humble in heart, and you will find rest for your souls. For my yoke is easy, and my burden is light." (Matt. 11:28-30)

Psalm

Psalm 145:8-14
God is full of compassion

Additional Readings

Zechariah 9:9-12
The king comes in peace

Romans 7:15-25a
The struggle within the self

Hymn: I Must Tell Jesus, TFF 183

You are great, O God, and greatly to be praised. You have made us for yourself, and our hearts are restless until they rest in you. Grant that we may believe in you, call upon you, know you, and serve you, through your Son, Jesus Christ, our Savior and Lord.

Monday, July 6, 2026

Time after Pentecost

Jan Hus, martyr, died 1415

Psalm 131

I rest like a weaned child on God

O Lord, my heart is not lifted up;
 my eyes are not raised too high;
I do not occupy myself with things
 too great and too marvelous for me.
But I have calmed and quieted my soul,
 like a weaned child with its mother;
 my soul is like the weaned child that is with me.

O Israel, hope in the Lord
 from this time on and forevermore. (Ps. 131:1-3)

Additional Readings

Jeremiah 27:1-11, 16-22
Jeremiah wears the evil yoke

Romans 1:18-25
The guilt of humankind

Hymn: When Peace like a River, ELW 785/TFF 194

O mysterious God, whose might created the universe and whose humility stooped low to lift us into your almighty arms, still our souls that we might find calm in your abiding presence and tranquility in your eternal embrace.

Tuesday, July 7, 2026

Time after Pentecost

Jeremiah 28:10-17

Hananiah breaks Jeremiah's yoke

Then the prophet Hananiah took the yoke from the neck of the prophet Jeremiah and broke it. And Hananiah spoke in the presence of all the people, saying, "Thus says the LORD: This is how I will break the yoke of King Nebuchadnezzar of Babylon from the neck of all the nations within two years." At this, the prophet Jeremiah went his way.

Sometime after the prophet Hananiah had broken the yoke from the neck of the prophet Jeremiah, the word of the LORD came to Jeremiah: Go, tell Hananiah, Thus says the LORD: You have broken wooden bars only to forge iron bars in place of them! For thus says the LORD of hosts, the God of Israel: I have put an iron yoke on the neck of all these nations so that they may serve King Nebuchadnezzar of Babylon, and they shall indeed serve him; I have even given him the wild animals. (Jer. 28:10-14)

Psalm

Psalm 131

I rest like a weaned child on God

Additional Reading

Romans 3:1-8

The faithfulness of God

Hymn: God, When Human Bonds Are Broken, ELW 603

O God of the prophets, who warns of fiery judgment for those who turn their backs on you, soften our hearts that we might again return to you and behold the gift of hope you so relentlessly offer to us.

Wednesday, July 8, 2026
Time after Pentecost

Jeremiah 13:1-11
Jeremiah's loincloth

Then the word of the LORD came to me: Thus says the LORD: Just so I will ruin the pride of Judah and the great pride of Jerusalem. This evil people, who refuse to hear my words, who stubbornly follow their own will and have gone after other gods to serve them and worship them, shall be like this loincloth, which is good for nothing. For as the loincloth clings to one's loins, so I made the whole house of Israel and the whole house of Judah cling to me, says the LORD, in order that they might be for me a people, a name, a praise, and a glory. But they would not listen. (Jer. 13:8-11)

Psalm
Psalm 131
I rest like a weaned child on God

Additional Reading
John 13:1-17
Jesus washes the disciples' feet

Hymn: When the Storms of Life Are Raging, TFF 198

Steadfast God, you draw near to us in all the seasons of life. Open our ears, that we might hear your heavenly footsteps come to earth as you seek to protect us from all harm and danger.

Thursday, July 9, 2026

Time after Pentecost

Psalm 65:[1-8] 9-13

Your paths overflow with plenty

You visit the earth and water it;
    you greatly enrich it;
the river of God is full of water;
    you provide the people with grain,
    for so you have prepared it.
You water its furrows abundantly,
    settling its ridges,
softening it with showers,
    and blessing its growth.
You crown the year with your bounty;
    your wagon tracks overflow with richness. (Ps. 65:9-11

Additional Readings

Isaiah 48:1-5
What God declared long ago

Romans 2:12-16
God judges the secret thoughts

Hymn: For the Fruit of All Creation, ELW 679

Astonishing God of fresh rain, brilliant sunshine, and gentle breeze, dazzle us with the glory of your creation throughout this day. Fill us with imaginative ways to protect all that you have made.

Friday, July 10, 2026

Time after Pentecost

Romans 15:14-21

Sanctified by the Holy Spirit

I myself feel confident about you, my brothers and sisters, that you yourselves are full of goodness, filled with all knowledge, and able to instruct one another. Nevertheless, on some points I have written to you rather boldly by way of reminder, because of the grace given me by God to be a minister of Christ Jesus to the gentiles in the priestly service of the gospel of God, so that the offering of the gentiles may be acceptable, sanctified by the Holy Spirit. In Christ Jesus, then, I have reason to boast of my work for God. (Rom. 15:14-17)

Psalm

Psalm 65:[1-8] 9-13

Your paths overflow with plenty

Additional Reading

Isaiah 48:6-11

You will hear new, hidden things

Hymn: Listen, God Is Calling, ELW 513/TFF 130

God of grace and glory, you invite us to be your faithful servants. Embolden us to proclaim your old, old story in daring new ways, that every suffering soul might experience gladness and encouragement in hearing your good news.

Saturday, July 11, 2026

Time after Pentecost

Benedict of Nursia, Abbot of Monte Cassino, died around 540

Isaiah 52:1-6

Sold, redeemed without money

For thus says the LORD: You were sold for nothing, and you shall be redeemed without money. For thus says the Lord GOD: Long ago, my people went down into Egypt to reside there as aliens; the Assyrian, too, has oppressed them without cause. Now therefore what am I doing here, says the LORD, seeing that my people are taken away without cause? Their rulers howl, says the LORD, and continually, all day long, my name is despised. Therefore my people shall know my name; on that day they shall know that it is I who speak—it is I! (Isa. 52:3-6)

Psalm

Psalm 65:[1-8] 9-13

Your paths overflow with plenty

Additional Reading

John 12:44-50

I have come as light into the world

Hymn: When Israel Was in Egypt's Land, TFF 87

Liberating God, you have freed your children from tyranny, wickedness, and oppression throughout the ages. Extend your liberating hand to all who long for freedom, and deliver them safely to your delightful land of milk and honey.

Sunday, July 12, 2026

Time after Pentecost

Nathan Söderblom, Bishop of Uppsala, died 1931

Matthew 13:1-9, 18-23

The parable of the sower and the seed

And [Jesus] told [the crowd] many things in parables, saying: "Listen! A sower went out to sow. And as he sowed, some seeds fell on a path, and the birds came and ate them up. Other seeds fell on rocky ground, where they did not have much soil, and they sprang up quickly, since they had no depth of soil. But when the sun rose, they were scorched, and since they had no root, they withered away. Other seeds fell among thorns, and the thorns grew up and choked them. Other seeds fell on good soil and brought forth grain, some a hundredfold, some sixty, some thirty. If you have ears, hear!" (Matt. 13:3-9)

Psalm

Psalm 65:[1-8] 9-13
Your paths overflow with plenty

Additional Readings

Isaiah 55:10-13
The growth of the word

Romans 8:1-11
Living according to the Spirit

Hymn: Almighty God, Your Word Is Cast, ELW 516

Almighty God, we thank you for planting in us the seed of your word. By your Holy Spirit help us to receive it with joy, live according to it, and grow in faith and hope and love, through Jesus Christ, our Savior and Lord.

Monday, July 13, 2026

Time after Pentecost

Psalm 92

The righteous as a tree

The righteous flourish like the palm tree
    and grow like a cedar in Lebanon.
They are planted in the house of the LORD;
    they flourish in the courts of our God.
In old age they still produce fruit;
    they are always green and full of sap,
showing that the LORD is upright;
    he is my rock, and there is no unrighteousness in him. (Ps. 92:12-15)

Additional Readings

Leviticus 26:3-20
A rich and a poor harvest

1 Thessalonians 4:1-8
A life pleasing to God

Hymn: I Shall Not Be Moved, TFF 147

Life-giving God, refresh us with your invigorating glad tidings, that all we do might blossom and flourish in your name. Inspire us to bear hope for the desperate, beauty for the tormented, and fruitfulness to the withering.

Tuesday, July 14, 2026

Time after Pentecost

Ephesians 4:17—5:2

The old life and the new

Let no evil talk come out of your mouths but only what is good for building up, as there is need, so that your words may give grace to those who hear. And do not grieve the Holy Spirit of God, with which you were marked with a seal for the day of redemption. Put away from you all bitterness and wrath and anger and wrangling and slander, together with all malice. Be kind to one another, tenderhearted, forgiving one another, as God in Christ has forgiven you. (Eph. 4:29-32)

Psalm

Psalm 92

The righteous as a tree

Additional Reading

Deuteronomy 28:1-14

The blessings of obedience

Hymn: When Long before Time, ELW 861

O God, whose word creates all that exists, grant that our every utterance may be chosen carefully, lovingly, and well, that in some small measure your creation may tilt in the direction of peace and understanding.

Wednesday, July 15, 2026

Time after Pentecost

Proverbs 11:23-30

The fruit of righteousness

Whoever diligently seeks good seeks favor,
    but evil comes to the one who searches for it.
Those who trust in their riches will wither,
    but the righteous will flourish like green leaves.
Those who trouble their households will inherit wind,
    and the fool will be servant to the wise.
The fruit of the righteous is a tree of life,
    and the wise capture souls. (Prov. 11:27-30)

Psalm

Psalm 92

The righteous as a tree

Additional Reading

Matthew 13:10-17

The purpose of parable

Hymn: If You But Trust in God to Guide You, ELW 769

O righteous God, you invite us to gather by your side, where there is everlasting delight. Sanctify our every thought, word, and deed, that we and those we encounter may experience your enduring joy forever and ever.

Thursday, July 16, 2026

Time after Pentecost

Psalm 86:11-17

Teach me your ways

Teach me your way, O LORD,
that I may walk in your truth;
give me an undivided heart to revere your name.
I give thanks to you, O Lord my God, with my whole heart,
and I will glorify your name forever.
For great is your steadfast love toward me;
you have delivered my soul from the depths of Sheol. (Ps. 86:11-13)

Additional Readings

Isaiah 41:21-29
The futility of idols

Hebrews 2:1-9
Warning to pay attention

Hymn: Lord, Speak to Us, That We May Speak, ELW 676

As you did with your Son Jesus, you invite us to a quiet place to rest and pray. In these moments of calm, soothe us with your heavenly balm, that we might live each day with dignity and kindness.

Friday, July 17, 2026

Time after Pentecost

Bartolomé de Las Casas, missionary to the Indies, died 1566

Hebrews 6:13-20

The certainty of God's promises

When God made a promise to Abraham, because he had no one greater by whom to swear, he swore by himself, saying, "I will surely bless you and multiply you." And thus Abraham, having patiently endured, obtained the promise. (Heb. 6:13-15)

Psalm

Psalm 86:11-17

Teach me your ways

Additional Reading

Isaiah 44:9-17

Those who make idols are nothing

Hymn: The God of Abraham Praise, ELW 831

O trustworthy God, at our baptism you call us by name, claim us as your own, and bring us out of death into life. May we live boldly in our baptismal promises, seeking abundance for all your dear children everywhere.

Saturday, July 18, 2026

Time after Pentecost

Isaiah 44:18-20

Idols do not know or comprehend

They do not know, nor do they comprehend, for their eyes are shut, so that they cannot see, and their minds as well, so that they cannot understand. No one considers, nor is there knowledge or discernment to say, "Half of it I burned in the fire; I also baked bread on its coals; I roasted meat and have eaten. Now shall I make the rest of it an abomination? Shall I fall down before a block of wood?" He feeds on ashes; a deluded mind has led him astray, and he cannot save himself or say, "Is not this thing in my right hand a fraud?" (Isa. 44:18-20)

Psalm

Psalm 86:11-17

Teach me your ways

Additional Reading

Matthew 7:15-20

A tree and its fruit

Hymn: I Was Sinking Deep in Sin, TFF 188

Gracious God, awaken us to your grandeur day by day, open our eyes to the breathtaking ways in which you lift us up, and fill our minds with imaginative means to proclaim your splendor in places longing for your manna come to earth.

Sunday, July 19, 2026

Time after Pentecost

Matthew 13:24-30, 36-43

The parable of the weeds

[Jesus] put before [the disciples] another parable: "The kingdom of heaven may be compared to someone who sowed good seed in his field, but while everybody was asleep an enemy came and sowed weeds among the wheat and then went away. So when the plants came up and bore grain, then the weeds appeared as well. And the slaves of the householder came and said to him, 'Master, did you not sow good seed in your field? Where, then, did these weeds come from?' He answered, 'An enemy has done this.' The slaves said to him, 'Then do you want us to go and gather them?' But he replied, 'No, for in gathering the weeds you would uproot the wheat along with them. Let both of them grow together until the harvest, and at harvest time I will tell the reapers, Collect the weeds first and bind them in bundles to be burned, but gather the wheat into my barn.' " (Matt. 13:24-30)

Psalm

Psalm 86:11-17

Teach me your ways

Additional Readings

Isaiah 44:6-8

There is no other God

Romans 8:12-25

The revealing of the children of God

Hymn: The Word of God Is Source and Seed, ELW 506

Faithful God, most merciful judge, you care for your children with firmness and compassion. By your Spirit nurture us who live in your kingdom, that we may be rooted in the way of your Son, Jesus Christ, our Savior and Lord.

Monday, July 20, 2026

Time after Pentecost

Psalm 75

God's judgment

We give thanks to you, O God;
    we give thanks; your name is near.
People tell of your wondrous deeds.

At the set time that I appoint,
    I will judge with equity.
When the earth totters, with all its inhabitants,
    it is I who keep its pillars steady. (Ps. 75:1-3)

Additional Readings

Nahum 1:1-13
The wrath and mercy of God

Revelation 14:12-20
The harvest at the end of time

Hymn: Oh, Praise the Gracious Power, ELW 651

God of wonder, place invigorating words of thanksgiving on our lips. Stir us to perceive every moment of our lives as an opportunity to echo your mighty acts to every person we encounter.

Tuesday, July 21, 2026

Time after Pentecost

Zephaniah 3:1-13

The wicked convert to God

For I will leave in the midst of you
a people humble and lowly.
They shall seek refuge in the name of the LORD—
the remnant of Israel;
they shall do no wrong
and utter no lies,
nor shall a deceitful tongue
be found in their mouths.
Then they will pasture and lie down,
and no one shall make them afraid. (Zeph. 3:12-13)

Psalm

Psalm 75

God's judgment

Additional Reading

Galatians 4:21—5:1

An allegory about those saved

Hymn: Come, Ye Disconsolate, ELW 607/TFF 186

O God, you summon us to champion life even in the valley of the shadow of death. Still our souls, that we might hear your familiar and soothing voice beseeching us to return to the safety of your almighty arms.

Wednesday, July 22, 2026

Mary Magdalene, Apostle

John 20:1-2, 11-18

Mary Magdalene meets Jesus in the garden

Jesus said to [Mary Magdalene], "Woman, why are you weeping? Whom are you looking for?" Supposing him to be the gardener, she said to him, "Sir, if you have carried him away, tell me where you have laid him, and I will take him away." Jesus said to her, "Mary!" She turned and said to him in Hebrew, "Rabbouni!" (which means Teacher). Jesus said to her, "Do not touch me, because I have not yet ascended to the Father. But go to my brothers and say to them, 'I am ascending to my Father and your Father, to my God and your God.' " Mary Magdalene went and announced to the disciples, "I have seen the Lord," and she told them that he had said these things to her. (John 20:15-18)

Psalm

Psalm 73:23-28
I will speak of all God's works

Additional Readings

Ruth 1:6-18
Ruth stays with Naomi

Acts 13:26-33a
The raising of Jesus fulfills God's promise

Hymn: For All the Faithful Women, ELW 419/TFF 219

Almighty God, your Son first entrusted the apostle Mary Magdalene with the joyful news of his resurrection. Following the example of her witness, may we proclaim Christ as our living Lord and one day see him in glory, for he lives and reigns with you and the Holy Spirit, one God, now and forever.

Thursday, July 23, 2026

Time after Pentecost

Birgitta of Sweden, renewer of the church, died 1373

Psalm 119:129-136

Light and understanding

Your decrees are wonderful;
therefore my soul keeps them.
The unfolding of your words gives light;
it imparts understanding to the simple.
With open mouth I pant,
because I long for your commandments.
Turn to me and be gracious to me,
as is your custom toward those who love your name.
Keep my steps steady according to your promise,
and never let iniquity have dominion over me. (Ps. 119:129-133)

Additional Readings

1 Kings 1:28-37
Solomon designated as king

1 Corinthians 4:14-20
Reign of God depends not on talk but power

Hymn: Day by Day, ELW 790

Steadfast God, cause us to hunger and thirst for your perfect word come down from heaven, and by your most excellent grace, inspire us to live in a manner that champions your divine plan for all creation.

Friday, July 24, 2026

Time after Pentecost

Acts 7:44-53

Solomon's temple cannot contain God

[Stephen spoke:] "Our ancestors had the tent of testimony in the wilderness, as God directed when he spoke to Moses, ordering him to make it according to the pattern he had seen. Our ancestors in turn brought it in with Joshua when they dispossessed the peoples whom God drove out before our ancestors. And it was there until the time of David, who found favor with God and asked that he might find a dwelling place for the house of Jacob. But it was Solomon who built a house for him. Yet the Most High does not dwell in houses made with human hands." (Acts 7:44-48a)

Psalm

Psalm 119:129-136

Light and understanding

Additional Reading

1 Kings 1:38-48

Solomon more famous than David

Hymn: Built on a Rock, ELW 652

Surprising God, you promise to be with us in the simple gifts of words and water, bread and wine. Open our ears and noses, tongues and fingers and eyes, that we may encounter unexpected happiness in your astonishing sacramental presence.

Saturday, July 25, 2026

James, Apostle

Mark 10:35-45

Whoever wishes to be great must serve

James and John, the sons of Zebedee, came forward to him and said to him, "Teacher, we want you to do for us whatever we ask of you." And he said to them, "What is it you want me to do for you?" And they said to him, "Appoint us to sit, one at your right hand and one at your left, in your glory." But Jesus said to them, "You do not know what you are asking. Are you able to drink the cup that I drink or be baptized with the baptism that I am baptized with?" They replied, "We are able." Then Jesus said to them, "The cup that I drink you will drink, and with the baptism with which I am baptized you will be baptized, but to sit at my right hand or at my left is not mine to appoint, but it is for those for whom it has been prepared." (Mark 10:35-40)

Psalm

Psalm 7:1-10
God, my shield and defense

Additional Readings

1 Kings 19:9-18
Elijah hears God amid silence

Acts 11:27—12:3a
James is killed by Herod

Hymn: Lord, Whose Love in Humble Service, ELW 712

Gracious God, we remember before you today your servant and apostle James, the first among the twelve to be martyred for the name of Jesus Christ. Pour out on the leaders of your church that spirit of self-denying service which is the true mark of authority among your people, through Jesus Christ our servant, who lives and reigns with you and the Holy Spirit, one God, now and forever.

Sunday, July 26, 2026

Time after Pentecost

Matthew 13:31-33, 44-52

Parables of the reign of heaven

[Jesus] told [the disciples] another parable: "The kingdom of heaven is like yeast that a woman took and mixed in with three measures of flour until all of it was leavened." . . .

"The kingdom of heaven is like treasure hidden in a field, which a man found and reburied; then in his joy he goes and sells all that he has and buys that field.

"Again, the kingdom of heaven is like a merchant in search of fine pearls; on finding one pearl of great value, he went and sold all that he had and bought it." (Matt. 13:33, 44-46)

Psalm

Psalm 119:129-136
Light and understanding

Additional Readings

1 Kings 3:5-12
Solomon's prayer for wisdom

Romans 8:26-39
Nothing can separate us from God's love

Hymn: Jesus, Priceless Treasure, ELW 775

Beloved and sovereign God, through the death and resurrection of your Son you bring us into your kingdom of justice and mercy. By your Spirit, give us your wisdom, that we may treasure the life that comes from Jesus Christ, our Savior and Lord.

Monday, July 27, 2026

Time after Pentecost

Psalm 119:121-128

Give me understanding

I am your servant; give me understanding,
    so that I may know your decrees.
It is time for the LORD to act,
    for your law has been broken.
Truly I love your commandments
    more than gold, more than fine gold.
Truly I direct my steps by all your precepts;
    I hate every false way. (Ps. 119:125-128)

Additional Readings

1 Kings 3:16-28
Solomon's wisdom in judgment

James 3:13-18
Two kinds of wisdom

Hymn: Will You Let Me Be Your Servant, ELW 659

Dear God, you call us to holiness all the days of our lives. Place your commandments on our hearts and minds, and when we fail to keep them, grant us forgiveness and the knowledge that you never forsake us.

Tuesday, July 28, 2026
Time after Pentecost

Johann Sebastian Bach, died 1750; Heinrich Schütz, died 1672;
George Frederick Handel, died 1759; musicians

1 Kings 4:29-34

God gave Solomon wisdom

God gave Solomon very great wisdom, discernment, and breadth of understanding as vast as the sand on the seashore, so that Solomon's wisdom surpassed the wisdom of all the people of the East and all the wisdom of Egypt. He was wiser than anyone else, wiser than Ethan the Ezrahite and Heman, Calcol, and Darda, children of Mahol; his fame spread throughout all the surrounding nations. He composed three thousand proverbs, and his songs numbered a thousand and five. He would speak of trees, from the cedar that is in the Lebanon to the hyssop that grows in the wall; he would speak of animals, and birds, and reptiles, and fish. People came from all the nations to hear the wisdom of Solomon, from all the kings of the earth who had heard of his wisdom. (1 Kings 4:29-34)

Psalm

Psalm 119:121-128
Give me understanding

Additional Reading

Ephesians 6:10-18
The allegory of the armor of God

Hymn: Be Thou My Vision, ELW 793

Magnificent God, source of all goodness and truth, fill us with your eternal wisdom. Let our thoughts and words, our deeds and songs reflect your glory and make the world shine brightly with your everlasting beauty.

Wednesday, July 29, 2026

Time after Pentecost

Mary, Martha, and Lazarus of Bethany
Olaf, King of Norway, martyr, died 1030

Proverbs 1:1-7, 20-33

The call of wisdom

Wisdom cries out in the street;
    in the squares she raises her voice.
At the busiest corner she cries out;
    at the entrance of the city gates she speaks:
"How long, O simple ones, will you love being simple?
How long will scoffers delight in their scoffing
    and fools hate knowledge?
Give heed to my reproof;
I will pour out my thoughts to you;
    I will make my words known to you." (Prov. 1:20-23)

Psalm

Psalm 119:121-128
Give me understanding

Additional Reading

Mark 4:30-34
Jesus' use of parables

Hymn: O God of Light, ELW 507

O tenderhearted God, you watch over your dear children night and day and provide them with all that is necessary and desirable. Teach us always to trust in your boundless generosity and to ever give thanks to you.

Thursday, July 30, 2026

Time after Pentecost

Psalm 145:8-9, 14-21

You open wide your hand

The LORD upholds all who are falling
    and raises up all who are bowed down.
The eyes of all look to you,
    and you give them their food in due season.
You open your hand,
    satisfying the desire of every living thing. (Ps. 145:14-16)

Additional Readings

Proverbs 10:1-5
The righteous will not go hungry

Philippians 4:10-15
Being well fed and yet hungry

Hymn: Praise to the Lord, the Almighty, ELW 858/859

Unfathomable God, your generosity surpasses our capacity to imagine or comprehend. Drench us with the longing to offer you unending praise and thanksgiving, that we may prove fervent witnesses to your stunning splendor.

Friday, July 31, 2026

Time after Pentecost

Isaiah 51:17-23

Drink no more from the bowl of wrath

Therefore hear this, you who are wounded,
who are drunk but not with wine:
Thus says your Sovereign, the LORD,
your God who pleads the cause of his people:
See, I have taken from your hand the cup of staggering;
you shall drink no more
from the cup of my wrath.
And I will put it into the hand of your tormentors,
who have said to you,
"Bow down, that we may walk on you,"
and you have made your back like the ground
and like the street for them to walk on. (Isa. 51:21-23)

Psalm

Psalm 145:8-9, 14-21
You open wide your hand

Additional Reading

Romans 9:6-13
True descendants of Abraham

Hymn: God of the Fertile Fields, ACS 1063

Giver of all good things, you take away what harms us and provide abundantly what we desperately need. Keep us attentive to the needs of others, and inspire our own giving. Match our actions with our best intentions.

Prayer List for August

Saturday, August 1, 2026

Time after Pentecost

Isaiah 44:1-5

God's blessing on Israel

But now hear, O Jacob my servant,
Israel whom I have chosen!
Thus says the Lord who made you,
who formed you in the womb and will help you:
Do not fear, O Jacob my servant,
Jeshurun whom I have chosen.
For I will pour water on the thirsty land
and streams on the dry ground;
I will pour my spirit upon your descendants
and my blessing on your offspring.
They shall spring up like a green tamarisk,
like willows by flowing streams. (Isa. 44:1-4)

Psalm

Psalm 145:8-9, 14-21
You open wide your hand

Additional Reading

Matthew 7:7-11
Bread and stones

Hymn: Christ Is the Life, ACS 927

Creator God, you are the source and sustenance of all life. Stir up within us the gifts of your Spirit. Remind us that we are your beloved children. Where the world is parched and disheartened, revive it with your love.

Sunday, August 2, 2026

Time after Pentecost

Matthew 14:13-21

Jesus feeds 5000

Then [Jesus] ordered the crowds to sit down on the grass. Taking the five loaves and the two fish, he looked up to heaven and blessed and broke the loaves and gave them to the disciples, and the disciples gave them to the crowds. And all ate and were filled, and they took up what was left over of the broken pieces, twelve baskets full. And those who ate were about five thousand men, besides women and children. (Matt. 14:19-21)

Psalm

Psalm 145:8-9, 14-21
You open wide your hand

Additional Readings

Isaiah 55:1-5
Eat and drink what truly satisfies

Romans 9:1-5
The glory of God's people in Israel

Hymn: The Church of Christ, in Every Age, ELW 729

Glorious God, your generosity waters the world with goodness, and you cover creation with abundance. Awaken in us a hunger for the food that satisfies both body and spirit, and with this food fill all the starving world; through your Son, Jesus Christ, our Savior and Lord.

Monday, August 3, 2026

Time after Pentecost

Psalm 78:1-8, 17-29

God fed the people with manna

Yet he commanded the skies above
    and opened the doors of heaven;
he rained down on them manna to eat
    and gave them the grain of heaven.
Mortals ate of the bread of angels;
    he sent them food in abundance. (Ps. 78:23-25)

Additional Readings

Deuteronomy 8:1-10
God will feed the people

Romans 1:8-15
A harvest among the gentiles

Hymn: Nothing Can Trouble, ACS 1033

God, you provide for our daily needs, transforming our fear of scarcity into trust in you. Help us recognize your grace in our lives so that we might share that same amazing grace with all whom we encounter this day.

Tuesday, August 4, 2026

Time after Pentecost

Acts 2:37-47

The believers breaking bread

Awe came upon everyone because many wonders and signs were being done through the apostles. All who believed were together and had all things in common; they would sell their possessions and goods and distribute the proceeds to all, as any had need. Day by day, as they spent much time together in the temple, they broke bread at home and ate their food with glad and generous hearts, praising God and having the goodwill of all the people. And day by day the Lord added to their number those who were being saved. (Acts 2:43-47)

Psalm

Psalm 78:1-8, 17-29
God fed the people with manna

Additional Reading

Deuteronomy 26:1-15
A tithe from God's harvest

Hymn: Commonwealth Is God's Commandment, ACS 1036

Awesome God, your will for all creation is abundant life. We thank and praise you for your wholehearted, all-encompassing love. Stretch our hearts and minds to share with our neighbors the resources you've entrusted to us.

Wednesday, August 5, 2026

Time after Pentecost

Exodus 16:2-15, 31-35

God feeds the people manna

The whole congregation of the Israelites complained against Moses and Aaron in the wilderness The Israelites said to them, "If only we had died by the hand of the LORD in the land of Egypt, when we sat by the pots of meat and ate our fill of bread, for you have brought us out into this wilderness to kill this whole assembly with hunger."

Then the LORD said to Moses, "I am going to rain bread from heaven for you, and each day the people shall go out and gather enough for that day. In that way I will test them, whether they will follow my instruction or not." (Exod. 16:2-4)

Psalm

Psalm 78:1-8, 17-29

God fed the people with manna

Additional Reading

Matthew 15:32-39

Jesus feeds 4000

Hymn: Sing Praise to God, the Highest Good, ELW 871

God, you lead your people to freedom. Even though we forget your goodness, you never forget us. Teach us to live as you would have us live, freed to love you and love our neighbors as ourselves.

Thursday, August 6, 2026

Time after Pentecost

Psalm 85:8-13

I will listen to God

Let me hear what God the LORD will speak,
for he will speak peace to his people,
to his faithful, to those who turn to him in their hearts.[a]
Surely his salvation is at hand for those who fear him,
that his glory may dwell in our land.

Steadfast love and faithfulness will meet;
righteousness and peace will kiss each other.
Faithfulness will spring up from the ground,
and righteousness will look down from the sky.
The LORD will give what is good,
and our land will yield its increase. (Ps. 85:8-12)

Additional Readings

1 Kings 18:1-16
God promises relief from drought

Acts 17:10-15
The good news is shared

Hymn: O Lord, Let Us See Your Kindness, TFF 8

God, the peace you offer surpasses all our human understanding. Turn us from hatred and division. Bring an end to war. Plant your peace in the fields of our hearts, that we might yield bountiful peace in all the world.

Friday, August 7, 2026

Time after Pentecost

Acts 18:24-28

A new disciple preaches

Now there came to Ephesus a Jew named Apollos from Alexandria. He was an eloquent man, well-versed in the scriptures. He had been instructed in the Way of the Lord, and he spoke with burning enthusiasm and taught accurately the things concerning Jesus, though he knew only the baptism of John. He began to speak boldly in the synagogue, but when Priscilla and Aquila heard him they took him aside and explained the Way of God to him more accurately. And when he wished to cross over to Achaia, the brothers and sisters encouraged him and wrote to the disciples to welcome him. On his arrival he greatly helped those who through grace had become believers, for he powerfully refuted the Jews in public, showing by the scriptures that the Messiah is Jesus. (Acts 18:24-28)

Psalm

Psalm 85:8-13
I will listen to God

Additional Reading

1 Kings 18:17-19, 30-40
God's flooded altar burns

Hymn: I Love to Tell the Story, ELW 661/TFF 228

God, you place people in our paths to support and encourage us as we heed your call to boldly share the good news of your love. Thank you for all who have uplifted us along the way.

Saturday, August 8, 2026

Time after Pentecost

Dominic, founder of the Order of Preachers (Dominicans), died 1221

1 Kings 18:41-46

From drought to heavy rain

Elijah said to Ahab, "Go up, eat and drink, for there is a sound of rushing rain." So Ahab went up to eat and to drink. Elijah went up to the top of Carmel; there he bowed himself down upon the earth and put his face between his knees. He said to his servant, "Go up now, look toward the sea." He went up and looked and said, "There is nothing." Then he said, "Go again seven times." At the seventh time he said, "Look, a little cloud no bigger than a person's hand is rising out of the sea." Then he said, "Go say to Ahab, 'Harness your chariot and go down before the rain stops you.'" In a little while the heavens grew black with clouds and wind; there was a heavy rain. Ahab rode off and went to Jezreel. But the hand of the LORD was on Elijah; he girded up his loins and ran in front of Ahab to the entrance of Jezreel. (1 Kings 18:41-46)

Psalm

Psalm 85:8-13

I will listen to God

Additional Reading

Matthew 16:1-4

The sign of Jonah

Hymn: Signs and Wonders, ELW 672

Sometimes we look for your power on display in our lives, O God, and we see nothing. Yet, you are daily working miracles and turning the smallest things into tremendous blessings. Help us perceive your power and passion.

Sunday, August 9, 2026

Time after Pentecost

Matthew 14:22-33

Jesus walking on the sea

Immediately [Jesus] made the disciples get into a boat and go on ahead to the other side, while he dismissed the crowds. And after he had dismissed the crowds, he went up the mountain by himself to pray. When evening came, he was there alone, but by this time the boat, battered by the waves, was far from the land, for the wind was against them. And early in the morning he came walking toward them on the sea. But when the disciples saw him walking on the sea, they were terrified, saying, "It is a ghost!" And they cried out in fear. But immediately Jesus spoke to them and said, "Take heart, it is I; do not be afraid." (Matt. 14:22-27)

Psalm

Psalm 85:8-13

I will listen to God

Additional Readings

1 Kings 19:9-18

Elijah on Mount Horeb

Romans 10:5-15

The word of faith

Hymn: Calm to the Waves, ELW 794

O God our defender, storms rage around and within us and cause us to be afraid. Rescue your people from despair, deliver your sons and daughters from fear, and preserve us in the faith of your Son, Jesus Christ, our Savior and Lord.

Monday, August 10, 2026

Time after Pentecost

Lawrence, deacon, martyr, died 258

Psalm 18:1-19

God saves from the waters

He reached down from on high; he took me;
he drew me out of mighty waters.
He delivered me from my strong enemy
and from those who hated me,
for they were too mighty for me.
They confronted me in the day of my calamity,
but the LORD was my support.
He brought me out into a broad place;
he delivered me because he delighted in me. (Ps. 18:16-19)

Additional Readings

Genesis 7:11—8:5
God saves Noah from the flood

2 Peter 2:4-10
God judges and rescues

Hymn: Thank You, Lord, ACS 1092/TFF 293

Mothering God, you fiercely protect and defend your children. We are yours, and you delight in us. Rescue all who are struck by hatred and violence this day. Be their strength, their confidence, and their certain salvation.

Tuesday, August 11, 2026

Time after Pentecost

Clare, Abbess of San Damiano, died 1253

Romans 9:14-29

God's wrath, God's mercy

What then are we to say? Is there injustice on God's part? By no means! For he says to Moses,

"I will have mercy on whom I have mercy,
and I will have compassion on whom I have compassion."

So it depends not on human will or exertion but on God who shows mercy. For the scripture says to Pharaoh, "I have raised you up for this very purpose, that I may show my power in you and that my name may be proclaimed in all the earth." So then he has mercy on whomever he chooses, and he hardens the heart of whomever he chooses. (Rom. 9:14-18)

Psalm

Psalm 18:1-19
God saves from the waters

Additional Reading

Genesis 19:1-29
God saves Lot

Hymn: Forgive Our Sins as We Forgive, ELW 605

God, our hope, in the life, death, and resurrection of Jesus you choose to exercise mercy and compassion. You judge the world, and your judgment is freedom, forgiveness, and death-defeating life. Help us love others as you have loved us.

Wednesday, August 12, 2026

Time after Pentecost

Matthew 8:23-27

Jesus stills the storm

And when he got into the boat, his disciples followed him. A windstorm suddenly arose on the sea, so great that the boat was being swamped by the waves, but he was asleep. And they went and woke him up, saying, "Lord, save us! We are perishing!" And he said to them, "Why are you afraid, you of little faith?" Then he got up and rebuked the winds and the sea, and there was a dead calm. They were amazed, saying, "What sort of man is this, that even the winds and the sea obey him?" (Matt. 8:23-27)

Psalm

Psalm 18:1-19

God saves from the waters

Additional Reading

Job 36:24-33; 37:14-24

The waters of God's creation

Hymn: Jesus, Savior, Pilot Me, ELW 755

God, sometimes it feels like the storms will never end. Sometimes it even feels like you don't care that we're drowning. When we feel fearful and alone, quiet the storms around us and hold us close to your heart.

Thursday, August 13, 2026

Time after Pentecost

Florence Nightingale, died 1910; Clara Maass, died 1901; renewers of society

Psalm 67

Let all the peoples praise God

May God be gracious to us and bless us
and make his face to shine upon us,
that your way may be known upon earth,
your saving power among all nations.
Let the peoples praise you, O God;
let all the peoples praise you.

Let the nations be glad and sing for joy,
for you judge the peoples with equity
and guide the nations upon earth.
Let the peoples praise you, O God;
let all the peoples praise you. (Ps. 67:1-5)

Additional Readings

Isaiah 45:20-25
All the ends of the earth shall be saved

Revelation 15:1-4
All nations will worship God

Hymn: Praise God, from Whom All Blessings Flow, ELW 884/885

The expansive radiance of your grace, O God, illumines all creation. Our hearts overflow with awe and wonder at the magnitude of your blessing. This day, and every day, we praise you and celebrate your saving power.

Friday, August 14, 2026

Time after Pentecost

Maximilian Kolbe, died 1941; Kaj Munk, died 1944; martyrs

Isaiah 63:15-19

A plea for God's attention

Why, O LORD, do you let us stray from your ways
and let our heart harden, so that we do not fear you?
Turn back for the sake of your servants,
the tribes that are your heritage.
Your holy people took possession for a little while,
but now our adversaries have trampled down your sanctuary.
We have long been like those whom you do not rule,
like those not called by your name. (Isa. 63:17-19)

Psalm

Psalm 67

Let all the peoples praise God

Additional Reading

Acts 14:19-28

God opens the door to gentiles

Hymn: O God, Why Are You Silent, ELW 703

What a complicated mess we create when we fail to fear, love, and trust you, dear God. Forgive us for turning from you. Assure us we can depend on you. You remain faithful no matter what. Thank you.

Saturday, August 15, 2026

Mary, Mother of Our Lord

Luke 1:46-55

Mary's thanksgiving

And Mary said,
"My soul magnifies the Lord,
and my spirit rejoices in God my Savior,
for he has looked with favor on the lowly state of his servant.
Surely from now on all generations will call me blessed,
for the Mighty One has done great things for me,
and holy is his name." (Luke 1:46-49)

Psalm

Psalm 34:1-9
O magnify the LORD with me

Additional Readings

Isaiah 61:7-11
God will cause righteousness to spring up

Galatians 4:4-7
We are no longer slaves, but children

Hymn: Canticle of the Turning, ELW 723

Almighty God, in choosing the virgin Mary to be the mother of your Son, you made known your gracious regard for the poor, the lowly, and the despised. Grant us grace to receive your word in humility, and so to be made one with your Son, Jesus Christ our Savior and Lord, who lives and reigns with you and the Holy Spirit, one God, now and forever.

Sunday, August 16, 2026

Time after Pentecost

Matthew 15:[10-20] 21-28

The Canaanite woman's daughter is healed

But [the Canaanite woman] came and knelt before him, saying, "Lord, help me." He answered, "It is not fair to take the children's food and throw it to the dogs." She said, "Yes, Lord, yet even the dogs eat the crumbs that fall from their masters' table." Then Jesus answered her, "Woman, great is your faith! Let it be done for you as you wish." And her daughter was healed from that moment. (Matt. 15:25-28)

Psalm

Psalm 67

Let all the peoples praise God

Additional Readings

Isaiah 56:1, 6-8

A house of prayer for all people

Romans 11:1-2a, 29-32

God's mercy to all, Jew and gentile

Hymn: Build a Longer Table, ACS 1062

God of all peoples, your arms reach out to embrace all those who call upon you. Teach us as disciples of your Son to love the world with compassion and constancy, that your name may be known throughout the earth, through Jesus Christ, our Savior and Lord.

Monday, August 17, 2026

Time after Pentecost

Psalm 87

Foreigners praise God in Zion

On the holy mount stands the city he founded;
the LORD loves the gates of Zion
more than all the dwellings of Jacob.
Glorious things are spoken of you,
O city of God.

Among those who know me I mention Rahab and Babylon;
Philistia, too, and Tyre, with Cush—
"This one was born there," they say.

And of Zion it shall be said,
"This one and that one were born in it,"
for the Most High himself will establish it. (Ps. 87:1-5)

Additional Readings

2 Kings 5:1-14
The foreigner Naaman is healed

Acts 15:1-21
The believing Jews accept the gentiles

Hymn: Glorious Things of You Are Spoken, ELW 647

God, the community you build is beautiful in its diversity. You call your people together from near and far, to be born anew in you. We live in confidence, trusting that you have created us to be a people of peace.

Tuesday, August 18, 2026

Time after Pentecost

Romans 11:13-29

God saves Jews and gentiles

I want you to understand this mystery, brothers and sisters, so that you may not claim to be wiser than you are: a hardening has come upon part of Israel until the full number of the gentiles has come in. And in this way all Israel will be saved, as it is written,

> "Out of Zion will come the Deliverer;
> he will banish ungodliness from Jacob."
> "And this is my covenant with them,
> when I take away their sins."

As regards the gospel they are enemies for your sake, but as regards election they are beloved for the sake of their ancestors, for the gifts and the calling of God are irrevocable. (Rom. 11:25-29)

Psalm

Psalm 87

Foreigners praise God in Zion

Additional Reading

Isaiah 43:8-13

Let all the nations gather

Hymn: God, We Gather as Your People, ACS 1038

God of mystery and revelation, you are both hidden and revealed to us. When we can't understand all that is changing around and within us, let us cling to the promise that your love for us is steadfast and forever.

Wednesday, August 19, 2026

Time after Pentecost

Matthew 8:1-13

Jesus heals many people

When [Jesus] entered Capernaum, a centurion came to him, appealing to him and saying, "Lord, my servant is lying at home paralyzed, in terrible distress." And he said to him, "I will come and cure him." The centurion answered, "Lord, I am not worthy to have you come under my roof, but only speak the word, and my servant will be healed. For I also am a man under authority, with soldiers under me, and I say to one, 'Go,' and he goes, and to another, 'Come,' and he comes, and to my slave, 'Do this,' and the slave does it." When Jesus heard him, he was amazed and said to those who followed him, "Truly I tell you, in no one in Israel have I found such faith." (Matt. 8:5-10)

Psalm

Psalm 87

Foreigners praise God in Zion

Additional Reading

Isaiah 66:18-23

All nations shall come to worship

Hymn: There Is a Longing in Our Hearts, ACS 1078

Trustworthy God, you are faithful to us. Your word both names us and saves us. Give us faith to approach you with confidence, knowing we can trust you to respond to us with hope and healing.

Thursday, August 20, 2026

Time after Pentecost

Bernard, Abbot of Clairvaux, died 1153

Psalm 138

Your love endures forever

I give you thanks, O Lord, with my whole heart;
before the gods I sing your praise;
I bow down toward your holy temple
and give thanks to your name for your steadfast love and your faithfulness,
for you have exalted your name and your word
above everything.
On the day I called, you answered me;
you increased my strength of soul.

All the kings of the earth shall praise you, O Lord,
for they have heard the words of your mouth.
They shall sing of the ways of the Lord,
for great is the glory of the Lord. (Ps. 138:1-5)

Additional Readings

Ezekiel 28:11-19
Disobedience and the loss of Eden

1 Corinthians 6:1-11
When believers disagree

Hymn: All Creatures, Worship God Most High! ELW 835

God of love and faithfulness, you are good. We cannot help but sing your praises, humming a tune of joy and thanksgiving as we dance through our days. Empower us to share your goodness with all creation.

Friday, August 21, 2026

Time after Pentecost

Ezekiel 31:15-18

Israel like the cedars of Lebanon

Thus says the Lord GOD: On the day it went down to Sheol I closed the deep over it and covered it; I restrained its rivers, and its mighty waters were checked. I clothed Lebanon in gloom for it, and all the trees of the field fainted because of it. I made the nations quake at the sound of its fall, when I cast it down to Sheol with those who go down to the Pit, and all the trees of Eden, the choice and best of Lebanon, all that were well watered, were consoled in the world below. They also went down to Sheol with it, to those killed by the sword, along with its allies, those who lived in its shade among the nations.

Which among the trees of Eden was like you in glory and in greatness? Now you shall be brought down with the trees of Eden to the world below; you shall lie among the uncircumcised, with those who are killed by the sword. This is Pharaoh and all his horde, says the Lord GOD. (Ezek. 31:15-18)

Psalm

Psalm 138

Your love endures forever

Additional Reading

2 Corinthians 10:12-18

Let those who boast, boast in the Lord

Hymn: O God, Who Gives Us Life, ACS 1086

God, you bring down those who need to be brought down, and you lift up those who need to be lifted. Dismantle all systems of injustice and oppression; help us live lives that are just and true to you.

Saturday, August 22, 2026

Time after Pentecost

Ezekiel 36:33-38

A desolate land becomes like Eden

Thus says the Lord GOD: On the day that I cleanse you from all your iniquities, I will cause the towns to be inhabited, and the waste places shall be rebuilt. The land that was desolate shall be tilled, instead of being the desolation that it was in the sight of all who passed by. And they will say, "This land that was desolate has become like the garden of Eden, and the waste and desolate and ruined towns are now inhabited and fortified." Then the nations that are left all around you shall know that I, the LORD, have rebuilt the ruined places and replanted that which was desolate; I, the LORD, have spoken, and I will do it. (Ezek. 36:33-36)

Psalm

Psalm 138

Your love endures forever

Additional Reading

Matthew 16:5-12

Bread as a sign of other things

Hymn: God Alone Be Praised, ACS 1023

God, your mercy transforms our lives. From the desolation of rock bottom, you come alongside your beloved and raise us to the beautiful freedom of new life. Make our faith communities places of flourishing forgiveness.

Sunday, August 23, 2026

Time after Pentecost

Matthew 16:13-20

The profession of Peter's faith

[Jesus] said to [the disciples], "But who do you say that I am?" Simon Peter answered, "You are the Messiah, the Son of the living God." And Jesus answered him, "Blessed are you, Simon son of Jonah! For flesh and blood has not revealed this to you but my Father in heaven. And I tell you, you are Peter, and on this rock I will build my church, and the gates of Hades will not prevail against it. I will give you the keys of the kingdom of heaven, and whatever you bind on earth will be bound in heaven, and whatever you loose on earth will be loosed in heaven." (Matt. 16:15-19)

Psalm

Psalm 138
Your love endures forever

Additional Readings

Isaiah 51:1-6
God's enduring salvation

Romans 12:1-8
One body in Christ, with gifts that differ

Hymn: My Hope Is Built on Nothing Less, ELW 596/TFF 192

O God, with all your faithful followers of every age, we praise you, the rock of our life. Be our strong foundation and form us into the body of your Son, that we may gladly minister to all the world, through Jesus Christ, our Savior and Lord.

Monday, August 24, 2026

Bartholomew, Apostle

John 1:43-51

Jesus says: Follow me

When Jesus saw Nathanael coming toward him, he said of him, "Here is truly an Israelite in whom there is no deceit!" Nathanael asked him, "Where did you get to know me?" Jesus answered, "I saw you under the fig tree before Philip called you." Nathanael replied, "Rabbi, you are the Son of God! You are the King of Israel!" Jesus answered, "Do you believe because I told you that I saw you under the fig tree? You will see greater things than these." And he said to him, "Very truly, I tell you, you will see heaven opened and the angels of God ascending and descending upon the Son of Man." (John 1:47-51)

Psalm

Psalm 12

A plea for help in evil times

Additional Readings

Exodus 19:1-6

Israel is God's priestly kingdom

1 Corinthians 12:27-31a

The body of Christ

Hymn: Will You Come and Follow Me, ELW 798

Almighty and everlasting God, you gave to your apostle Bartholomew grace truly to believe and courageously to preach your word. Grant that your church may proclaim the good news to the ends of the earth, through Jesus Christ, our Savior and Lord, who lives and reigns with you and the Holy Spirit, one God, now and forever.

Tuesday, August 25, 2026

Time after Pentecost

Psalm 18:1-3, 20-32

God the rock

I love you, O LORD, my strength.

The LORD is my rock, my fortress, and my deliverer,
my God, my rock in whom I take refuge,
my shield, and the horn of my salvation, my stronghold.
I call upon the LORD, who is worthy to be praised,
so I shall be saved from my enemies. (Ps. 18:1-3)

Additional Readings

Deuteronomy 32:18-20, 28-39
Praise the rock that is God

Romans 11:33-36
The riches, wisdom, and knowledge of God

Hymn: I Will Call Upon the Lord, TFF 277

God of all who seek refuge, you are a constant and steady presence in the life of this world you so love. Sheltered by your grace, may we become a source of strength and encouragement for others.

Wednesday, August 26, 2026

Time after Pentecost

Isaiah 28:14-22

God lays a cornerstone in Zion

Therefore hear the word of the LORD, you scoffers
who rule this people in Jerusalem.
Because you have said, "We have made a covenant with death,
and with Sheol we have an agreement;
when the overwhelming scourge passes through
it will not come to us,
for we have made lies our refuge,
and in falsehood we have taken shelter";
therefore thus says the Lord GOD,
"See, I am laying in Zion a foundation stone,
a tested stone,
a precious cornerstone, a sure foundation:
'One who trusts will not panic.'" (Isa. 28:14-16)

Psalm

Psalm 18:1-3, 20-32
God the rock

Additional Reading

Matthew 26:6-13
A woman anoints Jesus

Hymn: How Firm a Foundation, ELW 796

God of life, you alone are our shelter and refuge. When we are overwhelmed by death and surrounded by lies, restore us to trust in you. Provide mental health counselors, therapists, coaches, and guides for all in need.

Thursday, August 27, 2026

Time after Pentecost

Psalm 26:1-8

Your love is before my eyes

Vindicate me, O Lord,
for I have walked in my integrity,
and I have trusted in the Lord without wavering.
Prove me, O Lord, and try me;
test my heart and mind.
For your steadfast love is before my eyes,
and I walk in faithfulness to you. (Ps. 26:1-3)

Additional Readings

Jeremiah 14:13-18
Denunciation of lying prophets

Ephesians 5:1-6
Do not be deceived by empty words

Hymn: Just a Closer Walk with Thee, ELW 697/TFF 253

God, you lead and we follow. As you know the depths of our hearts and minds, we long to know and grow ever closer to you. Keep us with you on the path of hope, compassion, joy, and peace.

Friday, August 28, 2026

Time after Pentecost

Augustine, Bishop of Hippo, died 430
Moses the Black, monk, martyr, died around 400

2 Thessalonians 2:7-12

Refusal to love the truth

For the mystery of lawlessness is already at work, but only until the one who now restrains it is removed. And then the lawless one will be revealed, whom the Lord Jesus will destroy with the breath of his mouth, annihilating him by the manifestation of his coming. The coming of the lawless one is apparent in the working of Satan, who uses all power, signs, lying wonders, and every kind of wicked deception for those who are perishing because they refused to love the truth and so be saved. For this reason God sends them a powerful delusion, leading them to believe what is false, so that all who have not believed the truth but took pleasure in unrighteousness will be condemned. (2 Thess. 2:7-12)

Psalm

Psalm 26:1-8
Your love is before my eyes

Additional Reading

Jeremiah 15:1-9
The consequences of sin

Hymn: Come Now, O God, ACS 902

God of truth, your will for this world is life and salvation. Still, we fail to resist forces of death at work even in the church. Embolden your people to renounce sin and to live in love for our neighbors.

Saturday, August 29, 2026

Time after Pentecost

Jeremiah 15:10-14

Jeremiah's complaint to God

Woe is me, my mother, that you ever bore me, a man of strife and contention to the whole land! I have not lent, nor have I borrowed, yet all of them curse me. The LORD said: Surely I have intervened in your life for good; surely I have brought enemies upon you in a time of trouble and in a time of distress. Can one break iron, iron from the north, and bronze?

Your wealth and your treasures I will give as plunder, without price, for all your sins, throughout all your territory. I will make you serve your enemies in a land that you do not know, for in my anger a fire is kindled that shall burn against you. (Jer. 15:10-14)

Psalm

Psalm 26:1-8

Your love is before my eyes

Additional Reading

Matthew 8:14-17

Jesus heals many at Peter's house

Hymn: Sometimes Our Only Song Is Weeping, ACS 1050

Patient God, you remain with us always. You listen to our complaints. Even when our praise turns to blame, you refuse to abandon us. Free us to bring all our anger, resentment, pain, and frustration to you.

Sunday, August 30, 2026

Time after Pentecost

Matthew 16:21-28

The rebuke to Peter

From that time on, Jesus began to show his disciples that he must go to Jerusalem and undergo great suffering at the hands of the elders and chief priests and scribes and be killed and on the third day be raised. And Peter took him aside and began to rebuke him, saying, "God forbid it, Lord! This must never happen to you." But he turned and said to Peter, "Get behind me, Satan! You are a hindrance to me, for you are setting your mind not on divine things but on human things." (Matt. 16:21-23)

Psalm

Psalm 26:1-8

Your love is before my eyes

Additional Readings

Jeremiah 15:15-21

God fortifies the prophet

Romans 12:9-21

Live in harmony

Hymn: Jesus, Keep Me Near the Cross, ELW 335/TFF 73

O God, we thank you for your Son, who chose the path of suffering for the sake of the world. Humble us by his example, point us to the path of obedience, and give us strength to follow your commands, through Jesus Christ, our Savior and Lord.

Monday, August 31, 2026

Time after Pentecost

Psalm 17

The righteous shall see God

I call upon you, for you will answer me, O God;
    incline your ear to me; hear my words.
Wondrously show your steadfast love,
    O savior of those who seek refuge
    from their adversaries at your right hand.

Guard me as the apple of the eye;
    hide me in the shadow of your wings,
from the wicked who despoil me,
    my deadly enemies who surround me. (Ps. 17:6-9)

Additional Readings

2 Samuel 11:2-26
David sins

Revelation 3:1-6
Wake up to your faithlessness

Hymn: For the Beauty of the Earth, ELW 879

God, you are the steadfast lover of our souls. It is our deepest desire to walk with you in an honest and faithful fashion. Guide us in your ways, and hide us in the shadow of your wings.

Prayer List for September

Time after Pentecost

Autumn

The days of early autumn (September and October) herald the resumption of a more regular schedule: school begins, church education programs commence, and the steady rhythms of work are accompanied by cooling breezes and the changing colors of the landscape. During these months, various crops are harvested and appear on roadside stands and in grocery stores. In many countries the harvest days of September and October are marked with prayer, feasting, and special care for people who are poor and hungry.

Table Prayer for Autumn

We praise you and bless you, O God,
for bright autumn days
and for the gifts of this table.
Grant us grace to share your goodness
and to trust that there is more than enough for all of your people,
through Jesus Christ, who is abundance and mercy. Amen.

Tuesday, September 1, 2026

Time after Pentecost

Revelation 3:7-13

God blesses the humble

And to the angel of the church in Philadelphia write:
These are the words of the Holy One, the True One,
who has the key of David,
who opens and no one will shut,
who shuts and no one opens. . . .
Because you have kept my word of endurance, I will keep you from the hour of trial that is coming on the whole world to test the inhabitants of the earth. I am coming soon; hold fast to what you have, so that no one takes away your crown. If you conquer, I will make you a pillar in the temple of my God; you will never go out of it. I will write on you the name of my God and the name of the city of my God, the new Jerusalem that comes down from my God out of heaven, and my own new name. (Rev. 3:7, 10-12)

Psalm

Psalm 17

The righteous shall see God

Additional Reading

2 Samuel 11:27b—12:15

Nathan rebukes David

Hymn: O Christ, Our Light, O Radiance True, ELW 675

O Love Divine, you've watched over us from the beginning as we navigate this unpredictable world. You open doors and cover us with your love. As we face challenges and trials, help us stand firm in our faith.

Wednesday, September 2, 2026

Time after Pentecost

Nikolai Frederik Severin Grundtvig, bishop, renewer of the church, died 1872

Jeremiah 17:5-18

The vindication of the righteous

Thus says the LORD:
Cursed are those who trust in mere mortals
    and make mere flesh their strength,
    whose hearts turn away from the LORD.
They shall be like a shrub in the desert
    and shall not see when relief comes.
They shall live in the parched places of the wilderness,
    in an uninhabited salt land.

Blessed are those who trust in the LORD,
    whose trust is the LORD.
They shall be like a tree planted by water,
    sending out its roots by the stream.
It shall not fear when heat comes,
    and its leaves shall stay green;
in the year of drought it is not anxious,
    and it does not cease to bear fruit. (Jer. 17:5-8)

Psalm

Psalm 17

The righteous shall see God

Additional Reading

Matthew 12:22-32

Jesus comes to cast out Satan

Hymn: Blessed Assurance, ELW 638/TFF 118

God of comfort, we come before you with open hearts. As Jesus healed and cast out evil, we ask that you bring healing from anything that keeps us from you. Help us recognize the work of your Spirit.

Thursday, September 3, 2026

Time after Pentecost

Psalm 119:33-40

The path of your commandments

Teach me, O Lord, the way of your statutes,
  and I will observe it to the end.
Give me understanding, that I may keep your law
  and observe it with my whole heart.
Lead me in the path of your commandments,
  for I delight in it.
Turn my heart to your decrees
  and not to selfish gain. (Ps. 119:33-36)

Additional Readings

Ezekiel 24:1-14
God judges unrepentant Israel

2 Corinthians 12:11-21
Sinners warned but unrepentant

Hymn: Lord, Let My Heart Be Good Soil, ELW 512/TFF 131

Loving God, we praise you for imprinting your love upon our hearts. Teach us to walk in your ways, and give us understanding to follow you with our whole lives. Turn us from selfish desires to focus on what honors you.

Friday, September 4, 2026

Time after Pentecost

Romans 10:15b-21

God reaches out to erring Israel

As it is written, "How beautiful are the feet of those who bring good news!" But not all have obeyed the good news, for Isaiah says, "Lord, who has believed our message?" So faith comes from what is heard, and what is heard comes through the word of Christ. (Rom. 10:15b-17)

Psalm

Psalm 119:33-40

The path of your commandments

Additional Reading

Ezekiel 24:15-27

God opens the prophet's mouth

Hymn: O Word of God Incarnate, ELW 514

Gracious Lord, we thank you for the gift of your Word Incarnate. You are the lamp to our feet and a light to our path. Lead us toward your love and grace in the name of Jesus Christ.

Saturday, September 5, 2026

Time after Pentecost

Ezekiel 33:1-6

The prophet's vocation

The word of the LORD came to me: O Mortal, speak to your people and say to them: If I bring the sword upon a land and the people of the land take one of their number as their sentinel, and if the sentinel sees the sword coming upon the land and blows the trumpet and warns the people, then if any who hear the sound of the trumpet do not take warning and the sword comes and takes them away, their blood shall be upon their own heads. They heard the sound of the trumpet and did not take warning; their blood shall be upon themselves. But if they had taken warning, they would have saved their lives. But if the sentinel sees the sword coming and does not blow the trumpet so that the people are not warned, and the sword comes and takes any of them, they are taken away in their iniquity, but their blood I will require at the sentinel's hand. (Ezek. 33:1-6)

Psalm

Psalm 119:33-40

The path of your commandments

Additional Reading

Matthew 23:29-36

The martyrdom of the prophets

Hymn: You Are the Way, ELW 758

Merciful God, thank you for continuously fastening us to yourself. Grant us clarity as we navigate life's complexities, seeking understanding that leads to your abundance. Let our hearts bear witness to your love, encouraging others who seek your heavenly embrace.

Sunday, September 6, 2026

Time after Pentecost

Matthew 18:15-20

Reconciliation in the community of faith

[Jesus said to the disciples,] "If your brother or sister sins against you, go and point out the fault when the two of you are alone. If you are listened to, you have regained that one. But if you are not listened to, take one or two others along with you, so that every word may be confirmed by the evidence of two or three witnesses. If that person refuses to listen to them, tell it to the church, and if the offender refuses to listen even to the church, let such a one be to you as a gentile and a tax collector." (Matt. 18:15-17)

Psalm

Psalm 119:33-40
The path of your commandments

Additional Readings

Ezekiel 33:7-11
The prophet's responsibility

Romans 13:8-14
Live honorably as in the day

Hymn: Jesus, Savior, Pilot Me, ELW 755

O Lord God, enliven and preserve your church with your perpetual mercy. Without your help, we mortals will fail; remove far from us everything that is harmful and lead us toward all that gives life and salvation, through Jesus Christ, our Savior and Lord.

Monday, September 7, 2026

Time after Pentecost

Psalm 119:65-72

The law humbles me

You have dealt well with your servant,
O LORD, according to your word.
Teach me good judgment and knowledge,
for I believe in your commandments.
Before I was humbled I went astray,
but now I keep your word. (Ps. 119:65-67)

Additional Readings

Leviticus 4:27-31; 5:14-16
Atoning for sin in the community

1 Peter 2:11-17
Live as servants of God

Hymn: Let the Whole Creation Cry, ELW 876

Gracious Lord, thank you for opening the eyes of our hearts so that we may perceive the wondrous blessings of creation. Help us to offer ourselves into your hands, that we may live fully in your abundant life for us.

Tuesday, September 8, 2026

Time after Pentecost

Romans 13:1-7

Obeying authority

Let every person be subject to the governing authorities, for there is no authority except from God, and those authorities that exist have been instituted by God. Therefore whoever resists authority resists what God has appointed, and those who resist will incur judgment. For rulers are not a terror to good conduct but to bad. Do you wish to have no fear of the authority? Then do what is good, and you will receive its approval, for it is God's agent for your good. But if you do what is wrong, you should be afraid, for the authority does not bear the sword in vain! It is the agent of God to execute wrath on the wrongdoer. (Rom. 13:1-4)

Psalm

Psalm 119:65-72

The law humbles me

Additional Reading

Deuteronomy 17:2-13

Punishment for sin in community

Hymn: Precious Lord, Take My Hand, ELW 773/TFF 193

Breath of inspiration, we praise you for your divine mercy. As we seek to uphold justice and righteousness, inspire us to reflect your truth in all that we do. May our lives be a testament to your glory and wisdom.

Wednesday, September 9, 2026

Time after Pentecost

Peter Claver, priest, missionary to Colombia, died 1654

Matthew 21:18-22

Jesus teaches about praying in faith

In the morning, when [Jesus] returned to the city, he was hungry. And seeing a fig tree by the side of the road, he went to it and found nothing at all on it but leaves. Then he said to it, "May no fruit ever come from you again!" And the fig tree withered at once. When the disciples saw it, they were amazed, saying, "How did the fig tree wither at once?" Jesus answered them, "Truly I tell you, if you have faith and do not doubt, not only will you do what has been done to the fig tree, but even if you say to this mountain, 'Be lifted up and thrown into the sea,' it will be done. Whatever you ask for in prayer with faith, you will receive." (Matt. 21:18-22)

Psalm

Psalm 119:65-72

The law humbles me

Additional Reading

Leviticus 16:1-5, 20-28

The scapegoat cleanses the community

Hymn: Joy to the World, ELW 267

Almighty God, so many other voices tell us how and whose to be. Keep us in your steadfast love, and breathe grace on us in the silence of our hearts made tranquil by your presence.

Thursday, September 10, 2026

Time after Pentecost

Psalm 103:[1-7] 8-13

God's compassion and mercy

The LORD is merciful and gracious,
    slow to anger and abounding in steadfast love.
He will not always accuse,
    nor will he keep his anger forever.
He does not deal with us according to our sins
    nor repay us according to our iniquities.
For as the heavens are high above the earth,
    so great is his steadfast love toward those who fear him;
as far as the east is from the west,
    so far he removes our transgressions from us.
As a father has compassion for his children,
    so the LORD has compassion for those who fear him. (Ps. 103:8-13)

Additional Readings

Genesis 37:12-36
Joseph's brothers sin against him

1 John 3:11-16
Love one another

Hymn: Voices Raised to You, ELW 845

Merciful God, we praise you for your unfailing love and compassion. As you worked through our ancestors struggling to walk in your way, help us remember to love one another and follow your voice. Make us vessels of your grace.

Friday, September 11, 2026

Time after Pentecost

Genesis 41:53—42:17

Joseph acts harshly against his brothers

But Joseph said to [his brothers], "It is just as I have said to you; you are spies! Here is how you shall be tested: as Pharaoh lives, you shall not leave this place unless your youngest brother comes here! Let one of you go and bring your brother, while the rest of you remain in prison, in order that your words may be tested, whether there is truth in you, or else, as Pharaoh lives, surely you are spies." And he put them all together in prison for three days. (Gen. 42:14-17)

Psalm

Psalm 103:[1-7] 8-13

God's compassion and mercy

Additional Reading

Acts 7:9-16

Joseph's family is fed in Egypt

Hymn: Hope of the World, ACS 1085

Gracious God, we come before you with gratitude. You are compassionate and slow to anger, abounding in steadfast love. Help us embody your forgiveness and grace, extending your mercy to others.

Saturday, September 12, 2026

Time after Pentecost

Matthew 6:7-15

Forgiving one another

[Jesus taught his disciples,]
"Pray, then, in this way:
Our Father in heaven,
may your name be revered as holy.
May your kingdom come.
May your will be done
on earth as it is in heaven.
Give us today our daily bread.
And forgive us our debts,
as we also have forgiven our debtors.
And do not bring us to the time of trial,
but rescue us from the evil one." (Matt. 6:9-13)

Psalm

Psalm 103:[1-7] 8-13
God's compassion and mercy

Additional Reading

Genesis 45:1-20
Joseph forgives his brothers

Hymn: Restore in Us, O God, ELW 328

Reconciling, Lord, we come in prayer to align our hearts with your will and seek to approach you sincerely and humbly. May we remember your abundant mercy and compassion, and extend that same grace to those around us.

Sunday, September 13, 2026

Time after Pentecost

John Chrysostom, Bishop of Constantinople, died 407

Matthew 18:21-35

A parable of forgiveness

Then Peter came and said to him, "Lord, if my brother or sister sins against me, how often should I forgive? As many as seven times?" Jesus said to him, "Not seven times, but, I tell you, seventy-seven times." (Matt. 18:21-22)

Psalm

Psalm 103:[1-7] 8-13
God's compassion and mercy

Additional Readings

Genesis 50:15-21
Joseph reconciles with his brothers

Romans 14:1-12
When brothers and sisters judge each other

Hymn: Chief of Sinners Though I Be, ELW 609

O Lord God, merciful judge, you are the inexhaustible fountain of forgiveness. Replace our hearts of stone with hearts that love and adore you, that we may delight in doing your will, through Jesus Christ, our Savior and Lord.

Monday, September 14, 2026

Holy Cross Day

John 3:13-17

The Son of Man will be lifted up

[Jesus said to Nicodemus,] "No one has ascended into heaven except the one who descended from heaven, the Son of Man. And just as Moses lifted up the serpent in the wilderness, so must the Son of Man be lifted up, that whoever believes in him may have eternal life.

"For God so loved the world that he gave his only Son, so that everyone who believes in him may not perish but may have eternal life.

"Indeed, God did not send the Son into the world to condemn the world but in order that the world might be saved through him." (John 3:13-17)

Psalm

Psalm 98:1-4
The LORD has done marvelous things

Additional Readings

Numbers 21:4b-9
A bronze serpent in the wilderness

1 Corinthians 1:18-24
The cross is the power of God

Hymn: Lift High the Cross, ELW 660

Almighty God, your Son Jesus Christ was lifted high upon the cross so that he might draw the whole world to himself. To those who look upon the cross, grant your wisdom, healing, and eternal life, through Jesus Christ, our Savior and Lord, who lives and reigns with you and the Holy Spirit, one God, now and forever.

Tuesday, September 15, 2026

Time after Pentecost

Psalm 133

How good it is to live in unity

How very good and pleasant it is
when kindred live together in unity!
It is like the precious oil on the head,
running down upon the beard,
on the beard of Aaron,
running down over the collar of his robes.
It is like the dew of Hermon,
which falls on the mountains of Zion.
For there the LORD ordained his blessing,
life forevermore. (Ps. 133:1-3)

Additional Readings

Genesis 49:29—50:14
Honoring Jacob's burial wishes

Romans 14:13—15:2
Building each other up

Hymn: Send Me, Jesus, ELW 549/TFF 245

God of unity, in moments of grief and transition, may we find strength in our shared bonds and support one another. Help us to build each other up, putting aside judgments and focusing on love and understanding.

Wednesday, September 16, 2026

Time after Pentecost

Cyprian, Bishop of Carthage, martyr, died around 258

Genesis 50:22-26

Joseph dies

So Joseph remained in Egypt, he and his father's household, and Joseph lived one hundred ten years. Joseph saw Ephraim's children of the third generation; the children of Machir son of Manasseh were also born on Joseph's knees.

Then Joseph said to his brothers, "I am about to die, but God will surely come to you and bring you up out of this land to the land that he swore to Abraham, to Isaac, and to Jacob." So Joseph made the Israelites swear, saying, "When God comes to you, you shall carry up my bones from here." And Joseph died, being one hundred ten years old; he was embalmed and placed in a coffin in Egypt. (Gen. 50:22-26)

Psalm

Psalm 133

How good it is to live in unity

Additional Reading

Mark 11:20-25

Forgiveness for those who forgive

Hymn: Come, Join the Dance of Trinity, ELW 412

Triune God, you are the source of forgiveness and unity. Help us to be agents of forgiveness toward others and ourselves, even—by your power—for things we deem unforgivable, so that we may live in harmony with all.

Thursday, September 17, 2026

Time after Pentecost

Hildegard, Abbess of Bingen, died 1179

Psalm 145:1-8

God is slow to anger

One generation shall extol your works to another
    and shall declare your mighty acts.
They will recount the glorious splendor of your majesty,
    and on your wondrous works I will meditate.
They will proclaim the might of your awesome deeds,
    and I will declare your greatness.
They shall celebrate the fame of your abundant goodness
    and shall sing aloud of your righteousness. (Ps. 145:4-7)

Additional Readings

Nahum 1:1, 14—2:2
God's wrath toward Nineveh

2 Corinthians 13:1-4
Dissent among believers

Hymn: There Is a Balm in Gilead, ELW 614/TFF 185

Restorative God, soften our hearts of stone to and make of them a healing balm that helps us see your face in our siblings. Reveal how your light shines through all your children, that none may deny their identity in you.

Friday, September 18, 2026

Time after Pentecost

Dag Hammarskjöld, renewer of society, died 1961

2 Corinthians 13:5-10

Correction that builds up

But we pray to God that you may not do anything wrong—not that we may appear to have met the test but that you may do what is right, though we may seem to have failed. For we cannot do anything against the truth but only for the truth. For we rejoice when we are weak but you are strong. This is what we pray for, that you may be restored. So I write these things while I am away from you, so that when I come I may not have to be severe in using the authority that the Lord has given me for building up and not for tearing down. (2 Cor. 13:7-10)

Psalm

Psalm 145:1-8

God is slow to anger

Additional Reading

Nahum 2:3-13

Nineveh under siege

Hymn: O Christ, Our Hope, ELW 604

Beloved and merciful God, nobody and nothing is beyond your divine love. Where we have failed to recognize that truth, we ask that you bring us to our senses, lifting up every heart to your radical love and grace.

Saturday, September 19, 2026

Time after Pentecost

Zephaniah 2:13-15

Judgment on Nineveh

And he will stretch out his hand against the north
    and destroy Assyria,
and he will make Nineveh a desolation,
    a dry waste like the desert.
Herds shall lie down in it,
    every wild animal of the earth;
the desert owl and the screech owl
    shall lodge on its capitals;
the owl shall hoot at the window,
    the raven croak on the threshold,
    for its cedar work will be laid bare. (Zeph. 2:13-14)

Psalm

Psalm 145:1-8

God is slow to anger

Additional Reading

Matthew 19:23-30

The last will be first

Hymn: Baptized and Set Free, ELW 453

God of possibility, we know you are always with us in every hardship and turmoil. Make us not only pause to see and feel your presence but also be an active witness to this good news in the world.

Sunday, September 20, 2026

Time after Pentecost

Matthew 20:1-16

The parable of the vineyard workers

[Jesus said:] "But [the landowner] replied to one of [the laborers], 'Friend, I am doing you no wrong; did you not agree with me for a denarius? Take what belongs to you and go; I choose to give to this last the same as I give to you. Am I not allowed to do what I choose with what belongs to me? Or are you envious because I am generous?' So the last will be first, and the first will be last." (Matt. 20:13-16)

Psalm

Psalm 145:1-8
God is slow to anger

Additional Readings

Jonah 3:10—4:11
God's concern for Nineveh

Philippians 1:21-30
Standing firm in the gospel

Hymn: The Numberless Gifts of God's Mercies, ELW 683

Almighty and eternal God, you show perpetual lovingkindness to us, your servants. Because we cannot rely on our own abilities, grant us your merciful judgment and train us to embody the generosity of your Son, Jesus Christ, our Savior and Lord.

Monday, September 21, 2026

Matthew, Apostle and Evangelist

Matthew 9:9-13

Jesus calls to Matthew: Follow me

As Jesus was walking along, he saw a man called Matthew sitting at the tax-collection station, and he said to him, "Follow me." And he got up and followed him.

And as he sat at dinner in the house, many tax collectors and sinners came and were sitting with Jesus and his disciples. When the Pharisees saw this, they said to his disciples, "Why does your teacher eat with tax collectors and sinners?" But when he heard this, he said, "Those who are well have no need of a physician, but those who are sick. Go and learn what this means, 'I desire mercy, not sacrifice.' For I have not come to call the righteous but sinners." (Matt. 9:9-13)

Psalm

Psalm 119:33-40
Give me understanding

Additional Readings

Ezekiel 2:8—3:11
A prophet to the house of Israel

Ephesians 2:4-10
By grace you have been saved

Hymn: We Are an Offering, ELW 692

Almighty God, your Son our Savior called a despised tax collector to become one of his apostles. Help us, like Matthew, to respond to the transforming call of Jesus Christ, who lives and reigns with you and the Holy Spirit, one God, now and forever.

Tuesday, September 22, 2026

Time after Pentecost

Psalm 106:1-12

God's mercy

Praise the LORD!
O give thanks to the LORD, for he is good,
for his steadfast love endures forever.
Who can utter the mighty doings of the LORD
or declare all his praise?
Happy are those who observe justice,
who do righteousness at all times.

Remember us, O LORD, when you show favor to your people;
help us when you deliver them,
that we may see the prosperity of your chosen ones,
that we may rejoice in the gladness of your nation,
that we may glory in your heritage. (Ps. 106:1-5)

Additional Readings

Genesis 28:10-17
God blesses the runaway Jacob

Romans 16:17-20
A warning about troublemakers

Hymn: O Lord, Hear My Prayer, ELW 751

Giver of life, thank you for your steadfast love bestowed on us from generation to generation. Give us courage to commit to love, that we may no longer accept injustice when we see it in our world.

Wednesday, September 23, 2026

Time after Pentecost

Matthew 18:1-5

True greatness

At that time the disciples came to Jesus and asked, "Who is the greatest in the kingdom of heaven?" He called a child, whom he put among them, and said, "Truly I tell you, unless you change and become like children, you will never enter the kingdom of heaven. Whoever becomes humble like this child is the greatest in the kingdom of heaven. Whoever welcomes one such child in my name welcomes me." (Matt. 18:1-5)

Psalm

Psalm 106:1-12

God's mercy

Additional Reading

Isaiah 41:1-13

God will be with the last

Hymn: Go, My Children, with My Blessing, ELW 543/TFF 161

Comforting God, you open yourself to us with love and mercy, manifested among us in your Son Jesus Christ. Grant us tranquility through your Spirit, and lead us to still waters.

Thursday, September 24, 2026

Time after Pentecost

Psalm 25:1-9

God's compassion and love

Make me to know your ways, O LORD;
teach me your paths.
Lead me in your truth and teach me,
for you are the God of my salvation;
for you I wait all day long.

Be mindful of your mercy, O LORD, and of your steadfast love,
for they have been from of old.
Do not remember the sins of my youth or my transgressions;
according to your steadfast love remember me,
for the sake of your goodness, O LORD! (Ps. 25:4-7)

Additional Readings

Ezekiel 12:17-28
God's judgment is timely

James 4:11-16
We do not know what tomorrow will bring

Hymn: We Sing to You, O God, ELW 791

Everlasting God, you have been with us from the beginning. When we go astray, you bring us back home with compassion and forgiveness. Guide us once again to know your peace, in the name of your Son, Jesus Christ.

Friday, September 25, 2026

Time after Pentecost

Acts 13:32-41

Through Jesus forgiveness is proclaimed

[Paul said,] "For David, after he had served the purpose of God in his own generation, died, was laid beside his ancestors, and experienced corruption, but he whom God raised up experienced no corruption. Let it be known to you therefore, brothers and sisters, that through this man forgiveness of sins is proclaimed to you; by this Jesus everyone who believes is set free from all those sins from which you could not be freed by the law of Moses." (Acts 13:36-39)

Psalm

Psalm 25:1-9

God's compassion and love

Additional Reading

Ezekiel 18:5-18

Those who repent shall live

Hymn: O Master, Let Me Walk with You, ELW 818

Merciful God, we praise you for your abiding love, even in our sinfulness. In your compassion, grant us the courage to take responsibility when we fail to love your creations.

Saturday, September 26, 2026

Time after Pentecost

Ezekiel 18:19-24

A child does not suffer for a parent's sin

Yet you say, "Why should not the son suffer for the iniquity of the father?" When the son has done what is lawful and right and has been careful to observe all my statutes, he shall surely live. The person who sins shall die. A child shall not suffer for the iniquity of a parent nor a parent suffer for the iniquity of a child; the righteousness of the righteous shall be their own, and the wickedness of the wicked shall be their own. (Ezek. 18:19-20)

Psalm

Psalm 25:1-9

God's compassion and love

Additional Reading

Mark 11:27-33

Jesus' authority is questioned

Hymn: Listen, God Is Calling, ELW 513/TFF 130

You are gracious and just, O God! Your paths are loving and sure. May our eyes always be on you and only you. Call us back when we mistake the way. We ask this in the name of Jesus Christ.

Sunday, September 27, 2026

Time after Pentecost

Matthew 21:23-32

A parable of doing God's will

[Jesus said,] "What do you think? A man had two sons; he went to the first and said, 'Son, go and work in the vineyard today.' He answered, 'I will not,' but later he changed his mind and went. The father went to the second and said the same, and he answered, 'I go, sir,' but he did not go. Which of the two did the will of his father?" They said, "The first." Jesus said to them, "Truly I tell you, the tax collectors and the prostitutes are going into the kingdom of God ahead of you. For John came to you in the way of righteousness, and you did not believe him, but the tax collectors and the prostitutes believed him, and even after you saw it you did not change your minds and believe him." (Matt. 21:28-32)

Psalm

Psalm 25:1-9
God's compassion and love

Additional Readings

Ezekiel 18:1-4, 25-32
The fairness of God's way

Philippians 2:1-13
Christ humbled to the point of death

Hymn: Praise the Almighty! ELW 877

God of love, giver of life, you know our frailties and failings. Give us your grace to overcome them, keep us from those things that harm us, and guide us in the way of salvation, through Jesus Christ, our Savior and Lord.

Monday, September 28, 2026

Time after Pentecost

Psalm 28

Prayer to do God's will

Blessed be the LORD,
for he has heard the sound of my pleadings.
The LORD is my strength and my shield;
in him my heart trusts;
so I am helped, and my heart exults,
and with my song I give thanks to him.

The LORD is the strength of his people;
he is the saving refuge of his anointed.
O save your people and bless your heritage;
be their shepherd and carry them forever. (Ps. 28:6-9)

Additional Readings

Judges 14:1-20
Samson's riddle explained

Philippians 1:3-14
Paul prays for the Philippians

Hymn: Change My Heart, O God, ELW 801

O God, heart of our heart, you heed the cry of our spirit. You are our strength and our protection. Grace us with your presence, and keep us from all danger and harm.

Tuesday, September 29, 2026

Michael and All Angels

Revelation 12:7-12

Michael defeats Satan in a cosmic battle

And war broke out in heaven; Michael and his angels fought against the dragon. The dragon and his angels fought back, but they were defeated, and there was no longer any place for them in heaven. The great dragon was thrown down, that ancient serpent, who is called the devil and Satan, the deceiver of the whole world—he was thrown down to the earth, and his angels were thrown down with him. (Rev. 12:7-9)

Psalm

Psalm 103:1-5, 20-22
Bless the LORD, you angels

Additional Readings

Daniel 10:10-14; 12:1-3
Michael shall arise

Luke 10:17-20
Jesus gives his followers authority

Hymn: Come Down, O Love Divine, ELW 804

Everlasting God, you have wonderfully established the ministries of angels and mortals. Mercifully grant that as Michael and the angels contend against the cosmic forces of evil, so by your direction they may help and defend us here on earth, through your Son, Jesus Christ our Lord, who lives and reigns with you and the Holy Spirit, one God whom we worship and praise with angels and archangels and all the company of heaven, now and forever.

Wednesday, September 30, 2026

Time after Pentecost

Jerome, translator, teacher, died 420

Judges 16:23-31

Samson prays to do God's will

Then Samson called to the LORD and said, "Lord GOD, remember me and strengthen me only this once, O God, so that with this one act of revenge I may pay back the Philistines for my two eyes." And Samson grasped the two middle pillars on which the house rested, and he leaned his weight against them, his right hand on the one and his left hand on the other. Then Samson said, "Let me die with the Philistines." He strained with all his might, and the house fell on the lords and all the people who were in it. So those he killed at his death were more than those he had killed during his life. Then his kindred and all his family came down and took him and brought him up and buried him between Zorah and Eshtaol in the tomb of his father Manoah. He had judged Israel twenty years. (Judg. 16:28-31)

Psalm

Psalm 28

Prayer to do God's will

Additional Reading

Matthew 9:2-8

Jesus' authority to forgive and heal

Hymn: Let Us Ever Walk with Jesus, ELW 802

Cosmic God, nothing can compare to you. You provided the breath of life at creation. May we always cling to Jesus, in whom we find companionship, life-giving grace, and salvation.

Prayer List for October

Thursday, October 1, 2026

Time after Pentecost

Psalm 80:7-15

Look down from heaven, O God

Restore us, O God of hosts;
let your face shine, that we may be saved.

You brought a vine out of Egypt;
you drove out the nations and planted it.
You cleared the ground for it;
it took deep root and filled the land. (Ps. 80:7-9)

Additional Readings

Jeremiah 2:14-22
The choice vine becomes degenerate

Colossians 2:16-23
Hold fast to Christ, the head

Hymn: Lord, Take My Hand and Lead Me, ELW 767

Holy God, sometimes it feels like we have lost each other. Bring us back into your community. Remind us of all the ways you have been steadfast throughout our lives. Renew our faith.

Friday, October 2, 2026

Time after Pentecost

Philippians 2:14-18; 3:1-4a

Boast only in Jesus Christ

Do all things without murmuring and arguing, so that you may be blameless and innocent, children of God without blemish in the midst of a crooked and perverse generation, in which you shine like stars in the world, holding forth the word of life so that I can boast on the day of Christ that I did not run in vain or labor in vain.

But even if I am being poured out as a libation over the sacrifice and the service of your faith, I rejoice, and I rejoice together with all of you; in the same way also you should rejoice and rejoice together with me. (Phil. 2:14-18)

Psalm

Psalm 80:7-15

Look down from heaven, O God

Additional Reading

Jeremiah 2:23-37

Israel shall be shamed

Hymn: Have You Thanked the Lord? ELW 829/TFF 270

Gracious God, rejoicing can be hard amid the chaos of daily life. Even if just for a breath, help us to feel your joy and hope each day. You are with us, and for this we can give thanks.

Saturday, October 3, 2026

Time after Pentecost

Jeremiah 6:1-10

Gleaning a remnant from the vine

Thus says the LORD of hosts:
Glean thoroughly as a vine
    the remnant of Israel;
like a grape gatherer, pass your hand again
    over its branches.

To whom shall I speak and give warning,
    that they may hear?
See, their ears are closed;
    they cannot listen.
The word of the LORD is to them an object of scorn;
    they take no pleasure in it. (Jer. 6:9-10)

Psalm

Psalm 80:7-15

Look down from heaven, O God

Additional Reading

John 7:40-52

Some accept, others reject Jesus Christ

Hymn: Just As I Am, without One Plea, ELW 592

God of forgiveness, we haven't always been faithful. Forgive us for the ways that our actions, words, and thoughts have hurt others and hurt ourselves. Help us to grow in your grace each day.

Sunday, October 4, 2026

Time after Pentecost

Francis of Assisi, renewer of the church, died 1226

Theodor Fliedner, renewer of society, died 1864

See page 420 for a blessing of pets and animals, often used on or near the October 4 commemoration of Francis of Assisi.

Matthew 21:33-46

The parable of the vineyard owner's son

Jesus said to [the chief priests and the elders], "Have you never read in the scriptures:

'The stone that the builders rejected
has become the cornerstone;
this was the Lord's doing,
and it is amazing in our eyes'?

"Therefore I tell you, the kingdom of God will be taken away from you and given to a people that produces its fruits. The one who falls on this stone will be broken to pieces, and it will crush anyone on whom it falls."

When the chief priests and the Pharisees heard his parables, they realized that he was speaking about them. They wanted to arrest him, but they feared the crowds, because they regarded him as a prophet. (Matt. 21:42-46)

Psalm

Psalm 80:7-15
Look down from heaven, O God

Additional Readings

Isaiah 5:1-7
The song of the vineyard

Philippians 3:4b-14
Nothing surpasses knowing Christ

Hymn: God Alone Be Praised, ACS 1023

Beloved God, from you come all things that are good. Lead us by the inspiration of your Spirit to know those things that are right, and by your merciful guidance, help us to do them, through Jesus Christ, our Savior and Lord.

Monday, October 5, 2026

Time after Pentecost

Psalm 144

Prayer for blessing

Blessed be the LORD, my rock,
who trains my hands for war and my fingers for battle,
my rock and my fortress,
my stronghold and my deliverer,
my shield, in whom I take refuge,
who subdues the peoples under me.

O LORD, what are humans that you regard them,
or mortals that you think of them?
They are like a breath;
their days are like a passing shadow. (Ps. 144:1-4)

Additional Readings

Ezekiel 19:10-14
A lament for Israel the vine

1 Peter 2:4-10
Christ the cornerstone

Hymn: Praise God, from Whom All Blessings Flow, TFF 276

Immortal God, as the seasons change around us, remind us that you are beyond time. While our days may be like a blink of your eye, these years are precious to us. Thank you for the gift of life.

Tuesday, October 6, 2026

Time after Pentecost

William Tyndale, translator, martyr, died 1536

2 Corinthians 5:17-21

God reconciles us through Christ

So if anyone is in Christ, there is a new creation: everything old has passed away; look, new things have come into being! All this is from God, who reconciled us to himself through Christ and has given us the ministry of reconciliation; that is, in Christ God was reconciling the world to himself, not counting their trespasses against them, and entrusting the message of reconciliation to us. So we are ambassadors for Christ, since God is making his appeal through us; we entreat you on behalf of Christ: be reconciled to God. For our sake God made the one who knew no sin to be sin, so that in him we might become the righteousness of God. (2 Cor. 5:17-21)

Psalm

Psalm 144

Prayer for blessing

Additional Reading

Isaiah 27:1-6

God will save Israel the vine

Hymn: Beautiful Things, ACS 925

Holy Creator, you made the cosmos and each person, calling us good. As we age, grow, and change, you continue to work on us. Your forgiveness softens our rough edges. Your love expands our compassion. Always keep making us new.

Wednesday, October 7, 2026

Time after Pentecost

Henry Melchior Muhlenberg, pastor in North America, died 1787

John 11:45-57

Critics plan to silence Jesus

The chief priests and the Pharisees called a meeting of the council and said, "What are we to do? This man is performing many signs. If we let him go on like this, everyone will believe in him, and the Romans will come and destroy both our holy place and our nation." But one of them, Caiaphas, who was high priest that year, said to them, "You know nothing at all! You do not understand that it is better for you to have one man die for the people than to have the whole nation destroyed." He did not say this on his own, but being high priest that year he prophesied that Jesus was about to die for the nation, and not for the nation only, but to gather into one the dispersed children of God. (John 11:47-52)

Psalm

Psalm 144

Prayer for blessing

Additional Reading

Song of Songs 8:5-14

A love song for the vineyard

Hymn: When I Survey the Wondrous Cross, ELW 803/TFF 79

Saving Jesus, your love for the world is persistent. You find new ways to make your grace and mercy known among people. Nothing has stopped you from loving us, not even the cross. Thank you for your persistence and patience.

Thursday, October 8, 2026

Time after Pentecost

Psalm 23

You spread a table before me

Even though I walk through the darkest valley,
    I fear no evil,
for you are with me;
    your rod and your staff,
    they comfort me.

You prepare a table before me
    in the presence of my enemies;
you anoint my head with oil;
    my cup overflows.
Surely goodness and mercy shall follow me
    all the days of my life,
and I shall dwell in the house of the LORD
    my whole life long. (Ps. 23:4-6)

Additional Readings

Isaiah 22:1-8a
A futile cry to the mountains for help

1 Peter 5:1-5, 12-14
Stand fast, the chief shepherd is coming

Hymn: Shepherd Me, O God, ELW 780

Ever-attentive Lord, you watch over all people as a shepherd tends their sheep. You protect us. You sustain us. You find us when we're lost. At all times, keep us on your path and in your care.

Friday, October 9, 2026

Time after Pentecost

James 4:4-10

Humble yourselves before God

Submit yourselves therefore to God. Resist the devil, and he will flee from you. Draw near to God, and he will draw near to you. Cleanse your hands, you sinners, and purify your hearts, you double-minded. Lament and mourn and weep. Let your laughter be turned into mourning and your joy into dejection. Humble yourselves before the Lord, and he will exalt you. (James 4:7-10)

Psalm

Psalm 23

You spread a table before me

Additional Reading

Isaiah 22:8b-14

False joy instead of repentance

Hymn: Take My Life, That I May Be, ELW 583/685

Compassionate One, we need your mercy daily. Grant forgiveness for our sins. Help us understand the impact of our actions and have compassion for ourselves as well as for others as we seek reconciliation. May our bodies and minds reflect your love for the world.

Saturday, October 10, 2026

Time after Pentecost

Isaiah 24:17-23

God judges the earth from Mount Zion

On that day the LORD will punish
    the host of heaven in heaven
    and on earth the kings of the earth.
They will be gathered together
    like prisoners in a pit;
they will be shut up in a prison,
    and after many days they will be punished.
Then the moon will be abashed
    and the sun ashamed,
for the LORD of hosts will reign
    on Mount Zion and in Jerusalem,
and before his elders he will be glorified. (Isa. 24:21-23)

Psalm

Psalm 23

You spread a table before me

Additional Reading

Mark 2:18-22

No fasting when the bridegroom is present

Hymn: The Reign of God, like Farmer's Field, ACS 952

Holy Creator, all time is yours: The time before there was anything. This time when planets move, the oceans churn, and people walk. The time beyond death—your eternity. Hold us in this life and carry us to the next.

Sunday, October 11, 2026

Time after Pentecost

Matthew 22:1-14

The parable of the unwelcome guest

[Jesus concluded a parable:] "But when the king came in to see the guests, he noticed a man there who was not wearing a wedding robe, and he said to him, 'Friend, how did you get in here without a wedding robe?' And he was speechless. Then the king said to the attendants, 'Bind him hand and foot, and throw him into the outer darkness, where there will be weeping and gnashing of teeth.' For many are called, but few are chosen." (Matt. 22:11-14)

Psalm

Psalm 23
You spread a table before me

Additional Readings

Isaiah 25:1-9
The feast of victory

Philippians 4:1-9
Rejoice in the Lord always

Hymn: Bread of Life, Our Host and Meal, ELW 464

Lord of the feast, you have prepared a table before all peoples and poured out your life with abundance. Call us again to your banquet. Strengthen us by what is honorable, just, and pure, and transform us into a people of righteousness and peace, through Jesus Christ, our Savior and Lord.

Monday, October 12, 2026

Time after Pentecost

Day of Thanksgiving (Canada)

A Reading and Prayer for Thanksgiving Day is provided on page 360.

Psalm 34

Taste and see

O taste and see that the LORD is good;
    happy are those who take refuge in him.
O fear the LORD, you his holy ones,
    for those who fear him have no want.
The young lions suffer want and hunger,
    but those who seek the LORD lack no good thing. (Ps. 34:8-10)

Additional Readings

Exodus 19:7-20
God meets Moses on the mountain

Jude 17-25
Prepare for the Lord's coming

Hymn: Taste and See, ELW 493/TFF 126

God of provision, in the morning, help us to trust you. When we eat, remind us that all we have is from you. In the evening, show us your compassion. Be with us each hour of the day.

Tuesday, October 13, 2026

Time after Pentecost

Amos 9:5-15

Sweet wine from the mountains

The time is surely coming, says the LORD,
    when the one who plows shall catch up with the one who reaps
    and the treader of grapes with the one who sows the seed;
the mountains shall drip sweet wine,
    and all the hills shall flow with it.
I will restore the fortunes of my people Israel,
    and they shall rebuild the ruined cities and inhabit them;
they shall plant vineyards and drink their wine,
    and they shall make gardens and eat their fruit. (Amos 9:13-14)

Psalm

Psalm 34
Taste and see

Additional Reading

Philippians 3:13—4:1
Hold fast to Christ

Hymn: Wonderful Grace of Jesus, TFF 184

Mothering God, you are the healer of all people. Raise up those who have been put low. Repair the hearts that have been broken. Restore our faith in you. Remain with us always.

Wednesday, October 14, 2026

Time after Pentecost

John 6:25-35

God will feed the believer

When [the crowd] found him on the other side of the sea, they said to him, "Rabbi, when did you come here?" Jesus answered them, "Very truly, I tell you, you are looking for me not because you saw signs but because you ate your fill of the loaves. Do not work for the food that perishes but for the food that endures for eternal life, which the Son of Man will give you. For it is on him that God the Father has set his seal." Then they said to him, "What must we do to perform the works of God?" Jesus answered them, "This is the work of God, that you believe in him whom he has sent." (John 6:25-29)

Psalm

Psalm 34

Taste and see

Additional Reading

Song of Songs 7:10—8:4

Greed brings leprosy to GehaziNo fasting when the bridegroom is present

Hymn: The Rice of Life, ACS 965

Jesus, Bread of Life, we give thanks for all food that nourishes people: bread, rice, corn, potatoes. Each day may we be grateful both for our food from your hand and for your loving word that sustains us.

Thursday, October 15, 2026

Time after Pentecost

Teresa of Avila, teacher, renewer of the church, died 1582

Psalm 96:1-9 [10-13]

God's glory among the nations

O sing to the LORD a new song;
  sing to the LORD, all the earth.
Sing to the LORD; bless his name;
  tell of his salvation from day to day.
Declare his glory among the nations,
  his marvelous works among all the peoples.
For great is the LORD and greatly to be praised;
  he is to be revered above all gods. (Ps. 96:1-4)

Additional Readings

Judges 17:1-6
Before Israel had a king

3 John 9-12
Imitate what is good

Hymn: Ten Thousand Reasons, ACS 1097

Holy Spirit, today we join our voices with all creation to praise you. You give us hope through the colors of the changing seasons and in the rising dawn. Help us to always see and laud your beauty.

Friday, October 16, 2026

Time after Pentecost

1 Peter 5:1-5

Exemplary leadership

Now as an elder myself and a witness of the sufferings of Christ, as well as one who shares in the glory to be revealed, I exhort the elders among you to tend the flock of God that is in your charge, exercising the oversight, not under compulsion but willingly, as God would have you do it, not for sordid gain but eagerly. Do not lord it over those in your charge, but be examples to the flock. And when the chief shepherd appears, you will win the crown of glory that never fades away.
(1 Peter 5:1-4)

Psalm

Psalm 96:1-9 [10-13]
God's glory among the nations

Additional Reading

Deuteronomy 17:14-20
The limitations of royal authority

Hymn: We Are All One in Christ, ELW 643/TFF 221

God of expansive love, each person matters to you. Open our hearts to see your belovedness in everyone we meet, whoever they are. Help us to trust that your love is always with us too.

Saturday, October 17, 2026

Time after Pentecost

Ignatius, Bishop of Antioch, martyr, died around 115

Isaiah 14:3-11

The king of Babylon will fall

When the LORD has given you rest from your pain and turmoil and the hard service with which you were made to serve, you will take up this taunt against the king of Babylon:

How the oppressor has ceased!
    How his insolence has ceased!
The LORD has broken the staff of the wicked,
    the scepter of rulers,
that struck down the peoples in wrath
    with unceasing blows,
that ruled the nations in anger
    with unrelenting persecution. (Isa. 14:3-6)

Psalm

Psalm 96:1-9 [10-13]
God's glory among the nations

Additional Reading

Matthew 14:1-12
King Herod's misuse of power

Hymn: This Is My Song, ELW 887

God of all places, grant wisdom to all leaders of the nations. Tune their hearts to compassion and their minds to peace. May they use their power to care for humanity with grace and dignity.

Sunday, October 18, 2026

Time after Pentecost

Luke, Evangelist transferred to October 19

Matthew 22:15-22

A teaching about the emperor and God

But Jesus, aware of [the Pharisees'] malice, said, "Why are you putting me to the test, you hypocrites? Show me the coin used for the tax." And they brought him a denarius. Then he said to them, "Whose head is this and whose title?" They answered, "Caesar's." Then he said to them, "Give therefore to Caesar the things that are Caesar's and to God the things that are God's." When they heard this, they were amazed, and they left him and went away. (Matt. 22:18-22)

Psalm

Psalm 96:1-9 [10-13]
God's glory among the nations

Additional Readings

Isaiah 45:1-7
An earthly ruler works God's will

1 Thessalonians 1:1-10
Thanksgiving for the church at Thessalonica

Hymn: Let the Heavens Rejoice, TFF 10

Sovereign God, raise your throne in our hearts. Created by you, let us live in your image; created for you, let us act for your glory; redeemed by you, let us give you what is yours, through Jesus Christ, our Savior and Lord.

Monday, October 19, 2026

Luke, Evangelist (transferred)

Luke 1:1-4; 24:44-53

Luke witnesses to the ministry of Jesus

Since many have undertaken to compile a narrative about the events that have been fulfilled among us, just as they were handed on to us by those who from the beginning were eyewitnesses and servants of the word, I, too, decided, as one having a grasp of everything from the start, to write a well-ordered account for you, most excellent Theophilus, so that you may have a firm grasp of the words in which you have been instructed. (Luke 1:1-4)

Psalm

Psalm 124
Our help is in God

Additional Readings

Isaiah 43:8-13
You are my witness

2 Timothy 4:5-11
The good fight of faith

Hymn: By All Your Saints, ELW 421

Almighty God, you inspired your servant Luke to reveal in his gospel the love and healing power of your Son. Give your church the same love and power to heal, and to proclaim your salvation among the nations to the glory of your name, through Jesus Christ, your Son, our healer, who lives and reigns with you and the Holy Spirit, one God, now and forever.

Tuesday, October 20, 2026

Time after Pentecost

Psalm 98

God reigns over the nations

O sing to the LORD a new song,
for he has done marvelous things.
His right hand and his holy arm
have gotten him victory.
The LORD has made known his victory;
he has revealed his vindication in the sight of the nations.
He has remembered his steadfast love and faithfulness
to the house of Israel.
All the ends of the earth have seen
the victory of our God. (Ps. 98:1-3)

Additional Readings

Daniel 3:19-30
God saves three men in the furnace

Revelation 18:21-24
Babylon will be found no more

Hymn: Lord of All Hopefulness, ELW 765

Father God, your steadfast love and faithfulness are our source of hope and peace amid the anxieties of life. Ground us in your goodness each day so that we remember you're always with us wherever we are.

Wednesday, October 21, 2026

Time after Pentecost

Matthew 17:22-27

Jesus pays the temple tax

When [Jesus and the disciples] reached Capernaum, the collectors of the temple tax came to Peter and said, "Does your teacher not pay the temple tax?" He said, "Yes, he does." And when he came home, Jesus spoke of it first, asking, "What do you think, Simon? From whom do kings of the earth take toll or tribute? From their children or from others?" When Peter said, "From others," Jesus said to him, "Then the children are free. However, so that we do not give offense to them, go to the sea and cast a hook; take the first fish that comes up, and when you open its mouth you will find a coin; take that and give it to them for you and me." (Matt. 17:24-27)

Psalm

Psalm 98

God reigns over the nations

Additional Reading

Daniel 6:1-28

Daniel disobeys King Darius

Hymn: Caminemos con Jesús, ACS 1061

Holy God, empower us in faithfulness to you and in diligence in our love of neighbors, even when the world seems so unjust. Teach us to be generous with all that is ours and gracious in receiving the gifts of others.

Thursday, October 22, 2026

Time after Pentecost

Psalm 1

Their delight is in the law

Happy are those
  who do not follow the advice of the wicked
or take the path that sinners tread
  or sit in the seat of scoffers,
but their delight is in the law of the LORD,
  and on his law they meditate day and night.
They are like trees
  planted by streams of water,
which yield their fruit in its season,
  and their leaves do not wither.
In all that they do, they prosper. (Ps. 1:1-3)

Additional Readings

Numbers 5:5-10
Restitution for wronged neighbors

Titus 1:5-16
Troublemakers deny God

Hymn: We Shall Overcome, TFF 213

Sovereign Lord, your law teaches us what your love looks like when it is lived out. Forgive us when we are not able to abide by your commands. Teach us to use our words, actions, and voice for your justice.

Friday, October 23, 2026

Time after Pentecost

James of Jerusalem, martyr, died around 62

Titus 2:7-8, 11-15

A life devoted to good works

For the grace of God has appeared, bringing salvation to all, training us to renounce impiety and worldly passions and in the present age to live lives that are self-controlled, upright, and godly, while we wait for the blessed hope and the manifestation of the glory of our great God and Savior, Jesus Christ. He it is who gave himself for us that he might redeem us from all iniquity and purify for himself a people of his own who are zealous for good deeds. (Titus 2:11-14)

Psalm

Psalm 1
Their delight is in the law

Additional Reading

Deuteronomy 9:25—10:5
The second set of commandments

Hymn: Surely God Is My Salvation, ACS 926

Saving Christ, you are our salvation. You are our hope in this life and for the next. Thank you for your love shown through your life and on the cross.

Saturday, October 24, 2026

Time after Pentecost

John 5:39-47

Moses judges the disobedient

[Jesus said,] "You search the scriptures because you think that in them you have eternal life, and it is they that testify on my behalf. Yet you refuse to come to me to have life. I do not accept glory from humans. But I know that you do not have the love of God in you. I have come in my Father's name, and you do not accept me; if another comes in his own name, you will accept him. How can you believe when you accept glory from one another and do not seek the glory that comes from the one who alone is God? Do not think that I will accuse you before the Father; your accuser is Moses, on whom you have set your hope. If you believed Moses, you would believe me, for he wrote about me. But if you do not believe what he wrote, how will you believe what I say?" (John 5:39-47)

Psalm

Psalm 1

Their delight is in the law

Additional Reading

Proverbs 24:23-34

Rise above retribution

Hymn: Lord, I Lift Your Name on High, ELW 857

God of Moses and Miriam, you sent your Son to fulfill the law and the prophets of old. Open our minds to recognize the ways Jesus continues to speak in the world and to each of us.

Sunday, October 25, 2026

Time after Pentecost

Matthew 22:34-46

Loving God and neighbor

When the Pharisees heard that he had silenced the Sadducees, they gathered together, and one of them, an expert in the law, asked him a question to test him. "Teacher, which commandment in the law is the greatest?" He said to him, " 'You shall love the Lord your God with all your heart and with all your soul and with all your mind.' This is the greatest and first commandment. And a second is like it: 'You shall love your neighbor as yourself.' On these two commandments hang all the Law and the Prophets." (Matt. 22:34-40)

Psalm

Psalm 1

Their delight is in the law

Additional Readings

Leviticus 19:1-2, 15-18

Acts of justice

1 Thessalonians 2:1-8

The apostle's concern

Hymn: Now to the Holy Spirit Let Us Pray, ELW 743

O Lord God, you are the holy lawgiver, you are the salvation of your people. By your Spirit renew us in your covenant of love, and train us to care tenderly for all our neighbors, through Jesus Christ, our Savior and Lord.

Monday, October 26, 2026

Time after Pentecost

Philipp Nicolai, died 1608; Johann Heermann, died 1647;
Paul Gerhardt, died 1676; hymnwriters

Psalm 119:41-48

I will keep God's law

Let your steadfast love come to me, O LORD,
your salvation according to your promise.
Then I shall have an answer for those who taunt me,
for I trust in your word.
Do not take the word of truth utterly out of my mouth,
for my hope is in your ordinances.
I will keep your law continually,
forever and ever. (Ps. 119:41-44)

Additional Readings

Deuteronomy 6:1-9, 20-25
The great commandment

James 2:8-13
Fulfilling the royal law

Hymn: God, Be the Love to Search and Keep Me, ACS 1084

Lord of heaven, today and each day may our hearts be grounded in your grace, our minds filled with your wisdom, our strength inspired by your justice, and our actions guided by your love.

Tuesday, October 27, 2026

Time after Pentecost

James 2:14-26

Faith without works is dead

What good is it, my brothers and sisters, if someone claims to have faith but does not have works? Surely that faith cannot save, can it? If a brother or sister is naked and lacks daily food and one of you says to them, "Go in peace; keep warm and eat your fill," and yet you do not supply their bodily needs, what is the good of that? So faith by itself, if it has no works, is dead.

But someone will say, "You have faith, and I have works." Show me your faith apart from works, and I by my works will show you faith. (James 2:14-18)

Psalm

Psalm 119:41-48

I will keep God's law

Additional Reading

Deuteronomy 10:10-22

Moses urges the people to obey

Hymn: Let Us Ever Walk with Jesus, ELW 802

Holy Jesus, may the world know your love through our actions, hear it in our words, and feel it through our presence. Open our hearts to likewise know, hear, and feel your love through others.

Wednesday, October 28, 2026

Simon and Jude, Apostles

John 14:21-27

Those who love Jesus will keep his word

[Jesus said,] "They who have my commandments and keep them are those who love me, and those who love me will be loved by my Father, and I will love them and reveal myself to them." Judas (not Iscariot) said to him, "Lord, how is it that you will reveal yourself to us and not to the world?" Jesus answered him, "Those who love me will keep my word, and my Father will love them, and we will come to them and make our home with them. Whoever does not love me does not keep my words, and the word that you hear is not mine but is from the Father who sent me." (John 14:21-24)

Psalm

Psalm 11

Take refuge in God

Additional Readings

Jeremiah 26:[1-6] 7-16

Jeremiah promises the judgment of God

1 John 4:1-6

Do not believe every spirit of this world

Hymn: I Shall Not Be Moved, TFF 147

O God, we thank you for the glorious company of the apostles, and especially on this day for Simon and Jude. We pray that, as they were faithful and zealous in your mission, so we may with ardent devotion make known the love and mercy of our Savior Jesus Christ, who lives and reigns with you and the Holy Spirit, one God, now and forever.

Thursday, October 29, 2026

Time after Pentecost

Psalm 43

Send out your light and truth

O send out your light and your truth;
 let them lead me;
let them bring me to your holy hill
 and to your dwelling.
Then I will go to the altar of God,
 to God my exceeding joy,
and I will praise you with the harp,
 O God, my God. (Ps. 43:3-4)

Additional Readings

1 Samuel 2:27-36
Hope for a better priesthood

Romans 2:17-29
Real circumcision a matter of the heart

Hymn: If God My Lord Be for Me, ELW 788

Holy Spirit, when we are anxious, help us to find your peace. When we are ashamed, assure us of your grace. When we are angry, calm and direct our passion. In all things, guide our actions in your love.

Friday, October 30, 2026

Time after Pentecost

2 Peter 2:1-3

False prophets and their punishment

But false prophets also arose among the people, just as there will be false teachers among you, who will secretly bring in destructive opinions. They will even deny the Master who bought them—bringing swift destruction on themselves. Even so, many will follow their debaucheries, and because of these teachers the way of truth will be maligned. And in their greed they will exploit you with deceptive words. Their condemnation, pronounced against them long ago, has not been idle, and their destruction is not asleep. (2 Peter 2:1-3)

Psalm

Psalm 43

Send out your light and truth

Additional Reading

Ezekiel 13:1-16

False prophets condemned

Hymn: Goodness Is Stronger Than Evil, ELW 721

Almighty God, your ways bring faith, hope, love, and beauty into the world. May we always recognize you and not put trust in those who are driven by greed and power. You alone are our saving grace.

Saturday, October 31, 2026

Reformation Day

John 8:31-36

The truth will set you free

Then Jesus said to the Jews who had believed in him, "If you continue in my word, you are truly my disciples, and you will know the truth, and the truth will make you free." They answered him, "We are descendants of Abraham and have never been slaves to anyone. What do you mean by saying, 'You will be made free'?"

Jesus answered them, "Very truly, I tell you, everyone who commits sin is a slave to sin. The slave does not have a permanent place in the household; the son has a place there forever. So if the Son makes you free, you will be free indeed." (John 8:31-36)

Psalm

Psalm 46
The God of Jacob is our stronghold

Additional Readings

Jeremiah 31:31-34
I will write my law in their hearts

Romans 3:19-28
Justified by God's grace as a gift

Hymn: A Mighty Fortress Is Our God, ELW 503–505/TFF 133

Gracious Father, we pray for your holy catholic church. Fill it with all truth and peace. Where it is corrupt, purify it; where it is in error, direct it; where in anything it is amiss, reform it; where it is right, strengthen it; where it is in need, provide for it; where it is divided, reunite it; for the sake of your Son, Jesus Christ, our Savior, who lives and reigns with you and the Holy Spirit, one God, now and forever.

Prayer List for November

Time after Pentecost

November

We begin November by remembering the people who have died in Christ on All Saints Day. We speak their names and grieve their absence. But we also know that they are entrusted into the hands of God. The One who holds them, also holds us, and seeks to hold our attention long enough that hope for the future is born in us. We learn to trust in the support offered by the communion of saints, the faithful witnesses to the God of grace claimed by Jesus Christ.

November's Sunday and daily readings resonate with the harvests that happen during the fall in the Northern Hemisphere. The liturgical year ends with a relatively new Christian holiday, Christ the King or Reign of Christ Sunday. Pope Pius XI began this celebration in 1925. His hope was that Christians might cling to Jesus' way of ruling the world rather than offering their allegiance to earthly rulers.

As we get ready for the new church year, our celebration of Christ culminates by lifting up his transformative way of being in the world. We pledge our allegiance to the one who identifies with people who are hungry, thirsty, strangers, naked, sick, and imprisoned. We follow the one who was taunted as a king when he hung upon a cross. We live in the hope inspired by the crucified Christ whom God raised from the dead by the power of the Holy Spirit.

Table Prayer for November

Make yourself known to us, God of life,
as we share the bounty of this food and drink.

We give you thanks for those who have gone before us in faith,
revealing to us your gracious reign.
Feed those who hunger and
give us all a hunger for justice and peace.
We ask this through Christ our Lord. Amen.

Remembering Those Who Have Died

Use this prayer in the home or at the grave.

O God, our help in ages past and our hope for years to come:
We give you thanks for all your faithful people
who have followed the guiding light of your word throughout the centuries
into our time and place.

Here individual names may be spoken.

As we remember these people,
strengthen us to follow Christ through this world
until we are carried into the harvest of eternal life,
where suffering and death will be no more.
Hear our prayer in the name of the good and gracious shepherd,
Jesus Christ, our Savior and Lord. Amen.

or

With reverence and affection we remember before you,
O everlasting God,
all our departed friends and relatives.
Keep us in union with them here
through faith and love toward you,
that hereafter we may enter into your presence
and be numbered with those who serve you
and look upon your face in glory everlasting,
through your Son, Jesus Christ our Lord. Amen.

Sunday, November 1, 2026

All Saints Day

Matthew 5:1-12

Blessed are the poor in spirit

[Jesus said to his disciples,] "Blessed are those who are persecuted for the sake of righteousness, for theirs is the kingdom of heaven.

"Blessed are you when people revile you and persecute you and utter all kinds of evil against you falsely on my account. Rejoice and be glad, for your reward is great in heaven, for in the same way they persecuted the prophets who were before you." (Matt. 5:10-12)

Psalm

Psalm 34:1-10, 22
Fear the LORD, you saints

Additional Readings

Revelation 7:9-17
The multitude of heaven worship the Lamb

1 John 3:1-3
We are God's children

Hymn: Shall We Gather at the River, ELW 423/TFF 179

Almighty God, you have knit your people together in one communion in the mystical body of your Son, Jesus Christ our Lord. Grant us grace to follow your blessed saints in lives of faith and commitment, and to know the inexpressible joys you have prepared for those who love you, through Jesus Christ, our Savior and Lord, who lives and reigns with you and the Holy Spirit, one God, now and forever.

Monday, November 2, 2026

Time after Pentecost

Psalm 5

God blesses the righteous

Listen to my words, O Lord;
    attend to my sighing.
Listen to the sound of my cry,
    my King and my God,
    for to you I pray.
O Lord, in the morning you hear my voice;
    in the morning I plead my case to you and watch. . . .

Lead me, O Lord, in your righteousness
    because of my enemies;
    make your way straight before me. (Ps. 5:1-3, 8)

Additional Readings

Jeremiah 5:18-31
Prophets and priests who mislead

1 Thessalonians 2:13-20
Words to the church

Hymn: All Who Love and Serve Your City, ELW 724

God, both judge and redeemer, you gather us by grace when we cannot see you or hear you. Save us from the temptations of injustice, and let our hope and joy be found in the ones we serve.

Tuesday, November 3, 2026

Time after Pentecost

Martín de Porres, renewer of society, died 1639

Lamentations 2:13-17

When prophets see false visions

What can I say for you, to what compare you,
O daughter Jerusalem?
To what can I liken you, that I may comfort you,
O virgin daughter Zion?
For vast as the sea is your ruin;
who can heal you? . . .

All who pass along the way
clap their hands at you;
they hiss and wag their heads
at daughter Jerusalem:
"Is this the city that was called
the perfection of beauty,
the joy of all the earth?" (Lam. 2:13, 15)

Psalm

Psalm 5
God blesses the righteous

Additional Reading

Acts 13:1-12
Paul and Barnabas confront a false prophet

Hymn: Feed Us with Hunger for Justice, ACS 968

Healer of the forsaken, you make new what we have knocked down. In your persistence give us hope, that we may learn to repair and build up in the same way your love does.

Wednesday, November 4, 2026

Time after Pentecost

Proverbs 16:21-33

The wise heart and persuasive lips

The wise of heart is called perceptive,
    and pleasant speech increases persuasiveness.
Wisdom is a fountain of life to one who has it,
    but folly is the punishment of fools.
The mind of the wise makes their speech judicious
    and adds persuasiveness to their lips. (Prov. 16:21-23)

Psalm

Psalm 5

God blesses the righteous

Additional Reading

Matthew 15:1-9

Lips that misrepresent the heart

Hymn: Have You Got Good Religion? TFF 113

God of creation, you have shown us the mercy and wisdom of slowness and care. Teach us to value kindness in the search for what is right, that we may be blessed in heart, soul, mind, and strength.

Thursday, November 5, 2026

Time after Pentecost

Psalm 70

You are my helper and deliverer

Be pleased, O God, to deliver me.
　　O LORD, make haste to help me!
Let those be put to shame and confusion
　　who seek my life.
Let those be turned back and brought to dishonor
　　who desire to hurt me.
Let those who say, "Aha, Aha!"
　　turn back because of their shame.

Let all who seek you
　　rejoice and be glad in you.
Let those who love your salvation
　　say evermore, "God is great!" (Ps. 70:1-4)

Additional Readings

Amos 1:1—2:5
God judges Israel's neighbors

Revelation 8:6—9:12
The trumpet of God's judgment

Hymn: Jesus, Remember Me, ELW 616

God of truth, the wrong done by our hands and by others produces terrible, terrible things. Let wrong be stopped, remember the poor and needy, and may your justice guide us in work toward your goal of goodness for all.

Friday, November 6, 2026

Time after Pentecost

Amos 3:1-12

Israel's guilt and punishment

Proclaim to the strongholds in Ashdod
 and to the strongholds in the land of Egypt,
and say, "Assemble yourselves on Mount Samaria,
 and see what great tumults are within it
 and what oppressions are in its midst."
They do not know how to do right, says the LORD,
 those who store up violence and robbery in their strongholds.
Therefore thus says the Lord GOD:
An adversary shall surround the land
 and strip you of your defense,
 and your strongholds shall be plundered. (Amos 3:9-11)

Psalm

Psalm 70

You are my helper and deliverer

Additional Reading

Revelation 9:13-21

Unrepentant humankind persists in sin

Hymn: Our Father, We Have Wandered, ELW 606

Everlasting God, we stubbornly and arrogantly ignore your warning and wisdom, even in the face of death. In mercy, grant that the defining action of our lives might not be our own sin but your redeeming.

Saturday, November 7, 2026

Time after Pentecost

John Christian Frederick Heyer, died 1873; Bartholomaeus Ziegenbalg, died 1719; Ludwig Nommensen, died 1918; missionaries

Matthew 24:1-14

Jesus foretells the end

When [Jesus] was sitting on the Mount of Olives, the disciples came to him privately, saying, "Tell us, when will this be, and what will be the sign of your coming and of the end of the age?" Jesus answered them, "Beware that no one leads you astray. For many will come in my name, saying, 'I am the Messiah!' and they will lead many astray. And you will hear of wars and rumors of wars; see that you are not alarmed, for this must take place, but the end is not yet." (Matt. 24:3-6)

Psalm

Psalm 70

You are my helper and deliverer

Additional Reading

Amos 4:6-13

Israel, prepare to meet your God

Hymn: Beloved, God's Chosen, ELW 648

Giver of life, we see war, famines, and earthquakes, and we fear. Help us to remember our good purpose amid purposeless events, to love and not grow cold, that good news and life may be shared by all.

Sunday, November 8, 2026

Time after Pentecost

Matthew 25:1-13

Wise and foolish bridesmaids

[Jesus said to the disciples,] "Then the kingdom of heaven will be like this. Ten young women took their lamps and went to meet the bridegroom. Five of them were foolish, and five were wise. When the foolish took their lamps, they took no oil with them, but the wise took flasks of oil with their lamps." (Matt. 25:1-4)

Psalm

Psalm 70

You are my helper and deliverer

Additional Readings

Amos 5:18-24

Let justice roll down like waters

1 Thessalonians 4:13-18

The promise of the resurrection

Hymn: I Want to Walk as a Child of the Light, ELW 815

O God of justice and love, you illumine our way through life with the words of your Son. Give us the light we need, and awaken us to the needs of others, through Jesus Christ, our Savior and Lord.

Monday, November 9, 2026

Time after Pentecost

Psalm 63

God is a rich feast

My soul is satisfied as with a rich feast,
 and my mouth praises you with joyful lips
when I think of you on my bed
 and meditate on you in the watches of the night,
for you have been my help,
 and in the shadow of your wings I sing for joy.
My soul clings to you;
 your right hand upholds me. (Ps. 63:5-8)

Additional Readings

Amos 8:7-14
A famine of hearing God's word

1 Corinthians 14:20-25
They will not listen to me

Hymn: Listen Now for the Gospel, ACS 972

Creator God, you speak, and in your gracious words we live. Keep not your good word from us nor from our neighbors, and help us to listen to each other, that all may know your blessing and love.

Tuesday, November 10, 2026

Time after Pentecost

1 Thessalonians 3:6-13

Stand firm in the faith

Now may our God and Father himself and our Lord Jesus direct our way to you. And may the Lord make you increase and abound in love for one another and for all, just as we abound in love for you. And may he so strengthen your hearts in holiness that you may be blameless before our God and Father at the coming of our Lord Jesus with all his saints. (1 Thess. 3:11-13)

Psalm

Psalm 63

God is a rich feast

Additional Reading

Joel 1:1-14

Call to repentance

Hymn: Woman, Weeping in the Garden, ACS 935

God of every season, you gather us together in joy and in sorrow. Heal our divisions and bring justice to our wrongs, that we may find blessing in each other's presence.

Wednesday, November 11, 2026

Time after Pentecost

Martin, Bishop of Tours, died 397
Søren Aabye Kierkegaard, teacher, died 1855

Matthew 24:29-35

My words will not pass away

[Jesus said to the disciples,] "From the fig tree learn its lesson: as soon as its branch becomes tender and puts forth its leaves, you know that summer is near. So also, when you see all these things, you know that he is near, at the very gates. Truly I tell you, this generation will not pass away until all these things have taken place. Heaven and earth will pass away, but my words will not pass away." (Matt. 24:32-35)

Psalm

Psalm 63
God is a rich feast

Additional Reading

Joel 3:9-21
Promise of a glorious future

Hymn: Let the Whole Creation Cry, ELW 876

God of righteousness, justice sometimes comes with fear and trembling. Help us to learn from what we see and hear in your presence and to follow your ways, that we may find your coming a blessing.

Thursday, November 12, 2026

Time after Pentecost

Psalm 90:1-8 [9-11] 12

Number your days

LORD, you have been our dwelling place
in all generations.
Before the mountains were brought forth
or ever you had formed the earth and the world,
from everlasting to everlasting you are God.

You turn us back to dust
and say, "Turn back, you mortals."
For a thousand years in your sight
are like yesterday when it is past
or like a watch in the night. (Ps. 90:1-4)

Additional Readings

Ezekiel 6:1-14
Judgment on idolatrous Israel

Revelation 16:1-7
God's judgments are true and just

Hymn: Beautiful Things, ACS 925

Holy One, you who are and who were and who will be, our wrong is brought into the light. Let our confession honor your merciful listening, let our repentance glorify your grace, and let us embrace your good for all.

Friday, November 13, 2026

Time after Pentecost

Ezekiel 7:1-9

The end is upon us

The word of the LORD came to me: You, O mortal, thus says the Lord GOD to the land of Israel:

An end! The end has come
upon the four corners of the land.
Now the end is upon you;
I will let loose my anger upon you;
I will judge you according to your ways;
I will punish you for all your abominations.
My eye will not spare you; I will have no pity.
I will punish you for your ways
while your abominations are among you.
Then you shall know that I am the LORD. (Ezek. 7:1-4)

Psalm

Psalm 90:1-8 [9-11] 12
Number your days

Additional Reading

Revelation 16:8-21
The judged curse God

Hymn: Love Divine, All Loves Excelling, ELW 631

Alpha and Omega, the end is near, yet the story continues. Help us to end wrong by beginning what is right, and to end hate by beginning again in love. By your grace, make both our end and our beginning good.

Saturday, November 14, 2026

Time after Pentecost

Matthew 12:43-45

From bad to worse

[Jesus said,] "When the unclean spirit has gone out of a person, it wanders through waterless regions looking for a resting place, but it finds none. Then it says, 'I will return to my house from which I came.' When it returns, it finds it empty, swept, and put in order. Then it goes and brings along seven other spirits more evil than itself, and they enter and live there, and the last state of that person is worse than the first. So will it be also with this evil generation." (Matt. 12:43-45)

Psalm

Psalm 90:1-8 [9-11] 12

Number your days

Additional Reading

Ezekiel 7:10-27

You shall know that the LORD is God

Hymn: Come, Thou Fount of Every Blessing, ELW 807/TFF 108

God of cleansing waters, how often we track in sin where grace has just been. Help us to be mindful of your care and awed by your determined persistence. In time, may we become caretakers like you.

Sunday, November 15, 2026

Time after Pentecost

Matthew 25:14-30

The story of the slaves entrusted with talents

[Jesus spoke a parable:] "Then the one who had received the one talent also came forward, saying, 'Master, I knew that you were a harsh man, reaping where you did not sow and gathering where you did not scatter, so I was afraid, and I went and hid your talent in the ground. Here you have what is yours.' But his master replied, 'You wicked and lazy slave! You knew, did you, that I reap where I did not sow and gather where I did not scatter? Then you ought to have invested my money with the bankers, and on my return I would have received what was my own with interest. So take the talent from him, and give it to the one with the ten talents." (Matt. 25:24-28)

Psalm

Psalm 90:1-8 [9-11] 12
Number your days

Additional Readings

Zephaniah 1:7, 12-18
The day of the LORD

1 Thessalonians 5:1-11
Be alert for the day of the Lord

Hymn: Let Us Talents and Tongues Employ, ELW 674/TFF 232

Righteous God, our merciful master, you own the earth and all its peoples, and you give us all that we have. Inspire us to serve you with justice and wisdom, and prepare us for the joy of the day of your coming, through Jesus Christ, our Savior and Lord.

Monday, November 16, 2026

Time after Pentecost

Psalm 9:1-14

God's reward for the righteous

I will give thanks to the Lord with my whole heart;
  I will tell of all your wonderful deeds.
I will be glad and exult in you;
  I will sing praise to your name, O Most High.

When my enemies turned back,
  they stumbled and perished before you.
For you have maintained my just cause;
  you have sat on the throne giving righteous judgment. (Ps. 9:1-4)

Additional Readings

Zechariah 1:7-17
God's judgment and mercy

Romans 2:1-11
The righteous judgment of God

Hymn: Change My Heart, O God, ELW 801

God of wisdom, help us to learn and live the difference between vengeance and righteousness, between condoning injustice and practicing mercy, as we seek what is good for our neighbors and ourselves.

Tuesday, November 17, 2026

Time after Pentecost

Elizabeth of Hungary, renewer of society, died 1231

Zechariah 2:1-5; 5:1-4

Visions of mercy and judgment

I looked up and saw a man with a measuring line in his hand. Then I asked, "Where are you going?" He answered me, "To measure Jerusalem, to see how wide and how long it is." Then the angel who spoke with me came forward, and another angel came forward to meet him and said to him, "Run, say to that young man: Jerusalem shall be inhabited like unwalled villages because of the multitude of people and animals in it. For I will be a wall of fire all around it, says the LORD, and I will be the glory within it." (Zech. 2:1-5)

Psalm

Psalm 9:1-14

God's reward for the righteous

Additional Reading

1 Thessalonians 5:12-18

The Christian life

Hymn: Lord, I Hear of Showers of Blessings, TFF 120

God of blessing, you have more in store for us than we could ever ask or imagine. Let our hearts be inspired by the endless goodness of your nature, and may our limits show the infinite love found in you.

Wednesday, November 18, 2026

Time after Pentecost

Matthew 24:45-51

Parable of the unfaithful slave

[Jesus said,] "Who, then, is the faithful and wise slave whom his master has put in charge of his household, to give the other slaves their allowance of food at the proper time? Blessed is that slave whom his master will find at work when he arrives. Truly I tell you, he will put that one in charge of all his possessions." (Matt. 24:45-47)

Psalm

Psalm 9:1-14

God's reward for the righteous

Additional Reading

Job 16:1-21

A lament about unjust punishment

Hymn: Watch, O Lord, ACS 996

God of all goodness, help us to care for others as you have cared for us. Where we have been given your riches to steward, give us also wisdom. May we dwell in grace by giving and receiving in community.

Thursday, November 19, 2026

Time after Pentecost

Psalm 95:1-7a

We are the people of God's pasture

O come, let us sing to the LORD;
    let us make a joyful noise to the rock of our salvation!
Let us come into his presence with thanksgiving;
    let us make a joyful noise to him with songs of praise!
For the LORD is a great God
    and a great King above all gods.
In his hand are the depths of the earth;
    the heights of the mountains are his also.
The sea is his, for he made it,
    and the dry land, which his hands have formed. (Ps. 95:1-5)

Additional Readings

1 Kings 22:13-23
Israel like sheep without a shepherd

Revelation 14:1-11
Fear God and give God glory

Hymn: Wash, O God, Our Sons and Daughters, ELW 445/TFF 112

God, we trust in you for guidance, grace, and life. As we have been sealed by the Holy Spirit and marked with the cross of Christ forever, help us to share with all the way to your spring of blessing.

Friday, November 20, 2026

Time after Pentecost

Revelation 22:1-9

Worship God alone

Then the angel showed me the river of the water of life, bright as crystal, flowing from the throne of God and of the Lamb through the middle of the street of the city. On either side of the river is the tree of life with its twelve kinds of fruit, producing its fruit each month, and the leaves of the tree are for the healing of the nations. Nothing accursed will be found there any more. But the throne of God and of the Lamb will be in it, and his servants will worship him; they will see his face, and his name will be on their foreheads. And there will be no more night; they need no light of lamp or sun, for the Lord God will be their light, and they will reign forever and ever. (Rev. 22:1-5)

Psalm

Psalm 95:1-7a

We are the people of God's pasture

Additional Reading

1 Chronicles 17:1-15

David, shepherd and king of Israel

Hymn: My Shepherd, You Supply My Need, ELW 782

God of life and gladness, the healing and blessing you prepare for the nations is far greater than we can plan. Help us to leave room in our hearts and lives for unexpected and vast goodness.

Saturday, November 21, 2026

Time after Pentecost

Matthew 12:46-50

The true kindred of Jesus

While [Jesus] was still speaking to the crowds, his mother and his brothers were standing outside wanting to speak to him. Someone told him, "Look, your mother and your brothers are standing outside, wanting to speak to you." But to the one who had told him this, Jesus replied, "Who is my mother, and who are my brothers?" And pointing to his disciples, he said, "Here are my mother and my brothers! For whoever does the will of my Father in heaven is my brother and sister and mother." (Matt. 12:46-50)

Psalm

Psalm 95:1-7a

We are the people of God's pasture

Additional Reading

Isaiah 44:21-28

Cyrus, a shepherd for the Lord

Hymn: Children of the Heavenly Father, ELW 781

Loving God, today's wisdom tells us to narrow our care to a chosen few. Turn back our foolish ways. Broaden our care as wide as your remembrance, blessing us to call your Son our brother, and our neighbor our family.

Sunday, November 22, 2026

Christ the King

Matthew 25:31-46

The separation of sheep and goats

[Jesus concluded a parable:] "Then [the king] will say to those at his left hand, 'You who are accursed, depart from me into the eternal fire prepared for the devil and his angels, for I was hungry and you gave me no food, I was thirsty and you gave me nothing to drink, I was a stranger and you did not welcome me, naked and you did not give me clothing, sick and in prison and you did not visit me.' Then they also will answer, 'Lord, when was it that we saw you hungry or thirsty or a stranger or naked or sick or in prison and did not take care of you?' Then he will answer them, 'Truly I tell you, just as you did not do it to one of the least of these, you did not do it to me.' " (Matt. 25:41-45)

Psalm

Psalm 95:1-7a
We are the people of God's pasture

Additional Readings

Ezekiel 34:11-16, 20-24
God will shepherd Israel

Ephesians 1:15-23
The reign of Christ

Hymn: Lord of All Nations, Grant Me Grace, ELW 716

O God of power and might, your Son shows us the way of service, and in him we inherit the riches of your grace. Give us the wisdom to know what is right and the strength to serve the world you have made, through Jesus Christ, our Savior and Lord, who lives and reigns with you and the Holy Spirit, one God, now and forever.

Monday, November 23, 2026

Time after Pentecost

Clement, Bishop of Rome, died around 100
Miguel Agustín Pro, martyr, died 1927

Psalm 7

God the righteous judge

O let the evil of the wicked come to an end,
  but establish the righteous,
you who test the minds and hearts,
  O righteous God.
God is my shield,
  who saves the upright in heart.
God is a righteous judge
  and a God who has indignation every day. (Ps. 7:9-11)

Additional Readings

Esther 2:1-18
Lowly Esther becomes queen

2 Timothy 2:8-13
Those who endure with Christ reign with him

Hymn: I Will Call Upon the Lord, TFF 277

God of redirection, you raise your voice to the wrongs of the world, and in listening, we find your presence and care. Help us to share your passion for goodness, that we might embrace the fullness of life.

Tuesday, November 24, 2026
Time after Pentecost

Justus Falckner, died 1723; Jehu Jones, died 1852; William Passavant, died 1894; pastors in North America

Esther 8:3-17

Queen Esther saves her people

Then Esther spoke again to the king; she fell at his feet, weeping and pleading with him to avert the evil design of Haman the Agagite and the plot that he had devised against the Jews. The king held out the golden scepter to Esther, and Esther rose and stood before the king. She said, "If it pleases the king, and if I have won his favor, and if the thing seems right before the king, and I have his approval, let an order be written to revoke the letters devised by Haman son of Hammedatha the Agagite, which he wrote giving orders to destroy the Jews who are in all the provinces of the king. For how can I bear to see the calamity that is coming on my people? Or how can I bear to see the destruction of my kindred?" (Esther 8:3-6)

Psalm

Psalm 7
God the righteous judge

Additional Reading

Revelation 19:1-9
Praise of God's judgments

Hymn: Days Are Filled with Sorrow and Care, TFF 74

God of hope, we read of your saving action for your people and yearn for your saving action now. Be the keeper of all who are unjustly denied righteousness and care. Bless us, that we might follow your lead.

Wednesday, November 25, 2026

Time after Pentecost

Isaac Watts, hymnwriter, died 1748

John 5:19-40

The judgment of the Son

[Jesus said,] "Very truly, I tell you, the hour is coming and is now here when the dead will hear the voice of the Son of God, and those who hear will live. For just as the Father has life in himself, so he has granted the Son also to have life in himself, and he has given him authority to execute judgment because he is the Son of Man. Do not be astonished at this, for the hour is coming when all who are in their graves will hear his voice and will come out: those who have done good to the resurrection of life, and those who have done evil to the resurrection of condemnation." (John 5:25-29)

Psalm

Psalm 7

God the righteous judge

Additional Reading

Ezekiel 33:7-20

The righteous will live

Hymn: Spirit of God, Descend upon My Heart, ELW 800

Loving God, across time you have called us to your goodness. By grace we do good; yet still bound to sin, we struggle. Free us all from sin, that your goodness might flow in this life, at your day of judgment, and in eternity.

For Thanksgiving Day

Today we practice trusting God's provision like the Israelites in Exodus 16. When they saw a flaky white substance on the ground, they wondered what it was.

Moses said to them, "It is the bread that the LORD has given you to eat. This is what the LORD has commanded: 'Gather as much of it as each of you needs, an omer to a person according to the number of persons, all providing for those in their own tents.'" The Israelites did so, some gathering more, some less. But when they measured it with an omer, those who gathered much had nothing over, and those who gathered little had no shortage; they gathered as much as each of them needed. (Exod. 16:15-16)

On the heels of harvest, we give thanks for the labor, land, and seasons that prepare our food. We honor the wild and dormant places, the fruitful and fallow places. We remember that we are stewards of the earth and we are called to care for every living thing. We honor Indigenous peoples, generations past, present, and future, who care for creation with traditional wisdom.

We also acknowledge the ways we have failed to share the gifts of creation and the ways we have mistrusted God's promise of enough. We recognize the harm caused by those who colonized Indigenous peoples and forcefully occupied land in the name of God. We who are descendants of settlers confess that we benefit from broken promises, systems that hoard resources, and lies about who is valuable and what is enough. God calls us not to hoard for ourselves but to turn and recognize that all people and all creation are precious in God's sight. In God's abundance there is enough for us all.

Let us pray.
God who provides, your dreams for the world are revealed when communities are fed, promises are kept, and the vulnerable have what they need. May the tables we set in your name honor the fullness of your creation and your wide welcome. May your blessings move freely through us as delight that flows like rivers and waterways, signs of new life. Amen.

Thursday, November 26, 2026

Time after Pentecost

Day of Thanksgiving (USA)

Psalm 80:1-7, 17-19

We shall be saved

Give ear, O Shepherd of Israel,
    you who lead Joseph like a flock!
You who are enthroned upon the cherubim, shine forth
    before Ephraim and Benjamin and Manasseh.
Stir up your might,
    and come to save us!

Restore us, O God;
    let your face shine, that we may be saved. (Ps. 80:1-3)

Additional Readings

Zechariah 13:1-9
The coming day of God brings cleansing

Revelation 14:6-13
Hold fast to the faith

Hymn: Come, Ye Thankful People, Come, ELW 693

Creator and Redeemer, you call us to change, and change is so very hard. Thank you for your past blessings. In them give us hope for the future, and in this hope help us turn to your grace for all.

Friday, November 27, 2026

Time after Pentecost

1 Thessalonians 4:1-18

A life pleasing God to the end

But we do not want you to be uninformed, brothers and sisters, about those who have died, so that you may not grieve as others do who have no hope. For since we believe that Jesus died and rose again, even so, through Jesus, God will bring with him those who have died. For this we declare to you by the word of the Lord, that we who are alive, who are left until the coming of the Lord, will by no means precede those who have died. For the Lord himself, with a cry of command, with the archangel's call and with the sound of God's trumpet, will descend from heaven, and the dead in Christ will rise first. Then we who are alive, who are left, will be caught up in the clouds together with them to meet the Lord in the air, and so we will be with the Lord forever. (1 Thess. 4:13-17)

Psalm

Psalm 80:1-7, 17-19

We shall be saved

Additional Reading

Zechariah 14:1-9

God will come to rule

Hymn: Christ Is the Life, ACS 927

Ever-near God, we long for your coming. As you draw close, speak words of peace to us all. Be near, that we might be more loving and experience the goodness of your way.

Saturday, November 28, 2026

Time after Pentecost

Micah 2:1-13

God will gather all

I will surely gather all of you, O Jacob;
    I will gather the survivors of Israel;
I will set them together
    like sheep in a fold,
like a flock in its pasture;
    it will resound with people.
The one who breaks out will go up before them;
    they will break through and pass the gate,
    going out by it.
Their king will pass on before them,
    the LORD at their head. (Micah 2:12-13)

Psalm

Psalm 80:1-7, 17-19

We shall be saved

Additional Reading

Matthew 24:15-31

Be ready for that day

Hymn: You, Lord, Are Both Lamb and Shepherd, ACS 954

God who is good, so many messages tempt us away from your own. When false invitations to power and ease reach our hearts, help us instead to follow the way of your ever-widening love.

Advent

In the days of Advent, Christians prepare to celebrate the presence of God's Word among us in our own day. During these four weeks, we pray that the reign of God, which Jesus preached and lived, would come among us. We pray that God's justice would flourish in our land, that the people of the earth would live in peace, and that those who are weak, sick or hungry would be strengthened, healed, and fed with God's merciful presence.

During the last days of Advent, Christians welcome Christ with names inspired by the prophets: wisdom, liberator of the enslaved, mighty power, radiant dawn and sun of justice, the keystone of the arch of humanity, and Emmanuel—God with us.

The Advent Wreath

One of the best-known customs for the season is the Advent wreath. The wreath and winter candle-lighting in the midst of growing darkness strengthen some of the Advent images found in the Bible. The unbroken circle of greens is an image of everlasting life, a victory wreath, the crown of Christ, or the wheel of time itself. Christians use the wreath as a sign that Christ reaches into our time to lead us to the light of everlasting life. The four candles mark the progress of the four weeks of Advent and our growing expectation. Sometimes the wreath is embellished with natural dried flowers or fruit. Its evergreen branches lead the household and the congregation to the evergreen Christmas tree. In many homes, the family gathers for prayer around the wreath.

An Evening Service of Candlelight for Advent

This brief order may be used on any evening during the season of Advent. If the household has an Advent wreath (one candle for each of the four weeks of Advent) it may be lighted during this service. Alternatively, one simple candle (perhaps a votive candle) may be lighted instead.

Lighting the Advent Wreath

May this *candle/these candles* be a sign of the coming of Christ, our morning star.

One or more candles may be lighted.

Use this blessing when lighting the first candle.

Blessed are you, God of Jacob, for you promise to transform weapons of war into implements of planting and harvest and to teach us your way of peace; you promise that our night of sin is far gone and that your day of salvation is dawning.

As we light the first candle on this wreath, wake us from our sleep, wrap us in your warmth, empower us to live honorably, and guide us along your path of peace.

O house of Jacob, come,
let us walk in the light of the Lord. Amen.

Blessings for the second, third, and fourth weeks of Advent are provided on pages 376, 384, and 392, respectively.

Reading

Read one or more of the scripture passages appointed for the day in the dated pages that follow.

Hymn

One of the following, or the hymn suggested for the day, may be sung.

Light One Candle to Watch for Messiah, ELW 240
Come Now, O Prince of Peace/Ososo, ososo, ELW 247
People, Look East, ELW 248
My Soul Proclaims Your Greatness, ELW 251

During the final seven days of the Advent season (beginning on December 17), the hymn "O Come, O Come, Emmanuel" (ELW 257) is particularly appropriate. The stanzas of that hymn are also referred to as the "O Antiphons." The first stanza of the hymn could be sung each day during the final days before Christmas in addition to the stanza that is specifically appointed for the day.

First stanza

O come, O come, Emmanuel,
and ransom captive Israel,
that mourns in lonely exile here
until the Son of God appear.
Refrain Rejoice! Rejoice! Emmanuel shall come to you, O Israel.

December 17

O come, O Wisdom from on high,
embracing all things far and nigh:
in strength and beauty come and stay;
teach us your will and guide our way. *Refrain*

December 18

O come, O come, O Lord of might,
as to your tribes on Sinai's height
in ancient times you gave the law
in cloud, and majesty, and awe. *Refrain*

December 19

O come, O Branch of Jesse, free
your own from Satan's tyranny;
from depths of hell your people save,
and give them vict'ry o'er the grave. *Refrain*

December 20

O come, O Key of David, come,
and open wide our heav'nly home;
make safe the way that leads on high,
and close the path to misery. *Refrain*

December 21

O come, O Dayspring, come and cheer;
O Sun of justice, now draw near.
Disperse the gloomy clouds of night,
and death's dark shadow put to flight. *Refrain*

December 22

O come, O King of nations, come,
O Cornerstone that binds in one:
refresh the hearts that long for you;
restore the broken, make us new. *Refrain*

December 23

O come, O come, Emmanuel,
and ransom captive Israel,
that mourns in lonely exile here
until the Son of God appear. *Refrain*

Text: *Psalteriolum Cantionum Catholicarum,* Köln, 1710; tr. compositee

Table Prayer for Advent

For use when a meal follows.

Blessed are you, O Lord our God,
the one who is, who was, and who is to come.
At this table you fill us with good things.
May these gifts strengthen us
to share with the hungry and all those in need,
as we wait and watch for your coming among us
in Jesus Christ our Lord. Amen.

Candles may be extinguished now or after the meal, if one is to follow.

Sunday, November 29, 2026

First Sunday of Advent

Mark 13:24-37

The coming of the Son of Man

[Jesus said,] "But about that day or hour no one knows, neither the angels in heaven nor the Son, but only the Father. Beware, keep alert, for you do not know when the time will come. It is like a man going on a journey, when he leaves home and puts his slaves in charge, each with his work, and commands the doorkeeper to be on the watch. Therefore, keep awake, for you do not know when the master of the house will come, in the evening or at midnight or at cockcrow or at dawn, or else he may find you asleep when he comes suddenly. And what I say to you I say to all: Keep awake." (Mark 13:32-37)

Psalm

Psalm 80:1-7, 17-19
We shall be saved

Additional Readings

Isaiah 64:1-9
God will come with power and compassion

1 Corinthians 1:3-9
Gifts of grace sustain us

Hymn: Soon and Very Soon, ELW 439/TFF 38

Stir up your power, Lord Christ, and come. By your merciful protection awaken us to the threatening dangers of our sins, and keep us blameless until the coming of your new day, for you live and reign with the Father and the Holy Spirit, one God, now and forever.

Monday, November 30, 2026

Andrew, Apostle

John 1:35-42

Jesus calls Andrew

One of the two who heard John speak and followed [Jesus] was Andrew, Simon Peter's brother. He first found his brother Simon and said to him, "We have found the Messiah" (which is translated Anointed). He brought Simon to Jesus, who looked at him and said, "You are Simon son of John. You are to be called Cephas" (which is translated Peter). (John 1:40-42)

Psalm

Psalm 19:1-6
The heavens declare God's glory

Additional Readings

Ezekiel 3:16-21
A sentinel for the house of Israel

Romans 10:10-18
Faith comes from the word of Christ

Hymn: The Peace of the Lord, ELW 646

Almighty God, you gave your apostle Andrew the grace to obey the call of your Son and to bring his brother to Jesus. Give us also, who are called by your holy word, grace to follow Jesus without delay and to bring into his presence those who are near to us, for he lives and reigns with you and the Holy Spirit, one God, now and forever.

Prayer List for December

Tuesday, December 1, 2026
Week of Advent 1

Psalm 79
Prayer for deliverance

Do not remember against us the iniquities of our ancestors;
    let your compassion come speedily to meet us,
    for we are brought very low.
Help us, O God of our salvation,
    for the glory of your name;
deliver us and forgive our sins,
    for your name's sake.
Why should the nations say,
    "Where is their God?"
Let the avenging of the outpoured blood of your servants
    be known among the nations before our eyes. (Ps. 79:8-10)

Additional Readings
Micah 4:6-13
A promise of restoration after exile

Revelation 18:1-10
A liturgy of glory

Hymn: O Splendor of God's Glory Bright, ELW 559

O God of salvation in every age and for every generation, do not hold our ancestors' sins against us. Show us your compassion and mercy. Let all earth feel and see your power of love for all people.

Wednesday, December 2, 2026

Week of Advent 1

Micah 5:1-5a

A promise of a shepherd

But you, O Bethlehem of Ephrathah,
 who are one of the little clans of Judah,
from you shall come forth for me
 one who is to rule in Israel,
whose origin is from of old,
 from ancient days.
Therefore he shall give them up until the time
 when she who is in labor has brought forth;
then the rest of his kindred shall return
 to the people of Israel.
And he shall stand and feed his flock in the strength of the LORD,
 in the majesty of the name of the LORD his God.
And they shall live secure, for now he shall be great
 to the ends of the earth,
and he shall be the one of peace (Micah 5:2-5a)

Psalm

Psalm 79

Prayer for deliverance

Additional Reading

Luke 21:34-38

Be alert for that day

Hymn: O Little Town of Bethlehem, ELW 279

Creator God, you have been with us since the beginning of time. We are grateful for the promise of peace you made to the shepherds. Help us to bring your security and peace to all the earth.

Thursday, December 3, 2026

Week of Advent 1

Francis Xavier, missionary to Asia, died 1552

Psalm 85:1-2, 8-13

Righteousness and peace

Let me hear what God the LORD will speak,
for he will speak peace to his people,
to his faithful, to those who turn to him in their hearts.
Surely his salvation is at hand for those who fear him,
that his glory may dwell in our land.

Steadfast love and faithfulness will meet;
righteousness and peace will kiss each other.
Faithfulness will spring up from the ground,
and righteousness will look down from the sky.
The LORD will give what is good,
and our land will yield its increase. (Ps. 85:8-12)

Additional Readings

Hosea 6:1-6
Return to the God of life and love

1 Thessalonians 1:2-10
Paul thanks God for the Thessalonians

Hymn: Wake, Awake, for Night Is Flying, ELW 436

Gracious God, we thank you for your peace that speaks to our hearts. We rejoice in your steadfast love and faithfulness, which bring forth justice and joy. May your grace fill our world, and may we always seek your peace.

Friday, December 4, 2026

Week of Advent 1

John of Damascus, theologian and hymnwriter, died around 749

Jeremiah 1:4-10

God appoints a prophet

Now the word of the LORD came to me saying,
"Before I formed you in the womb I knew you,
and before you were born I consecrated you;
I appointed you a prophet to the nations."
Then I said, "Ah, Lord GOD! Truly I do not know how to speak, for I am only a boy." But the LORD said to me,
"Do not say, 'I am only a boy,'
for you shall go to all to whom I send you,
and you shall speak whatever I command you.
Do not be afraid of them,
for I am with you to deliver you,
says the LORD." (Jer. 1:4-8)

Psalm

Psalm 85:1-2, 8-13

Righteousness and peace

Additional Reading

Acts 11:19-26

The new community called "Christian"

Hymn: All Earth Is Hopeful, ELW 266/TFF 47

Living and loving Creator, you formed us in the womb, consecrated us, and appointed us to your work. Help us trust that our perceived flaws are no obstacle for you. Use us to bring forth your justice, peace, and love.

Saturday, December 5, 2026

Week of Advent 1

Ezekiel 36:24-28

A new heart and a new spirit

I will take you from the nations and gather you from all the countries and bring you into your own land. I will sprinkle clean water upon you, and you shall be clean from all your uncleannesses, and from all your idols I will cleanse you. A new heart I will give you, and a new spirit I will put within you, and I will remove from your body the heart of stone and give you a heart of flesh. I will put my spirit within you and make you follow my statutes and be careful to observe my ordinances. Then you shall live in the land that I gave to your ancestors, and you shall be my people, and I will be your God. (Ezek. 36:24-28)

Psalm

Psalm 85:1-2, 8-13

Righteousness and peace

Additional Reading

Mark 11:27-33

Jesus a prophet like John the Baptist

Hymn: Prepare the Royal Highway, ELW 264

Liberating God, you have given us new hearts. We ask that you continually free us from the sins of greed and idolatry. Guide us in creating a just world that honors the new spirit of peace you have given us.

Lighting the Advent Wreath

Use this blessing when lighting the first two candles.

Blessed are you, God of hope, for you promise to bring forth a shoot from the stump of Jesse who will bring justice to the poor, who will deliver the needy and crush the oppressor, who will stand as a signal of hope for all people.

As we light these candles, turn our wills to bear the fruit of repentance, transform our hearts to live in justice and harmony with one another, and fix our eyes on the root of Jesse, Jesus Christ, the hope of all nations.

O people of hope, come,
let us rejoice in the faithfulness of the Lord. Amen.

Sunday, December 6, 2026

Second Sunday of Advent

Nicholas, Bishop of Myra, died around 342

Mark 1:1-8

John appears from the wilderness

So John the baptizer appeared in the wilderness, proclaiming a baptism of repentance for the forgiveness of sins. And the whole Judean region and all the people of Jerusalem were going out to him and were baptized by him in the River Jordan, confessing their sins. Now John was clothed with camel's hair, with a leather belt around his waist, and he ate locusts and wild honey. He proclaimed, "The one who is more powerful than I is coming after me; I am not worthy to stoop down and untie the strap of his sandals. I have baptized you with water, but he will baptize you with the Holy Spirit." (Mark 1:4-8)

Psalm

Psalm 85:1-2, 8-13
Righteousness and peace

Additional Readings

Isaiah 40:1-11
God's coming to the exiles

2 Peter 3:8-15a
Waiting for the day of God

Hymn: There's a Voice in the Wilderness, ELW 255

Stir up our hearts, Lord God, to prepare the way of your only Son. By his coming strengthen us to serve you with purified lives; through Jesus Christ, our Savior and Lord, who lives and reigns with you and the Holy Spirit, one God, now and forever.

Monday, December 7, 2026
Week of Advent 2

Ambrose, Bishop of Milan, died 397

Psalm 27

God's level path

Teach me your way, O Lord,
    and lead me on a level path
    because of my enemies.
Do not give me up to the will of my adversaries,
    for false witnesses have risen against me,
    and they are breathing out violence.

I believe that I shall see the goodness of the Lord
    in the land of the living.
Wait for the Lord;
    be strong, and let your heart take courage;
    wait for the Lord! (Ps. 27:11-14)

Additional Readings

Isaiah 26:7-15
The way of the righteous is level

Acts 2:37-42
Baptism in the name of Jesus

Hymn: Wait for the Lord, ELW 262

O God, fortify us with your teachings. Help us to end the violence we have caused. Let us not lose heart, for in your goodness being done we see your realm coming to bless all. Give us courage to act with justice.

Tuesday, December 8, 2026

Week of Advent 2

Isaiah 4:2-6

God will wash Israel clean

On that day the branch of the LORD shall be beautiful and glorious, and the fruit of the land shall be the pride and glory of the survivors of Israel. Whoever is left in Zion and remains in Jerusalem will be called holy, everyone who has been recorded for life in Jerusalem, once the LORD has washed away the filth of the daughters of Zion and cleansed the bloodstains of Jerusalem from its midst by a spirit of judgment and by a spirit of burning. Then the LORD will create over the whole site of Mount Zion and over its places of assembly a cloud by day and smoke and the shining of a flaming fire by night. Indeed, over all the glory there will be a canopy. It will serve as a pavilion, a shade by day from the heat and a refuge and a shelter from the storm and rain. (Isa. 4:2-6)

Psalm

Psalm 27

God's level path

Additional Reading

Acts 11:1-18

John and Peter baptize

Hymn: Comfort, Comfort Now My People, ELW 256

God our Creator, wash away our greed, apathy, and cruelty. Purify us by your Spirit, making us a holy community in Christ. Let us flourish, radiant in your love that is a refuge for all. May we be united in your transforming grace.

Wednesday, December 9, 2026

Week of Advent 2

Luke 1:5-17

The messenger in the temple

But the angel said to [Zechariah], "Do not be afraid, Zechariah, for your prayer has been heard. Your wife Elizabeth will bear you a son, and you will name him John. You will have joy and gladness, and many will rejoice at his birth, for he will be great in the sight of the Lord. He must never drink wine or strong drink; even before his birth he will be filled with the Holy Spirit. He will turn many of the people of Israel to the Lord their God. With the spirit and power of Elijah he will go before him, to turn the hearts of parents to their children and the disobedient to the wisdom of the righteous, to make ready a people prepared for the Lord." (Luke 1:13-17)

Psalm

Psalm 27

God's level path

Additional Reading

Malachi 2:10—3:1

The coming messenger

Hymn: Blessed Be the God of Israel, ELW 250

You bring us joy and gladness, O God. But sometimes our contentment turns to fear. Release us from this anxiety as your angels bring good news into our lives. Help our hearts remain open to the Spirit.

Thursday, December 10, 2026

Week of Advent 2

Psalm 126

God does great things for us

When the LORD restored the fortunes of Zion,
we were like those who dream.
Then our mouth was filled with laughter
and our tongue with shouts of joy;
then it was said among the nations,
"The LORD has done great things for them."
The LORD has done great things for us,
and we rejoiced. (Ps. 126:1-3)

Additional Readings

Habakkuk 2:1-5
A vision concerning the end

Philippians 3:7-11
The righteousness that comes through faith

Hymn: Joy to the World, ELW 267

O God who smiles on creation, you rejoice in us, your children. Your transforming works through Christ Jesus have brought us laughter and filled our hearts with joy. Help us share this joy we have found with the whole world.

Friday, December 11, 2026

Week of Advent 2

Philippians 3:12-16

The prize of God's call in Christ

Not that I have already obtained this or have already reached the goal, but I press on to lay hold of that for which Christ has laid hold of me. Brothers and sisters, I do not consider that I have laid hold of it, but one thing I have laid hold of: forgetting what lies behind and straining forward to what lies ahead, I press on toward the goal, toward the prize of the heavenly call of God in Christ Jesus. Let those of us, then, who are mature think this way, and if you think differently about anything, this, too, God will reveal to you. Only let us hold fast to what we have attained. (Phil. 3:12-16)

Psalm

Psalm 126

God does great things for us

Additional Reading

Habakkuk 3:2-6

A prayer for God's glory and mercy

Hymn: Creator of the Stars of Night, ELW 245

O God, we press on, forgetting what lies behind. We are striving toward your call. Strengthen us to hold on to your truth revealed by your child, Jesus Christ. Aid us in reaching the prize.

Saturday, December 12, 2026

Week of Advent 2

Habakkuk 3:13-19

God's devastation, God's deliverance

Though the fig tree does not blossom
  and no fruit is on the vines;
though the produce of the olive fails
  and the fields yield no food;
though the flock is cut off from the fold
  and there is no herd in the stalls,
yet I will rejoice in the LORD;
  I will exult in the God of my salvation.
GOD, the Lord, is my strength;
  he makes my feet like the feet of a deer
  and makes me tread upon the heights. (Hab. 3:17-19)

Psalm

Psalm 126

God does great things for us

Additional Reading

Matthew 21:28-32

Resistance to God in the present generation

Hymn: Each Winter as the Year Grows Older, ELW 252

God of our weary years, there will be seasons in our lives when we bear no fruit. Keep us honest about our weariness in our relationships with you and each other, so that we may become fruitful once again.

Lighting the Advent Wreath

Use this blessing when lighting three candles.

Blessed are you, God of might and majesty, for you promise to make the desert rejoice and blossom, to watch over strangers, and to set prisoners free.

As we light these candles, satisfy our hunger with your good gifts, open our eyes to the great things you have done for us, and fill us with patience until the coming of the Lord Jesus.

O ransomed people of the Lord, come,
let us travel on God's holy way
and enter into Zion with singing. Amen.

Sunday, December 13, 2026

Third Sunday of Advent

Lucy, martyr, died 304

John 1:6-8, 19-28

A witness to the light

This is the testimony given by John when the Jews sent priests and Levites from Jerusalem to ask him, "Who are you?" He confessed and did not deny it, but he confessed, "I am not the Messiah." And they asked him, "What then? Are you Elijah?" He said, "I am not." "Are you the prophet?" He answered, "No." Then they said to him, "Who are you? Let us have an answer for those who sent us. What do you say about yourself?" He said,

"I am the voice of one crying out in the wilderness,
'Make straight the way of the Lord,'"

as the prophet Isaiah said. (John 1:19-23)

Psalm

Psalm 126
God does great things for us

Additional Readings

Isaiah 61:1-4, 8-11
Righteousness and praise flourish like a gardent

1 Thessalonians 5:16-24
Kept in faith until the coming of Christ

Hymn: On Jordan's Bank the Baptist's Cry, ELW 249

Stir up the wills of your faithful people, Lord God, and open our ears to the words of your prophets, that, anointed by your Spirit, we may testify to your light; through Jesus Christ, our Savior and Lord, who lives and reigns with you and the Holy Spirit, one God, now and forever.

Monday, December 14, 2026

Week of Advent 3

John of the Cross, renewer of the church, died 1591

Psalm 125

Prayer for blessing

Those who trust in the LORD are like Mount Zion,
which cannot be moved but abides forever.
As the mountains surround Jerusalem,
so the LORD surrounds his people
from this time on and forevermore.
For the scepter of wickedness shall not rest
on the land allotted to the righteous,
so that the righteous might not stretch out
their hands to do wrong.
Do good, O LORD, to those who are good
and to those who are upright in their hearts. (Ps. 125:1-4)

Psalm

Psalm 146:5-10
God lifts up those bowed down

Additional Reading

Isaiah 35:1-10
The desert blooms

Hymn: Come Now, O God, ACS 902

Creator of all things good, we trust in your love and protection, standing firm like Mount Zion. Guide us in prayer, and equip us with truth, righteousness, peace, and faith, so that we may stand against wicked powers and principalities.

Tuesday, December 15, 2026

Week of Advent 3

Acts 3:17—4:4

Peter preaches about the prophets

While Peter and John were speaking to the people, the priests, the captain of the temple, and the Sadducees came to them, much annoyed because they were teaching the people and proclaiming that in Jesus there is the resurrection of the dead. So they arrested them and put them in custody until the next day, for it was already evening. But many of those who heard the word believed, and they numbered about five thousand. (Acts 4:1-4)

Psalm

Psalm 125

Prayer for blessing

Additional Reading

2 Kings 2:9-22

Elisha receives Elijah's spirit

Hymn: I Want to Be Ready, TFF 41

Ready your people, inspiring God. Turn our hearts and minds to you. Let us boldly act and speak about the truth of your love, even in the face of opposition. Let your word awaken faith in all who believe.

Wednesday, December 16, 2026

Week of Advent 3

Mark 9:9-13

Questions about Elijah

As [Jesus, Peter, James, and John] were coming down the mountain, he ordered them to tell no one about what they had seen, until after the Son of Man had risen from the dead. So they kept the matter to themselves, questioning what this rising from the dead could mean. Then they asked him, "Why do the scribes say that Elijah must come first?" He said to them, "Elijah is indeed coming first to restore all things. How then is it written about the Son of Man, that he is to go through many sufferings and be treated with contempt? But I tell you that Elijah has come, and they did to him whatever they pleased, as it is written about him." (Mark 9:9-13)

Psalm

Psalm 125

Prayer for blessing

Additional Reading

Malachi 3:16—4:6

Elijah and the coming one

Hymn: Lost in the Night, ELW 243

O revealing Creator, guide us through confusion when we, like the disciples, do not understand your ways. Help us trust in your divine timing, the mystery of your death, and the assurance of your resurrection, even amid suffering and uncertainty.

Thursday, December 17, 2026

Week of Advent 3

Psalm 89:1-4, 19-26

I sing of your love

I will sing of your steadfast love, O LORD, forever;
with my mouth I will proclaim your faithfulness to all generations.
I declare that your steadfast love is established forever;
your faithfulness is as firm as the heavens.

You said, "I have made a covenant with my chosen one;
I have sworn to my servant David:
'I will establish your descendants forever
and build your throne for all generations.'" (Ps. 89:1-4)

Additional Readings

2 Samuel 6:1-11
The advent of the ark of the LORD

Hebrews 1:1-4
In the last days God speaks by a Son

Hymn: The King Shall Come, ELW 260

We thank you, God, for revealing yourself through your radiant Son, who reflects your glory and sustains all things. We proclaim your steadfast love and faithfulness through all generations, trusting in your enduring promises of life-giving grace.

Friday, December 18, 2026

Week of Advent 3

Hebrews 1:5-14

The advent of one higher than angels

Of the angels he says,
"He makes his angels winds
and his servants flames of fire."
But of the Son he says,
"Your throne, O God, is forever and ever,
and the scepter of righteousness is the scepter of your kingdom.
You have loved righteousness and hated lawlessness;
therefore God, your God, has anointed you
with the oil of gladness beyond your companions." (Heb. 1:7-9)

Psalm

Psalm 89:1-4, 19-26
I sing of your love

Additional Reading

2 Samuel 6:12-19
The ark of God enters Jerusalem

Hymn: He Came Down, ELW 253/TFF 37

God of earth, wind, and fire, we thank you for your Son. Anoint us with the oil of gladness and guide us with the rod of justice, that we may love what is good and reject all that opposes you.

Saturday, December 19, 2026

Week of Advent 3

John 7:40-52

The Messiah, David, and Bethlehem

When they heard [Jesus'] words, some in the crowd said, "This is really the prophet." Others said, "This is the Messiah." But some asked, "Surely the Messiah does not come from Galilee, does he? Has not the scripture said that the Messiah is descended from David and comes from Bethlehem, the village where David lived?" So there was a division in the crowd because of him. Some of them wanted to arrest him, but no one laid hands on him. (John 7:40-44)

Psalm

Psalm 89:1-4, 19-26
I sing of your love

Additional Reading

Judges 13:2-24
The birth of Samson

Hymn: Savior of the Nations, Come, ELW 263

God of mystery and truth, open our hearts to recognize your presence beyond our expectations. In moments of doubt, help us trust in your wisdom and purpose. Lead us to embrace the Messiah in unexpected places and with renewed faith.

Lighting the Advent Wreath

Use this blessing when lighting all four candles.

Blessed are you, God of hosts, for you promised to send a son, Emmanuel, who brought your presence among us; and you promise through your Son Jesus to save us from our sin.

As we light these candles, turn again to us in mercy; strengthen our faith in the word spoken by your prophets; restore us and give us life that we may be saved.

O house of David, come,
let us rejoice, for the Son of God, Emmanuel,
comes to be with us. Amen.

Sunday, December 20, 2026

Fourth Sunday of Advent

Katharina von Bora Luther, renewer of the church, died 1552

Luke 1:26-38

The angel appears to Mary

In the sixth month the angel Gabriel was sent by God to a town in Galilee called Nazareth, to a virgin engaged to a man whose name was Joseph, of the house of David. The virgin's name was Mary. And he came to her and said, "Greetings, favored one! The Lord is with you." But she was much perplexed by his words and pondered what sort of greeting this might be. The angel said to her, "Do not be afraid, Mary, for you have found favor with God. And now, you will conceive in your womb and bear a son, and you will name him Jesus." (Luke 1:26-31)

Psalm

Luke 1:46b-55
The Mighty One raises the lowly

Additional Readings

2 Samuel 7:1-11, 16
God's promise to David

Romans 16:25-27
The mystery revealed in Jesus Christ

Hymn: The Angel Gabriel from Heaven Came, ELW 265

Stir up your power, Lord Christ, and come. With your abundant grace and might, free us from the sin that would obstruct your mercy, that willingly we may bear your redeeming love to all the world, for you live and reign with the Father and the Holy Spirit, one God, now and forever.

Monday, December 21, 2026

Week of Advent 4

Luke 1:46b-55

The Lord lifts up the lowly

[Mary said:]
"My soul magnifies the Lord,
  and my spirit rejoices in God my Savior,
for he has looked with favor on the lowly state of his servant.
  Surely from now on all generations will call me blessed,
for the Mighty One has done great things for me,
  and holy is his name;
indeed, his mercy is for those who fear him
  from generation to generation.
He has shown strength with his arm;
  he has scattered the proud in the imagination of their hearts."
(Luke 1:46b-51)

Additional Readings

1 Samuel 1:1-18
Hannah is promised a child

Hebrews 9:1-14
Christ comes as high priest

Hymn: My Soul Proclaims Your Greatness, ELW 251

Loving Creator, we magnify your name and rejoice in your goodness. As you lift the lowly, guide us to serve with humility and grace, knowing that in this service we glorify you, the source of all mercy and compassion.

Tuesday, December 22, 2026

Week of Advent 4

Hebrews 8:1-13

The mediator replaces the sanctuary

Now the main point in what we are saying is this: we have such a high priest, one who is seated at the right hand of the throne of the Majesty in the heavens, a minister in the sanctuary and the true tent that the Lord, and not any mortal, has set up. For every high priest is appointed to offer gifts and sacrifices; hence it is necessary for this priest also to have something to offer. Now if he were on earth, he would not be a priest at all, since there are already those who offer gifts according to the law. They offer worship in a sanctuary that is a sketch and shadow of the heavenly one, just as Moses was warned when he was about to erect the tent. For, God said, "See that you make everything according to the pattern that was shown you on the mountain." But Jesus has now obtained a more excellent ministry, and to that degree he is the mediator of a better covenant, which has been enacted on the basis of better promises. For if that first covenant had been faultless, there would have been no need to look for a second one. (Heb. 8:1-7)

Psalm

Luke 1:46b-55

The Lord lifts up the lowly

Additional Reading

1 Samuel 1:19-28

Hannah presents Samuel to God

Hymn: Now the Heavens Start to Whisper, ACS 901

We are grateful for the new covenant, Living God. This renewed commitment is now written on our hearts through Jesus. Let us live in your promise, trusting in the grace that surpasses all earthly patterns of understanding.

Wednesday, December 23, 2026

Week of Advent 4

1 Samuel 2:1-10

Hannah's song

Hannah prayed and said,
"My heart exults in the Lord;
  my strength is exalted in my God.
My mouth derides my enemies
  because I rejoice in your victory. . . .

He will guard the feet of his faithful ones,
  but the wicked will perish in darkness,
  for not by might does one prevail.
The LORD! His adversaries will be shattered;
  the Most High will thunder in heaven.
The LORD will judge the ends of the earth;
  he will give strength to his king
  and exalt the power of his anointed." (1 Sam. 2:1, 9-10)

Psalm

Luke 1:46b-55

The Lord lifts up the lowly

Additional Reading

Mark 11:1-11

Jesus enters Jerusalem

Hymn: For All the Faithful Women, ELW 419/TFF 219

God of power and victory, we rejoice in your strength and trust in your justice. Guard the steps of your faithful ones, and let your truth prevail. Exalt the humble, and grant strength to all who seek your anointed path.

Christmas

During the Christmas season we celebrate Christ's coming in the flesh to sojourn among us. Each family and community marks this event in ways steeped in tradition. We adorn our homes, give one another gifts, and sing familiar carols. We meditate on the mystery of the incarnation as we look into the eyes of babies who have been born among us.

We do this at a time of year in the northern hemisphere when the days are shortest and the nights are longest. The darkness of this time is like that of a womb delivering us into new life. In the silence of these long nights, flames of hope come to light.

In the Christian church we not only celebrate the birth of Christ on Christmas Day, but for a season of twelve days. Christmas culminates with the Day of Epiphany on January 6. Through the Christmas season we remember the One born among us who has come to draw the whole world to God.

Table Prayer for the Twelve Days of Christmas

O God, with joy we celebrate the birth of your Son.
Born of Mary, he came to live among us
and is with us now at this table.
May Christ also be born in us
that we might bear his love to all the world,
and offer each other grace upon grace.
In Jesus' name we pray.
Amen.

Lighting the Christmas Tree

Use this prayer when you first illumine the tree or when you gather at the tree.

Holy God,
we praise you as we light this tree.
It casts beauty and warmth in this place
just as you illuminate our lives through Jesus,
the light of the world.

God of all,
we thank you for your love,
the love that has come to us in Jesus.
Be with us now as we remember that gift of love
and help us to share that love with a yearning world.

Creator God,
you made the stars in the heavens.
Thank you for the hope that shines on us in Jesus,
the bright morning star.
Amen.

Blessing of the Nativity Scene

This blessing may be used when figures are added to the nativity scene and throughout the days of Christmas.

Bless us, O God, as we remember Jesus' birth. With each angel and shepherd we place here before you, show us the wonder found in a stable. In song and prayer, silence and awe, we adore your gift of love, Christ Jesus our Savior.
Amen.

Thursday December 24, 2026

Nativity of Our Lord

Christmas Eve

Luke 2:1-14 [15-20]

God with us

When the angels had left them and gone into heaven, the shepherds said to one another, "Let us go now to Bethlehem and see this thing that has taken place, which the Lord has made known to us." So they went with haste and found Mary and Joseph and the child lying in the manger. When they saw this, they made known what had been told them about this child, and all who heard it were amazed at what the shepherds told them, and Mary treasured all these words and pondered them in her heart. The shepherds returned, glorifying and praising God for all they had heard and seen, just as it had been told them. (Luke 2:15-20)

Psalm

Psalm 96

Let the heavens rejoice and the earth be glad

Additional Readings

Isaiah 9:2-7

Light shines: a child is born for us

Titus 2:11-14

The grace of God has appeared

Hymn: Angels We Have Heard on High, ELW 289

Almighty God, you made this holy night shine with the brightness of the true Light. Grant that here on earth we may walk in the light of Jesus' presence and in the last day wake to the brightness of his glory; through your Son, Jesus Christ our Lord, who lives and reigns with you and the Holy Spirit, one God, now and forever.

Friday, December 25, 2026

Nativity of Our Lord
Christmas Day

John 1:1-14

The Word became flesh

In the beginning was the Word, and the Word was with God, and the Word was God. He was in the beginning with God. All things came into being through him, and without him not one thing came into being. What has come into being in him was life, and the life was the light of all people. The light shines in the darkness, and the darkness did not overtake it. (John 1:1-5)

Psalm

Psalm 98
The victory of our God

Additional Readings

Isaiah 52:7-10
Heralds announce God's salvation

Hebrews 1:1-4 [5-12]
God has spoken by a Son

Hymn: Jesus, the Light of the World, ACS 914/TFF 59

Almighty God, you gave us your only Son to take on our human nature and to illumine the world with your light. By your grace adopt us as your children and enlighten us with your Spirit, through Jesus Christ, our Redeemer and Lord, who lives and reigns with you and the Holy Spirit, one God, now and forever.

Saturday, December 26, 2026

Stephen, Deacon and Martyr

Acts 6:8—7:2a, 51-60

Stephen is stoned to death

But filled with the Holy Spirit, [Stephen] gazed into heaven and saw the glory of God and Jesus standing at the right hand of God. "Look," he said, "I see the heavens opened and the Son of Man standing at the right hand of God!" But they covered their ears, and with a loud shout all rushed together against him. Then they dragged him out of the city and began to stone him, and the witnesses laid their coats at the feet of a young man named Saul. While they were stoning Stephen, he prayed, "Lord Jesus, receive my spirit." Then he knelt down and cried out in a loud voice, "Lord, do not hold this sin against them." When he had said this, he died. (Acts 7:55-60)

Psalm

Psalm 17:1-9, 15

I call upon you, O God

Additional Readings

2 Chronicles 24:17-22

Zechariah is stoned to death

Matthew 23:34-39

Jesus laments that Jerusalem kills her prophets

Hymn: Founded on Faith, ACS 1048

We give you thanks, O Lord of glory, for the example of Stephen the first martyr, who looked to heaven and prayed for his persecutors. Grant that we also may pray for our enemies and seek forgiveness for those who hurt us, through Jesus Christ, our Savior and Lord, who lives and reigns with you and the Holy Spirit, one God, now and forever.

Sunday, December 27, 2026

First Sunday of Christmas

John, Apostle and Evangelist transferred to December 29

Luke 2:22-40

The presentation of the child

Now there was a man in Jerusalem whose name was Simeon; this man was righteous and devout, looking forward to the consolation of Israel, and the Holy Spirit rested on him. It had been revealed to him by the Holy Spirit that he would not see death before he had seen the Lord's Messiah. Guided by the Spirit, Simeon came into the temple, and when the parents brought in the child Jesus to do for him what was customary under the law, Simeon took him in his arms and praised God. (Luke 2:25-28a)

Psalm

Psalm 148
God's splendor is over earth and heaven

Additional Readings

Isaiah 61:10—62:3
Clothed in garments of salvation

Galatians 4:4-7
Children and heirs of God

Hymn: Jesus, What a Wonderful Child, ELW 297/TFF 51

Almighty God, you wonderfully created the dignity of human nature and yet more wonderfully restored it. In your mercy, let us share the divine life of the one who came to share our humanity, Jesus Christ, your Son, our Lord, who lives and reigns with you and the Holy Spirit, one God, now and forever.

Monday, December 28, 2026

The Holy Innocents, Martyrs

Matthew 2:13-18

Herod kills innocent children

Now after [the magi] had left [Bethlehem], an angel of the Lord appeared to Joseph in a dream and said, "Get up, take the child and his mother, and flee to Egypt, and remain there until I tell you, for Herod is about to search for the child, to destroy him." Then Joseph got up, took the child and his mother by night, and went to Egypt and remained there until the death of Herod. This was to fulfill what had been spoken by the Lord through the prophet, "Out of Egypt I have called my son."

When Herod saw that he had been tricked by the magi, he was infuriated, and he sent and killed all the children in and around Bethlehem who were two years old or under, according to the time that he had learned from the magi. (Matt. 2:13-16)

Psalm

Psalm 124
We have escaped like a bird

Additional Readings

Jeremiah 31:15-17
Rachel weeps for her children

1 Peter 4:12-19
Continue to do good while suffering

Hymn: All My Heart Again Rejoices, ELW 273

We remember today, O God, the slaughter of the innocent children of Bethlehem by order of King Herod. Receive into the arms of your mercy all innocent victims. By your great might frustrate the designs of evil tyrants and establish your rule of justice, love, and peace, through Jesus Christ, our Savior and Lord, who lives and reigns with you and the Holy Spirit, one God, now and forever.

Tuesday, December 29, 2026

John, Apostle and Evangelist (transferred)

John 21:20-25

The beloved disciple remains with Jesus

Peter turned and saw the disciple whom Jesus loved following them; he was the one who had reclined next to Jesus at the supper and had said, "Lord, who is it that is going to betray you?" When Peter saw him, he said to Jesus, "Lord, what about him?" Jesus said to him, "If it is my will that he remain until I come, what is that to you? Follow me!" So the rumor spread among the brothers and sisters that this disciple would not die. Yet Jesus did not say to him that he would not die, but, "If it is my will that he remain until I come, what is that to you?"

This is the disciple who is testifying to these things and has written them, and we know that his testimony is true. But there are also many other things that Jesus did; if every one of them were written down, I suppose that the world itself could not contain the books that would be written. (John 21:20-25)

Psalm

Psalm 116:12-19
The death of faithful servants

Additional Readings

Genesis 1:1-5, 26-31
Humankind is created by God

1 John 1:1—2:2
Jesus, the word of life

Hymn: Let Our Gladness Have No End, ELW 291

Merciful God, through John the apostle and evangelist you have revealed the mysteries of your Word made flesh. Let the brightness of your light shine on your church, so that all your people, instructed in the holy gospel, may walk in the light of your truth and attain eternal life, through Jesus Christ, our Savior and Lord, who lives and reigns with you and the Holy Spirit, one God, now and forever.

Wednesday, December 30, 2026

Sixth Day of Christmas

2 Peter 3:8-13

A thousand years as one day

But do not ignore this one fact, beloved, that with the Lord one day is like a thousand years, and a thousand years are like one day. The Lord is not slow about his promise, as some think of slowness, but is patient with you, not wanting any to perish but all to come to repentance. But the day of the Lord will come like a thief, and then the heavens will pass away with a loud noise, and the elements will be destroyed with fire, and the earth and everything that is done on it will be disclosed. (2 Peter 3:8-10)

Psalm

Psalm 148

God's splendor is over earth and heaven

Additional Reading

Proverbs 9:1-12

Your days will be multiplied

Hymn: Hark! The Herald Angels Sing, ELW 270

Forgiving God, you call us to repent so that we may be reconciled to you. Help us live each day in readiness, trusting in your promises. Guide us to seek transformation, knowing that your patience is offered to lead us to salvation.

Thursday, December 31, 2026

Seventh Day of Christmas

John 8:12-19

I am the light

Again Jesus spoke to [the scribes and Pharisees], saying, "I am the light of the world. Whoever follows me will never walk in darkness but will have the light of life." Then the Pharisees said to him, "You are testifying on your own behalf; your testimony is not valid." Jesus answered, "Even if I testify on my own behalf, my testimony is valid because I know where I have come from and where I am going, but you do not know where I come from or where I am going. You judge by human standards; I judge no one. Yet even if I do judge, my judgment is valid, for it is not I alone who judge but I and the Father who sent me. In your law it is written that the testimony of two witnesses is valid. I testify on my own behalf, and the Father who sent me testifies on my behalf." Then they said to him, "Where is your Father?" Jesus answered, "You know neither me nor my Father. If you knew me, you would know my Father also." (John 8:12-19)

Psalm

Psalm 148

God's splendor is over earth and heaven

Additional Reading

1 Kings 3:5-14

God grants a discerning mind

Hymn: This Little Light of Mine, ELW 677/TFF 65

Illuminating Creator, on this last day of the year, lead us with the light of Christ. May we always follow the radiance of your presence, knowing that you guided our past, guide us today, and will guide us tomorrow.

Lesser Festivals and Commemorations

For more see Gail Ramshaw's *More Days for Praise: Festivals and Commemorations in Evangelical Lutheran Worship* (Augsburg Fortress, 2016).

January 1—Name of Jesus Every Jewish boy was circumcised and formally named on the eighth day of his life. Already in his infancy, Jesus bore the mark of a covenant that he made new through the shedding of his blood on the cross.

January 2—Johann Konrad Wilhelm Loehe Wilhelm Loehe was a pastor in nineteenth-century Germany. From the small town of Neuendettelsau he sent pastors to North America, Australia, New Guinea, Brazil, and Ukraine.

January 15—Martin Luther King Jr. Martin Luther King Jr. is remembered as an American prophet of justice among races and nations. Many churches hold commemorations near Dr. King's birth date of January 15, in conjunction with the American civil holiday honoring him.

January 17—Antony of Egypt Antony was one of the earliest Egyptian desert fathers. He became the head of a group of monks who lived in a cluster of huts and devoted themselves to communal prayer, worship, and manual labor.

January 17—Pachomius Another of the desert fathers, Pachomius was born in Egypt about 290. He organized hermits into a religious community in which the members prayed together and held their goods in common.

January 18—Confession of Peter; *Week of Prayer for Christian Unity begins* The Week of Prayer for Christian Unity is framed by two commemorations, the Confession of Peter and the Conversion of Paul. On this day the church remembers that Peter was led by God's grace to acknowledge Jesus as "the Christ, the Son of the living God" (Matt. 16:16).

January 19—Henry When Erik, king of Sweden, determined to invade Finland for the purpose of converting the people there to Christianity, Henry went with him. Henry is recognized as the patron saint of Finland.

January 21—Agnes Agnes was a girl of about thirteen living in Rome, who had chosen a life of service to Christ as a virgin, despite the Roman emperor Diocletian's ruling that had outlawed all Christian activity. She gave witness to her faith and was put to death as a result.

January 25—Conversion of Paul; *Week of Prayer for Christian Unity ends* As the Week of Prayer for Christian Unity comes to an end, the church remembers how a man of Tarsus named Saul, a former persecutor of the early Christian church, was led to become one of its chief preachers.

January 26—Timothy, Titus, Silas On the two days following the celebration of the Conversion of Paul, his companions are remembered. Timothy, Titus, and Silas were missionary coworkers with Paul.

January 27—Lydia, Dorcas, Phoebe On this day the church remembers three women who were companions in Paul's ministry.

January 28—Thomas Aquinas Thomas Aquinas was a brilliant and creative theologian who immersed himself in the thought of Aristotle and worked to explain Christian beliefs amid the philosophical culture of the day.

February 2—Presentation of Our Lord Forty days after the birth of Christ, the church marks the day Mary and Joseph presented him in the temple in accordance with Jewish law. Simeon greeted Mary and Joseph, responding with a canticle that begins "Now, Lord, you let your servant go in peace" (see ELW S113).

February 3—Ansgar Ansgar was a monk who led a mission to Denmark and later to Sweden. His work ran into difficulties with the rulers of the day, and he was forced to withdraw into Germany, where he served as a bishop in Hamburg.

February 5—The Martyrs of Japan In the sixteenth century, Jesuit missionaries, followed by Franciscans, introduced the Christian faith in Japan. By 1630, Christianity was driven underground. This day commemorates the first martyrs of Japan, twenty-six missionaries and converts, who were killed by crucifixion.

February 14—Cyril, Methodius These brothers from a noble family in Thessalonika in northeastern Greece were priests who are regarded as the founders of Slavic literature. Their work in preaching and worshiping in the language of the people is honored by Christians in both East and West.

February 18—Martin Luther On this day Luther died at the age of sixty-two. For a time, he was an Augustinian monk, but it is primarily for his work as a biblical scholar, translator of the Bible, reformer of the liturgy, theologian, educator, and father of German vernacular literature that he is remembered.

February 23—Polycarp Polycarp was bishop of Smyrna and a link between the apostolic age and the church at the end of the second century. At the age of eighty-six he was martyred for his faith.

February 25—Elizabeth Fedde Fedde was born in Norway and trained as a deaconess. Among her notable achievements is the establishment of the Deaconess House in Brooklyn and the Deaconess House and Hospital of the Lutheran Free Church in Minneapolis.

March 1—George Herbert Herbert was ordained a priest in 1630 and served the little parish of St. Andrew Bremerton until his death. He is best remembered, however, as a writer of poems and hymns, such as "Come, My Way, My Truth, My Life" and "The King of Love My Shepherd Is."

March 2—John Wesley, Charles Wesley The Wesleys were leaders of a revival in the Church of England. Their spiritual methods of frequent communion, fasting, and advocacy for the poor earned them the name "Methodists."

March 7—Perpetua, Felicity In the year 202 the emperor Septimius Severus forbade conversions to Christianity. Perpetua, a noblewoman; Felicity, an enslaved woman; and other companions were all catechumens at Carthage in North Africa, where they were imprisoned and sentenced to death.

March 10—Harriet Tubman, Sojourner Truth Harriet Tubman helped about three hundred enslaved people escape via the Underground Railroad until slavery was abolished in the United States. After slavery was abolished in New York in 1827, Sojourner Truth became deeply involved in Christianity, and in later life she was a popular speaker against slavery and for women's rights.

March 12—Gregory the Great Gregory held political office and at another time lived as a monk, all before he was elected to the papacy. He also established a school to train church musicians; thus Gregorian chant is named in his honor.

March 17—Patrick Patrick went to Ireland from Britain to serve as a bishop and missionary. He made his base in the north of Ireland and from there made many missionary journeys, with much success.

March 19—Joseph The Gospel of Luke shows Joseph acting in accordance with both civil and religious law by returning to Bethlehem for the census and by presenting the child Jesus in the temple on the fortieth day after his birth.

March 21—Thomas Cranmer Cranmer's lasting achievement is contributing to and overseeing the creation of the *Book of Common Prayer,* which remains (in revised form) the worship book of the Anglican Communion. He was burned at the stake under Queen Mary for his support of the Protestant Reformation.

March 22—Jonathan Edwards Edwards was a minister in Connecticut and has been described as the greatest of the New England Puritan preachers. Edwards carried out mission work among the Housatonic Indians of Massachusetts and became president of the College of New Jersey, later to be known as Princeton University.

March 24—Oscar Arnulfo Romero Romero is remembered for his advocacy on behalf of the poor in El Salvador, though it was not a characteristic of his early priesthood. After several years of threats to his life, Romero was assassinated while presiding at the eucharist.

March 25—Annunciation of Our Lord Nine months before Christmas, the church celebrates the annunciation. In Luke the angel Gabriel announces to Mary that she will give birth to the Son of God, and she responds, "Here am I, the servant of the Lord" (Luke 1:38).

March 29—Hans Nielsen Hauge Hans Nielsen Hauge was a layperson who began preaching in Norway and Denmark after a mystical experience that he believed called him to share the assurance of salvation with others. At the time, itinerant preaching and religious gatherings held without the supervision of a pastor were illegal, and Hauge was arrested several times.

March 31—John Donne This priest of the Church of England is commemorated for his poetry and spiritual writing. Most of his poetry was written before his ordination and is sacred and secular, intellectual and sensuous.

April 4—Benedict the African Benedict's fame as a confessor brought many visitors to him, and he was eventually named superior of a Franciscan community.

April 6—Albrecht Dürer, Matthias Grünewald, Lucas Cranach These great artists revealed through their work the mystery of salvation and the wonder of creation. Though Dürer remained a Roman Catholic, at his death Martin Luther wrote to a friend, "Affection bids us mourn for one who was the best." Several religious works are included in Grünewald's small surviving corpus, the most famous being the Isenheim Altarpiece. Cranach was widely known for his woodcuts, some of which illustrated the first German printing of the New Testament.

April 9—Dietrich Bonhoeffer In 1933, and with Hitler's rise to power, Bonhoeffer became a leading spokesman for the Confessing Church, a resistance movement against the Nazis. After leading a worship service on April 8, 1945, at Schönberg prison, he was taken away to be hanged the next day.

April 10—Mikael Agricola Agricola began a reform of the Finnish church along Lutheran lines. He translated the New Testament, the prayer book, hymns, and the mass into Finnish and through this work set the rules of orthography that are the basis of modern Finnish spelling.

April 19—Olavus Petri, Laurentius Petri These two brothers are commemorated for their introduction of the Lutheran movement to the Church of Sweden after studying at the University of Wittenberg. Together the brothers published a complete Bible in Swedish and a revised liturgy in 1541.

April 21—Anselm This eleventh-century Benedictine monk stands out as one of the greatest theologians between Augustine and Thomas Aquinas. He is perhaps best known for his "satisfaction" theory of atonement, in which God takes on human nature in Jesus Christ in order to make the perfect payment for sin.

April 23—Toyohiko Kagawa Toyohiko Kagawa's vocation to help the poor led him to live among them. He was arrested for his efforts to reconcile Japan and China after the Japanese attack of 1940.

April 25—Mark Though Mark himself was not an apostle, it is likely that he was a member of one of the early Christian communities. The gospel attributed to him is brief and direct and is considered by many to be the earliest gospel.

April 29—Catherine of Siena Catherine was a member of the Order of Preachers (Dominicans), and among Roman Catholics she was the first woman to receive the title Doctor of the Church. She also advised popes and any uncertain persons who told her their problems.

May 1—Philip, James Philip and James are commemorated together because the remains of these two saints were placed in the Church of the Apostles in Rome on this day in 561.

May 2—Athanasius At the Council of Nicea in 325 and when he himself served as bishop of Alexandria, Athanasius defended the full divinity of Christ against the Arian position held by emperors, magistrates, and theologians.

May 4—Monica Almost everything known about Monica comes from Augustine's *Confessions*, his autobiography. Her dying wish was that her son remember her at the altar of the Lord, wherever he was.

May 8—Julian of Norwich Julian was most likely a Benedictine nun living in an isolated cell attached to the Carrow Priory in Norwich, England. When she was about thirty years old, she reported visions that she later compiled into a book, *Sixteen Revelations of Divine Love*, which is a classic of medieval mysticism.

May 9—Nicolaus Ludwig von Zinzendorf Drawn from an overly intellectual

Lutheran faith to Pietism, at the age of twenty-two Count Zinzendorf permitted a group of Moravians to live on his lands. Zinzendorf participated in worldwide missions emanating from this community and is also remembered for writing hymns characteristic of his Pietistic faith.

May 14—Matthias After Christ's ascension, the apostles met in Jerusalem to choose a replacement for Judas. Though little is known about him, Matthias had traveled among the disciples from the time of Jesus' baptism until his ascension.

May 18—Erik Erik, long considered the patron saint of Sweden, ruled there from 1150 to 1160. He is honored for efforts to bring peace to the nearby pagan kingdoms and for his crusades to spread the Christian faith in Scandinavia.

May 21—Helena Helena was the mother of Constantine, a man who later became the Roman emperor. Helena is remembered for traveling through Palestine and building churches on the sites she believed to be where Jesus was born, where he was buried, and from which he ascended.

May 24—Nicolaus Copernicus, Leonhard Euler Copernicus formally studied astronomy, mathematics, Greek, Plato, law, medicine, and canon law and is chiefly remembered for his work as an astronomer and his idea that the sun, not the earth, is the center of the solar system. Euler is regarded as one of the founders of the science of pure mathematics and made important contributions to mechanics, hydrodynamics, astronomy, optics, and acoustics.

May 27—John Calvin Having embraced the views of the Reformation by his mid-twenties, John Calvin was a preacher in Geneva, was banished once, and later returned to reform the city with a rigid, theocratic discipline. Calvin is considered the father of the Reformed churches.

May 29—Jiří Tranovský Jiří Tranovský is considered the "Luther of the Slavs" and the father of Slovak hymnody. He produced a translation of the Augsburg Confession and published his hymn collection *Cithara Sanctorum (Lyre of the Saints)*, also known as the Tranoscius, which is the foundation of Slovak Lutheran hymnody.

May 31—Visit of Mary to Elizabeth Sometime after the annunciation, Mary visited her cousin Elizabeth, who greeted Mary with the words "Blessed are you among women" (Luke 1:42), and Mary responded with her famous song, the Magnificat.

June 1—Justin Justin was a teacher of philosophy and engaged in debates about the truth of the Christian faith. Having been arrested and jailed for practicing an unauthorized religion, he refused to renounce his faith, and he and six of his students were beheaded.

June 3—The Martyrs of Uganda King Mwanga of Uganda was angered by Christian members of the court whose first allegiance was not to him but to Christ. On this date in 1886, thirty-two young men were burned to death for refusing to renounce Christianity. Their persecution led to a much stronger Christian presence in the country.

June 3—John XXIII Despite the expectation upon his election that the seventy-seven-year-old John XXIII would be a transitional pope, he had great energy and spirit. He convened the Second Vatican Council in order to "open the windows" of the church. The council brought about great changes in Roman Catholic worship and ecumenical relationships.

June 5—Boniface Boniface led large numbers of Benedictine monks and nuns in establishing churches, schools, and seminaries. Boniface was preparing a group for confirmation on the eve of Pentecost when he and others were killed by a band of pagans.

June 7—Seattle The city of Seattle was named after Noah Seattle against his wishes. After Chief Seattle became a Roman Catholic, he began the practice of morning and evening prayer in the tribe, a practice that continued after his death.

June 9—Columba, Aidan, Bede These three monks from the British Isles were pillars among those who kept alive the light of learning and devotion during the Middle Ages. Columba founded three monasteries, including one on the island of Iona, off the coast of Scotland. Aidan, who helped bring Christianity to the Northumbria area of England, was known for his pastoral style and ability to stir people to charity and good works. Bede was a Bible translator and scripture scholar who wrote a history of the English church and was the first historian to date events "anno Domini" (AD), the "year of our Lord."

June 11—Barnabas Though Barnabas was not among the Twelve mentioned in the gospels, the book of Acts gives him the title of apostle. When Paul came to Jerusalem after his conversion, Barnabas took him in over the fears of the other apostles who doubted Paul's discipleship.

June 14—Basil the Great, Gregory of Nyssa, Gregory of Nazianzus, Macrina The three men in this group are known as the Cappadocian fathers; all three explored the mystery of the Holy Trinity. Basil's Longer Rule and Shorter Rule for monastic life are the basis for Eastern monasticism to this day, and express a preference for communal monastic life over that of hermits. Gregory of Nazianzus defended Orthodox trinitarian and christological doctrines, and his preaching won over the city of Constantinople. Gregory of Nyssa is remembered as a writer on spiritual life and the contemplation of God in worship and sacraments. Macrina was the older sister of Basil and Gregory of Nyssa, and her teaching was influential within the early church.

June 17—Emanuel Nine On June 17, 2015, Clementa C. Pinckney, Cynthia Marie Graham Hurd, Susie Jackson, Ethel Lee Lance, DePayne Middleton-Doctor, Tywanza Sanders, Daniel Lee Simmons, Sharonda Coleman-Singleton, and Myra Thompson were murdered by a self-professed white supremacist while they were gathered for Bible study and prayer at the Emanuel African Methodist Episcopal Church (often referred to as Mother Emanuel) in Charleston, South Carolina. A resolution to commemorate June 17 as a day of repentance for the martyrdom of the Emanuel Nine was adopted by the Churchwide Assembly of the Evangelical Lutheran Church in America on August 8, 2019.

June 21—Onesimos Nesib Nesib, an Ethiopian, was captured by slave traders and taken from his homeland to Eritrea, where he was bought, freed, and educated by Swedish missionaries. He translated the Bible into Oromo and returned to his homeland to preach the gospel there.

June 24—John the Baptist The birth of John the Baptist is celebrated exactly six months before Christmas Eve. For Christians in the northern hemisphere, these two dates are deeply symbolic, since John said that he must decrease as Jesus increased. John was born as the days are longest and then steadily decrease, while Jesus was born as the days are shortest and then steadily increase.

June 25—Presentation of the Augsburg Confession On this day in 1530 the German and Latin editions of the Augsburg Confession were presented to Emperor Charles of the Holy Roman Empire. The Augsburg Confession was written by Philipp Melanchthon and endorsed by Martin Luther and consists of a brief summary of points in which the reformers saw their teaching as either agreeing with or differing from that of the Roman Catholic Church of the time.

June 25—Philipp Melanchthon Though he died on April 19, Philipp Melanchthon is commemorated today because of his connection with the Augsburg Confession. Colleague and co-reformer with Martin Luther, Melanchthon was a brilliant scholar, known as "the teacher of Germany."

June 27—Cyril Remembered as an outstanding theologian, Cyril defended the Orthodox teachings about the person of Christ against Nestorius, who was at that time bishop of Constantinople. Eventually it was decided that Cyril's interpretation that Christ's person included both divine and human natures was correct.

June 28—Irenaeus Irenaeus believed that only Matthew, Mark, Luke, and John were trustworthy gospels. As a result of his battles with the Gnostics, he was one of the first to speak of the church as "catholic," meaning that congregations did not exist by themselves but were linked to one another throughout the whole church.

June 29—Peter, Paul One of the things that unites Peter and Paul is the tradition that says they were martyred together on this date in 67 or 68 CE. What unites them even more closely is their common confession of Jesus Christ.

July 1—Catherine Winkworth, John Mason Neale Many of the most beloved hymns in the English language are the work of these gifted poets. Catherine Winkworth devoted herself to the translation of German hymns into English, while John Mason Neale specialized in translating many ancient Latin and Greek hymns.

July 3—Thomas Alongside the doubt for which Thomas is famous, the Gospel according to John shows Thomas moving from doubt to deep faith. Thomas makes one of the strongest confessions of faith in the New Testament, "My Lord and my God!" (John 20:28).

July 6—Jan Hus Jan Hus was a Bohemian priest who spoke against abuses in the church of his day in many of the same ways Luther would a century later. The followers of Hus became known as the Czech Brethren and later became the Moravian Church.

July 11—Benedict of Nursia Benedict is known as the father of Western monasticism. Benedict encouraged a generous spirit of hospitality. Visitors to Benedictine communities are to be welcomed as Christ himself.

July 12—Nathan Söderblom In 1930 this Swedish theologian, ecumenist, and social activist received the Nobel Peace Prize. Söderblom organized the Universal Christian Council on Life and Work, which was one of the organizations that in 1948 came together to form the World Council of Churches.

July 17—Bartolomé de Las Casas Bartolomé de Las Casas was a Spanish priest and a missionary in the Western Hemisphere. Throughout the Caribbean and Central America, he worked to stop the enslavement of Indigenous peoples, to halt the brutal treatment of women by military forces, and to promote laws that humanized the process of colonization.

July 22—Mary Magdalene The gospels report that Mary Magdalene was one of the women of Galilee who followed Jesus. As the first person to whom the risen Lord appeared, she returned to the disciples with the news and has been called "the apostle to the apostles" for her proclamation of the resurrection.

July 23—Birgitta of Sweden Birgitta's devotional commitments led her to give to the poor and needy all that she owned while she began to live a more ascetic life. She founded an order of monks and nuns, the Order of the Holy Savior (Birgittines), whose superior was a woman.

July 25—James James was one of the sons of Zebedee and is counted as one of the twelve disciples. James was the first of the Twelve to suffer martyrdom and is the only apostle whose martyrdom is recorded in scripture.

July 28—Johann Sebastian Bach, Heinrich Schütz, George Frederick Handel These three composers did much to enrich the worship life of the church. Johann Sebastian Bach drew on the Lutheran tradition of hymnody and wrote about two hundred cantatas, including at least two for each Sunday and festival day in the Lutheran calendar of his day. George Frederick Handel was not primarily a church musician, but his great work *Messiah* is a musical proclamation of the scriptures. Heinrich Schütz wrote choral settings of biblical texts and paid special attention to ways his composition would underscore the meaning of the words.

July 29—Mary, Martha, Lazarus of Bethany Mary and Martha are remembered for the hospitality and refreshment they offered Jesus in their home. Following the characterization drawn by Luke, Martha represents the active life, and Mary, the contemplative.

July 29—Olaf Olaf is considered the patron saint of Norway. While at war in the Baltic and in Normandy, he became a Christian; then he returned to Norway and declared himself king, and from then on Christianity was the dominant religion of the realm.

August 8—Dominic Dominic believed that a stumbling block to restoring heretics to the church was the wealth of clergy, so he formed an itinerant religious order, the Order of Preachers (Dominicans), who lived in poverty, studied philosophy and theology, and preached against heresy.

August 10—Lawrence Lawrence was one of seven deacons of the congregation at Rome and, like the deacons appointed in Acts, was responsible for financial matters in the church and for the care of the poor.

August 11—Clare At age eighteen, Clare of Assisi heard Francis preach a sermon. With Francis's help she and a growing number of companions established a women's Franciscan community called the Order of Poor Ladies, or Poor Clares.

August 13—Florence Nightingale, Clara Maass Nightingale led a group of thirty-eight nurses to serve in the Crimean War, where they worked in appalling conditions. She returned to London as a hero and there resumed her work for hospital reform. Clara Maass was born in New Jersey and served as a nurse in the Spanish-American War, where she encountered the horrors of yellow fever. Later responding to a call for subjects in research on yellow fever, Maass contracted the disease and died.

August 14—Maximilian Kolbe, Kaj Munk Confined in Auschwitz, Father Kolbe was a Franciscan priest who gave generously of his meager resources and finally volunteered to be starved to death in place of another man who was a husband and father. Kaj Munk, a Danish Lutheran pastor and playwright, was an outspoken critic of the Nazis. His plays frequently highlighted the eventual victory of the Christian faith despite the church's weak and ineffective witness.

August 15—Mary, Mother of Our Lord The honor paid to Mary as mother of our Lord goes back to biblical times, when Mary herself sang, "From now on all generations will call me blessed" (Luke 1:48). Mary's song speaks of reversals in the reign of God: the mighty are cast down, the lowly are lifted up, the hungry are fed, and the rich are sent away empty-handed.

August 20—Bernard of Clairvaux Bernard was a Cistercian monk who became an abbot of great spiritual depth. Through translation his several devotional writings and hymns are still read and sung today.

August 24—Bartholomew Bartholomew is mentioned as one of Jesus' disciples in Matthew, Mark, and Luke. Except for his name on these lists of the Twelve, little is known about him.

August 28—Augustine As an adult, Augustine came to see Christianity as a religion appropriate for a philosopher. Augustine was baptized by Ambrose at the Easter Vigil in 387, was made bishop of Hippo in 396, and was one of the greatest theologians of the Western church.

August 28—Moses the Black A man of great strength and rough character, Moses the Black was converted to Christian faith toward the close of the fourth century. The change in his heart and life had a profound impact on his native Ethiopia.

September 2—Nikolai Frederik Severin Grundtvig Grundtvig was a prominent Danish theologian of the nineteenth century. From his university days, he was convinced that poetry spoke to the human spirit better than prose, and he wrote more than a thousand hymns.

September 9—Peter Claver Peter Claver was born into Spanish nobility and was persuaded to become a Jesuit missionary. He served in Cartagena (in what is now Colombia) by teaching and caring for enslaved people.

September 13—John Chrysostom John was a priest in Antioch and an outstanding preacher. His eloquence earned him the nickname Chrysostom ("golden mouth"), but he also preached against corruption among the royal court, whereupon the empress sent him into exile.

September 14—Holy Cross Day The celebration of Holy Cross Day commemorates the dedication of the Church of the Resurrection in 335 CE on the location believed to be where Christ was buried.

September 16—Cyprian During Cyprian's time as bishop, many people had denied the faith under duress. In contrast to some who held the belief that the church should not receive these people back, Cyprian believed they ought to be welcomed into full communion after a period of penance.

September 17—Hildegard, Abbess of Bingen Hildegard lived virtually her entire life in convents yet was widely influential. She advised and reproved kings and popes, wrote poems and hymns, and produced treatises in medicine, theology, and natural history.

September 18—Dag Hammarskjöld Dag Hammarskjöld was a Swedish diplomat and humanitarian who served as secretary general of the United Nations. The depth of Hammarskjöld's Christian faith was unknown until his private journal, *Markings*, was published following his death.

September 21—Matthew Matthew was a tax collector, an occupation that was distrusted, because tax collectors were frequently dishonest and worked as agents for the occupying Roman government; yet it was these outcasts to whom Jesus showed his love. Since the second century, tradition has attributed the first gospel to him.

September 29—Michael and All Angels The scriptures speak of angels who worship God in heaven, and in both testaments angels are God's messengers on earth. Michael is an angel whose name appears in Daniel as the heavenly being who leads the faithful dead to God's throne on the day of resurrection, while in the book of Revelation, Michael fights in a cosmic battle against Satan.

September 30—Jerome Jerome translated the scriptures into the Latin that was spoken and written by the majority of people in his day. His translation is known as the Vulgate, which comes from the Latin word for "common."

October 4—Francis of Assisi Francis renounced wealth and future inheritance and devoted himself to serving the poor. Since Francis had a spirit of gratitude for all of God's creation, this commemoration has been a traditional time to bless pets and animals, creatures Francis called his brothers and sisters.

October 4—Theodor Fliedner Fliedner's work was instrumental in the revival of the ministry of deaconesses among Lutherans. Fliedner's deaconess motherhouse in Kaiserswerth, Germany, inspired Lutherans all over the world to commission deaconesses to serve in parishes, schools, prisons, and hospitals.

October 6—William Tyndale Tyndale's plan to translate the scriptures into English met opposition from Henry VIII. Though Tyndale completed work on the New Testament in 1525 and worked on a portion of the Old Testament, he was tried for heresy and burned at the stake.

October 7—Henry Melchior Muhlenberg Muhlenberg was prominent in setting the course for Lutheranism in the United States by helping Lutheran churches make the transition from the state churches of Europe to independent churches of America. Among other things, he established the first Lutheran synod in America and developed an American Lutheran liturgy.

October 15—Teresa of Avila Teresa of Avila (also known as Teresa de Jesús) chose the life of a Carmelite nun after reading the letters of Jerome. Teresa's writings on devotional life are widely read by members of various denominations.

October 17—Ignatius Ignatius was the second bishop of Antioch in Syria. When his own martyrdom approached, he wrote in one of his letters, "I prefer death in Christ Jesus to power over the farthest limits of the earth. . . . Do not stand in the way of my birth to real life."

October 18—Luke Luke, as author of both Luke and Acts, was careful to place the events of Jesus' life in both their social and religious contexts. Some of the most loved parables and canticles are found only in this gospel.

October 23—James of Jerusalem James is described in the New Testament as the brother of Jesus, and the secular historian Josephus called him "the brother of Jesus, the so-called Christ." Little is known about James, but Josephus reported that the Pharisees respected him for his piety and observance of the law.

October 26—Philipp Nicolai, Johann Heermann, Paul Gerhardt These three outstanding hymnwriters all worked in Germany in the seventeenth century during times of war and plague. Philipp Nicolai's hymns "Wake, Awake, for Night Is Flying" and "O Morning Star, How Fair and Bright!" were included in a series of meditations he wrote to comfort his parishioners during the plague. The style of Johann Heermann's hymns (including "Ah, Holy Jesus") moved away from the more objective style of Reformation hymnody toward expressing the emotions of faith. Paul Gerhardt, whom some have called the greatest of Lutheran hymnwriters, lost a preaching position at St. Nicholas's Church in Berlin because he refused to sign a document stating he would not make theological arguments in his sermons.

October 28—Simon, Jude Little is known about Simon and Jude. In New Testament lists of the apostles, Simon the Zealot is mentioned, but he is never mentioned apart from these lists. Jude, sometimes called Thaddaeus, is also mentioned in lists of the Twelve.

October 31—Reformation Day By the end of the seventeenth century, many Lutheran churches celebrated a festival commemorating Martin Luther's posting of the 95 Theses, a summary of abuses in the church of his time. At the heart of the reform movement was the gospel, the good news that it is by grace through faith that we are justified and set free.

November 1—All Saints Day The custom of commemorating all of the saints of the church on a single day goes back at least to the third century. All Saints Day celebrates the baptized people of God, living and dead, who make up the body of Christ.

November 3—Martín de Porres Martín was a lay brother in the Order of Preachers (Dominicans) and engaged in many charitable works. He is recognized as an advocate for Christian charity and interracial justice.

November 7—John Christian Frederick Heyer, Bartholomaeus Ziegenbalg, Ludwig Nommensen Heyer was the first missionary sent out by American Lutherans, and he became a missionary in the Andhra region of India. Ziegenbalg was a missionary to the Tamils of Tranquebar on the southeast coast of India. Nommensen worked among the Batak people, who had previously not seen Christian missionaries.

November 11—Martin of Tours In 371 Martin was elected bishop of Tours. As bishop he developed a reputation for intervening on behalf of prisoners and heretics who had been sentenced to death.

November 11—Søren Aabye Kierkegaard Kierkegaard, a nineteenth-century Danish theologian whose writings reflect his Lutheran heritage, was the founder of modern existentialism. Kierkegaard's work attacked the established church of his day—its complacency, its tendency to intellectualize faith, and its desire to be accepted by polite society.

November 17—Elizabeth of Hungary This Hungarian princess gave away large sums of money, including her dowry, for relief of the poor and sick. She founded hospitals, cared for 392 orphans, and used the royal food supplies to feed the hungry.

November 23—Clement Clement is best remembered for a letter he wrote to the Corinthian congregation still having difficulty with divisions in spite of Paul's canonical letters. Clement's letter is also a witness to early understandings of church government and the way each office in the church works for the good of the whole.

November 23—Miguel Agustín Pro Miguel Agustín Pro grew up amid oppression in Mexico and worked on behalf of the poor and homeless. Miguel and his two brothers were arrested, falsely accused of throwing a bomb at the car of a government official, and executed by a firing squad.

November 24—Justus Falckner, Jehu Jones, William Passavant Not only was Falckner the first Lutheran pastor to be ordained in North America, but he published a catechism that was the first Lutheran book published on the continent. Jones was the Lutheran Church's first African American pastor and carried out missionary work in Philadelphia, which led to the formation there of the first African American Lutheran congregation (St. Paul's). William Passavant helped to establish hospitals and orphanages in a number of cities and was the first to introduce deaconesses to the work of hospitals in the United States.

November 25—Isaac Watts Watts wrote about six hundred hymns, many of them in a two-year period beginning when he was twenty years old. When criticized for writing hymns not taken from scripture, he responded that if we can pray prayers that are not from scripture but written by us, then surely we can sing hymns that we have made up ourselves.

November 30—Andrew Andrew was the first of the Twelve. As a part of his calling, he brought other people, including Simon Peter, to meet Jesus.

December 3—Francis Xavier Francis Xavier became a missionary to India, Southeast Asia, Japan, and the Philippines. Together with Ignatius Loyola and five others, Francis formed the Society of Jesus (Jesuits).

December 4—John of Damascus John left a career in finance and government to become a monk in an abbey near Jerusalem. He wrote many hymns as well as theological works, including *The Fount of Wisdom*, a work that touches on philosophy, heresy, and the orthodox faith.

December 6—Nicholas Nicholas was a bishop in what is now Turkey. Legends that surround Nicholas tell of his love for God and neighbor, especially the poor.

December 7—Ambrose Ambrose was baptized, ordained, and consecrated a bishop all on the same day. While bishop, he gave away his wealth and lived in simplicity.

December 13—Lucy Lucy was a young Christian of Sicily who was martyred during the persecutions under Emperor Diocletian. Her celebration became particularly important in Sweden and Norway, perhaps because the feast of Lucia (whose name means "light") originally fell on the shortest day of the year.

December 14—John of the Cross John was a monk of the Carmelite religious order who met Teresa of Avila when she was working to reform the Carmelite Order and return it to a stricter observance of its rules. His writings, like Teresa's, reflect a deep interest in mystical thought and meditation.

December 20—Katharina von Bora Luther Katharina took vows as a nun, but around age twenty-four she and several other nuns who were influenced by the writings of Martin Luther left the convent. When she later became Luther's wife, she proved herself a gifted household manager and became a trusted partner.

December 26—Stephen Stephen, a deacon and the first martyr of the church, was one of those seven upon whom the apostles laid hands after they had been chosen to serve widows and others in need. Later, Stephen's preaching angered the temple authorities, and they ordered him to be put to death by stoning.

December 27—John John, a son of Zebedee, was a fisherman and one of the Twelve. Tradition has attributed authorship of the gospel and the three epistles bearing his name to the apostle John.

December 28—The Holy Innocents The infant martyrs commemorated on this day were the children of Bethlehem, two years old and younger, who were killed by Herod, who worried that his reign was threatened by the birth of a new king named Jesus.

Anniversary of Baptism (abbreviated)

This order is intended for use in the home. It may be adapted for use in another context, such as a Christian education setting. When used in the home, a parent or sponsor may be the leader. A more expanded version of this order appears in *Evangelical Lutheran Worship Pastoral Care* (pp. 128–135).

A bowl of water may be placed in the midst of those who are present.

Gathering

A baptismal hymn or acclamation (see Evangelical Lutheran Worship *#209–217, 442–459) may be sung.*

The sign of the cross may be made by all in remembrance of their baptism as the leader begins.

In the name of the Father, and of the + Son, and of the Holy Spirit.
Amen.

The candle received at baptism or another candle may be used. As it is lighted, the leader may say:

Jesus said, I am the light of the world.
Whoever follows me will have the light of life.

Reading

One or more scripture readings follow. Those present may share in reading.

A reading from Mark: People were bringing little children to Jesus in order that he might touch them; and the disciples spoke sternly to them. But when Jesus saw this, he was indignant and said, "Let the little children come to me; do not stop them; for it is to such as these that the kingdom of God belongs."... And he took them up in his arms, laid his hands on them, and blessed them. *(Mark 10:13-14, 16)*

A reading from Second Corinthians: If anyone is in Christ, there is a new creation: everything old has passed away; see, everything has become new! (*2 Corinthians 5:17*)

A reading from First John: Beloved, let us love one another, because love is from God; everyone who loves is born of God and knows God. (*1 John 4:7*)

Those present may share experiences related to baptism and their lives as baptized children of God. A portion of the Small Catechism (Evangelical Lutheran Worship, *pp. 1160–1167) may be read as part of this conversation.*

A baptismal hymn or acclamation may be sung.

Baptismal Remembrance

A parent or sponsor may trace a cross on the forehead of the person celebrating a baptismal anniversary. Water from a bowl placed in the midst of those present may be used. These or similar words may be said.

Name, when you were baptized, you were marked with the cross of Christ forever.
Remember your baptism with thanksgiving and joy.

Prayers

Prayers may include the following or other appropriate prayers. Others who are present may place a hand on the head or shoulder of the one who is celebrating the anniversary.

Let us pray.
Gracious God, we thank you for the new life you give us through holy baptism. Especially, we ask you to bless *name* on the anniversary of *her/his* baptism. Continue to strengthen *name* with the Holy Spirit, and increase in *her/him* your gifts of grace: the spirit of wisdom and understanding, the spirit of counsel and might, the spirit of knowledge and the fear of the Lord, the spirit of joy in your presence; through Jesus Christ, our Savior and Lord.

Amen.

Other prayers may be added. Those present may offer petitions and thanksgivings.

The prayers may conclude with the Lord's Prayer.

Our Father in heaven,
hallowed be your name, your kingdom come,
your will be done, on earth as in heaven.
Give us today our daily bread.
Forgive us our sins
as we forgive those who sin against us.
Save us from the time of trial and deliver us from evil.
For the kingdom, the power, and the glory are yours,
now and forever. Amen.

Blessing

The order may conclude with this or another suitable blessing.

Almighty God, who gives us a new birth by water and the Holy Spirit and forgives us all our sins, strengthen us in all goodness and by the power of the Holy Spirit keep us in eternal life through Jesus Christ our Lord.

Amen.

The greeting of peace may be shared by all.

Other suggested readings for this service:

John 3:1-8: *Born again from above*
Romans 6:3-11: *Raised with Christ in baptism*
Galatians 3:26-28: *All are one in Christ*
Ephesians 4:1-6: *There is one body and one Spirit*
Colossians 1:11-13: *Claimed by Christ, heirs of light*
1 Peter 2:2-3: *Long for spiritual food*
1 Peter 2:9: *Chosen in baptism to tell about God*
Revelation 22:1-2: *The river of the water of life*

Prayers for Various Situations

A prayer to begin the work day

May the graciousness of the Lord our God be upon us;
prosper the work of our hands. (Ps. 90:17, *ELW*)
Generous God, you call us to lives of service.
In my words and actions this day, move me to serve in Christ's name.
When I lack energy, inspire me. When I lack courage, strengthen me.
When I lack compassion, be merciful to me.

You may make the sign of the cross.

In all things, O God, you are our way, our truth, and our life. Reveal through me your life-giving work, that I love my neighbors as myself. I ask this in Jesus' name. Amen.

A prayer to begin the school day

Show me your ways, O LORD, and teach me your paths. (Ps. 25:4, *ELW*)
Christ be with me: in you I am never alone.
Christ within me: your Spirit is at work in me.
Christ behind me: reassure me when I struggle.
Christ before me: lead me when I am uncertain.
Christ beneath me: support me when I am weak.
Christ above me: encourage me to do my best.
Christ in quiet: I listen for the sound of your voice.
Christ in danger: I will not fear, for you are with me.

You may make the sign of the cross.

In all things, O God, you are our way, our truth, and our life.
Teach me to love you and my neighbors as myself.
I ask this in Jesus' name. Amen.
(Based on the Prayer of St. Patrick)

Meal time

Every good and perfect gift comes from you, O God. Bless this food, and help us to receive it with thankful hearts. By your Spirit nourish our love for one another and for our neighbor in need; through Jesus Christ, our Savior and Lord. Amen.

Living alone

Gracious God, none who trust in your Son can be separated from your love. Give to all who live alone peace and contentment in their solitude, hope and fulfillment in their love of you, and joy and companionship in their relations with others; through Jesus Christ our Lord. Amen.

Blessing for pets and animals

Use this prayer on St. Francis Day, October 4, or whenever it is appropriate.

Gracious God,
in your love you created us in your image
and made us stewards of the animals
that live in the skies, the earth, and the sea.
Bless us in our care for our *pet/s* (*animal/s*) (*names may be added here*).
Help us recognize your power and wisdom
in the variety of creatures that live in our world,
and hear our prayer for all that suffer overwork, hunger, and ill-treatment.
Protect your creatures and guard them from all evil, now and forever. Amen.

Time of conflict, crisis, disaster

O God, where hearts are fearful and constricted, grant courage and hope. Where anxiety is infectious and widening, grant peace and reassurance. Where impossibilities close every door and window, grant imagination and resistance. Where distrust twists our thinking, grant healing and illumination. Where spirits are daunted and weakened, grant soaring wings and strengthened dreams. All these things we ask in the name of Jesus Christ, our Savior and Lord. Amen.

Health of body and soul

By your power, great God, our Lord Jesus healed the sick and gave new hope to the hopeless. Though we cannot command or possess your power, we pray for those who want to be healed. Mend their wounds, soothe fevered brows, and make broken people whole again. Help us to welcome every healing as a sign that, though death is against us, you are for us, and have promised renewed and risen life in Jesus Christ the Lord. Amen.

Time of grief

Merciful Creator, your Holy Spirit intercedes for us even when we do not know how to pray. Send your Spirit now to comfort us in these days of need and loss, and help us to commend (*name*) to your merciful care; through Jesus Christ, our Savior and Lord. Amen.

Those suffering from addiction

O blessed Jesus, you ministered to all who came to you. Look with compassion upon all who through addiction have lost their health and freedom. Restore to them the assurance of your unfailing mercy; remove the fears that attack them; strengthen those who are engaged in the work of recovery; and to those who care for them, give honesty, understanding, and persevering love; for your mercy's sake. Amen.

The chronically ill and those who support them

Loving God, your heart overflows with compassion for your whole creation. Pour out your Spirit on all people living with illness for which there is no cure, as well as their families and loved ones. Help them to know that you claim them as your own and deliver them from fear and pain; for the sake of Jesus Christ, our healer and Lord. Amen.

Living with mental illness

Mighty God, in Jesus Christ you know the spirits that cloud our minds and set us against ourselves. Comfort those who are torn by conflict, cast down, or lost in worlds of illusion. By your power, drive from us the powers that shake confidence and shatter love. Tame unruly forces within us, and bring us to your truth, so that we may know peace and accept ourselves as your beloved children in Jesus Christ. Amen.

A prayer attributed to Francis of Assisi

Lord, make us instruments of your peace. Where there is hatred, let us sow love; where there is injury, pardon; where there is discord, union; where there is doubt, faith; where there is despair, hope; where there is darkness, light; where there is sadness, joy. Grant that we may not so much seek to be consoled as to console; to be understood as to understand; to be loved as to love. For it is in giving that we receive; it is in pardoning that we are pardoned; and it is in dying that we are born to eternal life. Amen.

A prayer of Catherine of Siena

Power of the eternal Father, help me. Wisdom of the Son, enlighten the eye of my understanding. Tender mercy of the Holy Spirit, unite my heart to yourself. Eternal God, restore health to the sick and life to the dead. Give us a voice, your own voice, to cry out to you for mercy for the world. You, light, give us light. You, wisdom, give us wisdom. You, supreme strength, strengthen us. Amen.

A prayer of Julian of Norwich

In you, Father all-mighty, we have our preservation and our bliss. In you, Christ, we have our restoring and our saving. You are our mother, brother, and savior. In you, our Lord the Holy Spirit, is marvelous and plenteous grace. You are our clothing; for love you wrap us and embrace us. You are our maker, our lover, our keeper. Teach us to believe that by your grace all shall be well, and all shall be well, and all manner of things shall be well. Amen.

A prayer of Martin Luther

Behold, Lord, an empty vessel that needs to be filled. My Lord, fill it. I am weak in the faith; strengthen me. I am cold in love; warm me and make me fervent, that my love may go out to my neighbor. I do not have a strong and firm faith; at times I doubt and am unable to trust you altogether. O Lord, help me. Strengthen my faith and trust in you. In you I have sealed the treasure of all I have. I am poor; you are rich and came to be merciful to the poor. I am a sinner; you are upright. With me, there is an abundance of sin; in you is the fullness of righteousness. Therefore I will remain with you, of whom I can receive, but to whom I may not give. Amen.

Prayers on pages 419–422 from *Evangelical Lutheran Worship, All Creation Sings,* and *Pastoral Care.*

Morning Blessing

You may make the sign of the cross.

I am a beloved child of God, marked with the cross of Christ forever.

Your mercies are new every morning. *(Based on Lam. 3:23)*

Thank you, gracious God, for the gift of this new day.
Awaken me to your abiding presence;
open my eyes to your creation;
open my ears to your promises;
open my heart to the needs of others.
Fill me with your Spirit and guide me this day
in works of kindness, justice, and mercy.
I ask this in the name of Jesus, the light and life of the world.
Amen.

A Simplified Form for Morning Prayer

Opening

O Lord, open my lips,
and my mouth shall proclaim your praise.
Glory to the Father, and to the Son,
and to the Holy Spirit:
as it was in the beginning, is now,
and will be forever. Amen.

The alleluia is omitted during Lent.

Alleluia.

Psalmody

The psalmody may begin with Psalm 63, Psalm 67, Psalm 95, Psalm 100, or another psalm appropriate for morning. Psalms provided in this book for each day may be used instead of or in addition to the psalms mentioned.

A time of silence follows.

A hymn may follow (see the suggested hymn for each day).

Readings

One or more readings for each day may be selected from those provided in this book. The reading of scripture may be followed by silence for reflection.

The reflection may conclude with these or similar words.

Long ago God spoke to our ancestors
in many and various ways by the prophets,
but in these last days God has spoken to us by the Son.

Gospel Canticle

The song of Zechariah may be sung or said.

Blessed are you, Lord, the God of Israel,
you have come to your people and set them free.
You have raised up for us a mighty Savior,
born of the house of your servant David.
Through your holy prophets, you promised of old
to save us from our enemies,
from the hands of all who hate us,
to show mercy to our forebears,
and to remember your holy covenant.
This was the oath you swore to our father Abraham:
to set us free from the hands of our enemies,
free to worship you without fear,
holy and righteous before you, all the days of our life.
And you, child, shall be called the prophet of the Most High,
for you will go before the Lord to prepare the way,
to give God's people knowledge of salvation
by the forgiveness of their sins.
In the tender compassion of our God
the dawn from on high shall break upon us,
to shine on those who dwell in darkness and the shadow of death,
and to guide our feet into the way of peace.

Prayers

Various intercessions may be spoken at this time. The prayer provided in this book for each day may also be used.

The following prayer is especially appropriate for morning.

Almighty and everlasting God,
you have brought us in safety to this new day.
Preserve us with your mighty power,
that we may not fall into sin

nor be overcome in adversity.
In all we do, direct us to the fulfilling of your purpose;
through Jesus Christ our Lord.
Amen.

The Lord's Prayer

Our Father in heaven,
hallowed be your name,
your kingdom come,
your will be done, on earth as in heaven.
Give us today our daily bread.
Forgive us our sins
as we forgive those who sin against us.
Save us from the time of trial
and deliver us from evil.
For the kingdom, the power, and the glory are yours,
now and forever. Amen.

Blessing

Let us bless the Lord.
Thanks be to God.

Almighty God,
the Father, + the Son, and the Holy Spirit,
bless and preserve us.
Amen.

Additional materials for daily prayer are available in Evangelical Lutheran Worship *(pp. 295–331) and may supplement this simple order.*

A Simplified Form for Evening Prayer

Opening

Jesus Christ is the light of the world,
the light no darkness can overcome.
Stay with us, Lord, for it is evening,
and the day is almost over.
Let your light scatter the darkness
and illumine your church.

Psalmody

The psalmody may begin with Psalm 141, Psalm 121, or another psalm appropriate for evening. Psalms provided in this book for each day may be used instead of or in addition to the psalms mentioned.

A time of silence follows.

A hymn may follow (see the suggested hymn for each day).

Readings

One or more readings for each day may be selected from those provided in this book. The reading of scripture may be followed by silence for reflection.

The reflection may conclude with these or similar words.

Jesus said, I am the light of the world.
Whoever follows me will never walk in darkness.

Gospel Canticle

The song of Mary may be sung or said.

My soul proclaims the greatness of the Lord,
my spirit rejoices in God my Savior,
for you, Lord, have looked with favor on your lowly servant.
From this day all generations will call me blessed:
you, the Almighty, have done great things for me,
and holy is your name.
You have mercy on those who fear you,
from generation to generation.
You have shown strength with your arm
and scattered the proud in their conceit,
casting down the mighty from their thrones
and lifting up the lowly.
You have filled the hungry with good things
and sent the rich away empty.
You have come to the aid of your servant Israel,
to remember the promise of mercy,
the promise made to our forebears,
to Abraham and his children forever.

Prayers

Various intercessions may be spoken at this time. The prayer provided in this book for each day may also be used.

The following prayer is especially appropriate for evening.

We give thanks to you, heavenly Father,
through Jesus Christ your dear Son,
that you have graciously protected us today.
We ask you to forgive us all our sins, where we have done wrong,
and graciously to protect us tonight.
For into your hands we commend ourselves:
our bodies, our souls, and all that is ours.

Let your holy angels be with us,
so that the wicked foe may have no power over us.
Amen.

The Lord's Prayer

Our Father in heaven,
hallowed be your name,
your kingdom come,
your will be done, on earth as in heaven.
Give us today our daily bread.
Forgive us our sins
as we forgive those who sin against us.
Save us from the time of trial
and deliver us from evil.
For the kingdom, the power, and the glory are yours,
now and forever. Amen.

Blessing

Let us bless the Lord.
Thanks be to God.

The peace of God,
which surpasses all understanding,
keep our hearts and our minds in Christ Jesus.
Amen.

Additional materials for daily prayer are available in Evangelical Lutheran Worship *(pp. 295–331) and may supplement this simple order.*

Evening Blessing

You may make the sign of the cross.

I am a beloved child of God, marked with the cross of Christ forever.
Come to me, all you that are weary . . . and I will give you rest.
(Matt. 11:28)

Thank you, gracious God, for the gift of this coming night.
Restore me with your right spirit. Calm my mind. Quiet my heart.
Enfold me with your bountiful mercy.
Protect me from all harm,
that I sleep assured of the peace found in you alone.
I ask this in the name of Jesus, who gives us rest. Amen.

Night Prayers with Children

Dear Jesus, as a hen covers her chicks with her wings to keep them safe, protect us this night under your golden wings; for your mercy's sake. Amen.

We bless you, God, for the day just spent,
for laughter, tears, and all you've sent.
Grant us, Good Shepherd, through this night,
a peaceful sleep till morning light.

A parent or caregiver may trace the cross on the child's forehead or heart and say one of these blessings:

God the Father, Son, and Holy Spirit watch over you.
May God protect you through the night.
May the Lord Jesus keep you in his love.

Suggestions for Daily Reflection

God's word for me this day is:

God's word will shape my day by:

I will share God's word with others through:

My prayers today will include:

- Jesus' church throughout the whole earth and all the ways it serves the gospel

- The safeguarding and restoration of God's creation

- Peace and justice in our community, our nation, and our world

- All who suffer from poverty, oppression, sickness, grief, or loneliness

- All who suffer in body, mind, or spirit

- Specific concerns today